C000060837

The
HIDDEN PLACES
of
SOUTH WALES

Edited by
Barbara Vesey

Published by:
Travel Publishing Ltd
7a Apollo House, Calleva Park
Aldermaston, Berks, RG7 8TN

ISBN 1-902-00719-0

© Travel Publishing Ltd 1999

First Published:	1989
Second Edition:	1994
Third Edition:	1999

Regional Titles in the Hidden Places Series:

Cambridgeshire & Lincolnshire	Channel Islands
Cheshire	Chilterns
Cornwall	Devon
Dorset, Hants & Isle of Wight	Essex
Gloucestershire	Highlands & Islands
Kent	Lake District & Cumbria
Lancashire	Norfolk
Northeast Yorkshire	Northumberland & Durham
North Wales	Nottinghamshire
Peak District	Potteries
Somerset	South Wales
Suffolk	Surrey
Sussex	Thames Valley
Warwickshire & W Midlands	Welsh Borders
Wiltshire	Yorkshire Dales

National Titles in the Hidden Places Series:

England	Ireland
Scotland	Wales

Printing by: Ashford Press, Gosport

Maps by: © MAPS IN MINUTES ™ (1998)

Line Drawings: Sarah Bird

Editor: Barbara Vesey

Cover : Clare Hackney

Born in 1961, Clare was educated at West Surrey College of Art and Design as well as studying at Kingston University. She runs her own private water-colour school based in Surrey and has exhibited both in the UK and internationally. The cover is taken from an original water-colour of the Carew Castle.

FOREWORD

The Hidden Places series is a collection of easy to use travel guides taking you, in this instance, on a relaxed but informative tour through South Wales describing the pastoral green countryside, the natural beauty of the coastline, the enchantment of the mountains and valleys and of course the strong industrial and cultural heritage.

Our books contain a wealth of interesting information on the history, the countryside, the towns and villages and the more established places of interest in the area. But they also promote the more secluded and little known visitor attractions and places to stay, eat and drink many of which are easy to miss unless you know exactly where you are going.

We include hotels, inns, restaurants, public houses, teashops, various types of accommodation, historic houses, museums, gardens, garden centres, craft centres and many other attractions throughout South Wales, all of which are comprehensively indexed. Most places have an attractive line drawing and are cross-referenced to coloured maps found at the rear of the book. We do not award merit marks or rankings but concentrate on describing the more interesting, unusual or unique features of each place with the aim of making the reader's stay in the local area an enjoyable and stimulating experience.

Whether you are visiting the area for business or pleasure or in fact are living in the area we do hope that you enjoy reading and using this book. We are always interested in what readers think of places covered (or not covered) in our guides so please do not hesitate to use the reader reaction forms provided to give us your considered comments. We also welcome any general comments which will help us improve the guides themselves. Finally if you are planning to visit any other corner of the British Isles we would like to refer you to the list of other *Hidden Places* titles to be found at the rear of the book.

Travel Publishing

CONTENTS

FOREWORD   iii

CONTENTS   v

GEOGRAPHICAL AREAS:

South Powys   1
Ceredigion   37
Pembrokeshire   65
Carmarthenshire   99
Gower Peninsula & The Heritage Coast   125
The Valleys of Southeast Wales   159

INDEXES AND LISTS:

List of Tourist Information Centres   187
Index of Towns and Villages   193
Index of Places to Stay, Eat, Drink and Shop   199
Index of Places of Interest   205

ADDITIONAL INFORMATION:

Order Form   217
Reader Comment Forms   219

MAPS:

Key to Maps   221
Maps   223

1 South Powys

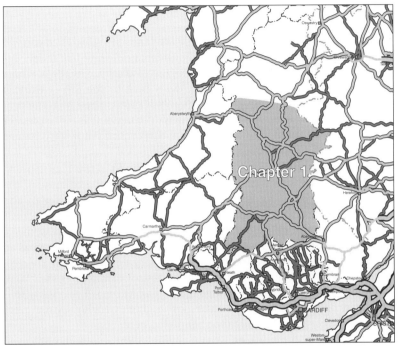

© MAPS IN MINUTES ™ (1998)

The Brecon Beacons and Heart of Wales region is steeped in history - evident in the ruined castles such as those at Builth Wells, Painscastle, Clyro and at Bronllys near Talgarth, and the numerous Celtic standing stones and stone circles dotted on the landscape.

This area offers a wide and varied range of sporting, recreational and entertainment facilities. From hang-gliding to concerts and festivals, visitors will find it here, amid some spectacular rural scenery. Pony-trekking centres can be found in abundance throughout the area, with many centres offering riding holidays. The area also has an excellent reputation for fishing; all the necessary permits can be obtained locally.

Radnorshire is an area of rolling mountains, secret valleys and tranquil beauty. The River Wye, famous for its salmon fishing, meanders through this part of South Wales. Every corner boasts a picture-postcard scene and is a dream location for walkers and cyclists.

This is also Red Kite country. Once on the verge of extinction, these birds are now on the increase thanks to the success of local feeding centres such as Gigrin Farm where, from special hides and with the use of video surveillance, visitors can view these magnificent birds of prey feeding.

RHAYADER

Rhayader is known as the gateway to the lakelands of Wales. Here you will find an impressive collection of dams in the magnificent Elan Valley. The dams were built to supply water to the English Midlands. The town, whose name means 'Waterfall of the Wye', dates back to the 5th century. It stands above the river, though the falls all but disappeared with the construction of the bridge in 1780. The town's centrepoint is its impressive clocktower. Four main streets radiate from this central point, each named after a point of a compass.

The town's castle, built here by Rhys ap Gruffydd in the 12th century, was destroyed by civil war. The town was also the scene of some of the Rebecca Riots protesting against toll gates. Men dressed as women and nicknamed Rebecca's Daughters destroyed turnpikes in protest at the high toll charges. Many tall tales have grown up around these riots, some of them to do with Rebecca herself. Some tell of how she would appear as an old blind woman who would pause at the tollgate saying, *'My children, something is in my way.'* The first gate to be destroyed was at Yr Efail Wen, where 'Rebecca' proved to be a huge man called Thomas Rees. Many tollgates were demolished, until in 1844 most of them were legally removed. In Tudor times, an assize judge was murdered here.

Rhayader's Friday livestock market is considered one of the most important in the region, known for its sheep fairs and also popular with holiday-makers for its walks, fishing and pony-trekking in the surrounding area.

On the outskirts of the town visitors will find **Gigrin Farm**. Here, Red Kites can be seen and fed. This 17th-century longhouse, with original oak beams and cosy atmosphere, has a nature trail and an abundance of farm animals. Live cameras reveal the life of badgers during spring and summer evenings.

Welsh Royal Crystal is the principality's own complete manufacturer of hand-crafted lead crystal tableware and gift items. Visitors can enjoy a tour of the manufacturing process which features glass-blowing, cutting, decoration of the glass shape and final polishing. The well-stocked shop offers a plethora of Welsh Royal Crystal products.

Liverpool House is a large and attractive double-fronted guest house offering bed and breakfast accommodation. It is situated just 200 metres from the heart of the handsome market town of Rhayader, a lovely place

Liverpool House, East Street, Rhayader, Powys LD6 5EA
Tel: 01597 810706 Fax: 01597 810964
email: info@liverpoolhouse.net website: www.liverpoolhouse.net

surrounded on all sides with the finest scenery: mountains, waterfalls and moorland woods abound. There are eight charming guest bedrooms, five ensuite, three with private bath. Some have four-poster beds for that extra bit of luxury. Single, double, twin and family rooms are available, either in the main house or its delightful annex. Each room is unique in size and decor. There are two comfortable and cosy guest lounges. Owner Ann Griffiths is a friendly and welcoming host who makes every effort to ensure that guests have an enjoyable and relaxing stay. Breakfasts are hearty and delicious - a great way to start a day of touring, walking or birdwatching in this peaceful and very picturesque area.

AROUND RHAYADER

ST HARMON   MAP 3 REF H4
3 miles NE of Rhayader off the A470

Gilfach is a lovingly restored Welsh longhouse at the centre of a 418 acre nature reserve. Tumbling upland river, sessile oak woodland, meadows and upland moorland feature at the reserve, providing visitors with the opportunity to explore nature's rich diversity. At the longhouse visitors can watch live filming of wildlife from the reserve, and learn more of Gilfach's wildlife and history.

ELAN VILLAGE
MAP 3 REF H4

3 miles SW of Rhayader off the B4518

Elan village is surrounded by the beautiful reservoirs of the Elan Valley along whose waters stand a magnificent series of dams. Nearby you'll find a group of distinguished spa towns, popular during the 18th and 19th centuries, clustered round a grouping of natural springs. The Elan Valley is an area rich in manmade lakes set in wonderful rural countryside.

The reservoirs themselves are a string of five dammed lakes, together roughly nine miles long, which were constructed between 1892 and 1903. The Elan dams were opened in 1904 by King Edward VII and Queen Alexandra. The Claerwen dam, four miles long, was completed in 1952. Built to supply water to Birmingham and parts of South and Mid Wales, they are the oldest and most natural-looking of mid-Wales' many manmade lakes. The **Elan Valley Visitor Centre**, as well as incorporating a tourist information office, also has an exhibition telling the story behind the building of the reservoirs and of the dreadful conditions in 19th-century Birmingham. Countryside Rangers run an extensive programme of birdwatching trips, guided walks and special events, and are always on hand to give information and advice to visitors.

Percy Bysshe Shelley and his wife Harriet stayed at a house called Nant Gwyllt in 1812. Now submerged under the waters of **Caben Coch** reservoir, when the water is low the walls to the garden can still be seen. This house provided the inspiration for Francis Brett Young's novel *The House Under the Water*. Cwm Elan, the house Shelley stayed in after being kicked out of Oxford in 1811, is also submerged.

LLANWRTHWL
MAP 3 REF H5

3 miles S of Rhayader off the A470

St Gwrthwl, an early Christian holy man, built a church here which has since been succeeded by the present church. It is likely that the ancient stone which stands in the churchyard near the porch dates from pre-Christian times.

LLANDRINDOD WELLS

Although only a scattered hamlet until a hotel was built in 1749, for a time Llandrindod Wells had a reputation as the haunt of gamblers and rakes, but the historical roots of the town reach deeper than this. The Romans had a fort at nearby **Castell Collen** - the earthworks are clearly detectable to this day. **Holy Trinity Church**, which gives the town its name, dates from the 12th century.

Llandrindod Wells emerged as a thriving spa town in the late 17th century. The influx of people coming to take the waters continued to grow right through the 19th century, enhanced by the coming of the railway. At its peak some 80,000 visitors a year came to try the sulphur waters. Today the town retains a spacious Edwardian style.

Llandrindod Wells' tall houses with their turrets, ornamental ironwork and balconies reflect the Victorians' enthusiasm for the town. The annual Victorian Festival is held every August, at which time the whole town is transformed by locals and visitors alike dressed in period costumes. Street entertainments are held throughout the week of the festival.

The town's lake offers opportunities for boating and fishing. Other recreational activities available here include golfing at the 18-hole golf course overlooking the town as well as green bowls and indoor bowls centres, which are among the finest in Wales.

The Heart of Wales railway line passes through the town on its way to Shropshire in the north or Swansea in the south. **Llandrindod Wells and Radnorshire Museum**, off Temple Street, houses exhibits on old Radnorshire, focusing on rural family life and Llandrindod's development as a spa town, together with many finds from the Roman fort site. The Red Kite centre occupies the top floor of the museum, with demonstrations of local feeding centres.

The **National Cycle Exhibition** is housed in the Tom Norton Automobile Palace on Temple Street. This unique exhibition covers more than 100 years of cycling history, with a collection of over 120 bicycles and tricycles dating back as far as 1867. Displays include a Victorian cycle shop, lamp collection and Edwardian cycle shop. Modern-day models such as the exciting M-Trax 450, as ridden by Team Raleigh, can also be found here.

The Rock Spa was one of the most famous spas in Llandrindod during its heyday as a spa town, and remains today a healing and treatment centre where the waters can be taken at the 19th-century Pump Room. It is located in Rock Park, west of the town centre.

Here in the handsome Victorian spa town of Llandrindod Wells, surrounded by the spectacular mid-Wales countryside, **Ty Clyd Guest House** is a handsome three-storey Victorian brick-built terraced residence offering bed and breakfast accommodation. This charming establishment is furnished throughout with comfort and convenience in mind. The seven guest bedrooms are cosy and attractive. The clientele is a mix of guests from the UK and around the world, here to make this homely B&B a touring base while they sample the delights of the town and the opportunities for walking, fishing, cycling, birdwatching and other outdoor pursuits offered in the area. Owners Bryn and Judith Griffiths are caterers by profession, and have been running this appealing guest house since 1996; they bring the benefit of their experience to offering high standards of service and

**Ty Clyd Guest House, 4 Park Terrace, Llandrindod Wells
Powys LD1 6AY Tel: 01597 822122.**

efficiency. Evening meals are available if required, and everything on the
evening and breakfast menus makes use of fresh ingredients. All dietary
needs are catered for.

AROUND LLANDRINDOD WELLS

LLANBISTER   MAP 3 REF I4
7½ miles NE of Llandrindod Wells off the A483/B4356

This small Radnorshire village is steeped in history. The local church is
13th century, but ecclesiastical records date the village back to the 6th
century.

The Lion Hotel in Llanbister is a strikingly attractive brick-built hotel.
Dating back to 1897, it has been excellently maintained and boasts a wealth
of original features, as well as all the modern conveniences guests have
come to expect. Comfort is the byword in this homely and elegant establishment. Proprietors Janet and Ray Thomas have been here since 1993.
They are a mine of information about local history, and are happy to help
and advise walkers on routes and the many places of special interest in the
area. This handsome hotel boasts three ensuite guest bedrooms, as well as
one self-contained flat. Adorned with lots of old pictures and memorabilia, the rooms also command wonderful views over the surrounding

**The Lion Hotel, Llanbister, Llandrindod Wells, Powys LD1 6TN
Tel: 01597 840244.**

countryside. To the rear there are extensive and beautifully kept gardens. The hotel's menu boasts very good, home-prepared and home-cooked dishes using the freshest ingredients, locally produced where possible. Special dietary needs are catered for. Children and pets welcome.

CROSSGATES
Map 3 ref I4

3 miles NE of Llandrindod Wells off the A483

Just to the north of this village in the Clywedog Valley are the ruins of **Abbeycwmhir**, where the remains of the last Prince of Wales, Llewelyn, are buried. Cwmhir Abbey was founded in 1143 for Cistercians. Twice destroyed in its history, first by Henry III in 1231 and then by Owain Glyndwr in 1402 (who took the monks to be English in disguise), by the time of the Dissolution the Abbey was home to only three monks. A blackthorn marks the spot where Llewelyn's remains are believed to lie.

LLANDEGLEY
Map 3 ref I5

5 miles E of Llandrindod Wells off the A44

This beautiful village lies among some of the most scenic countryside in Wales, in the heart of sheep-rearing country. The church here has a 15th-century screen and a blocked priest's doorway with a curious and interesting seven-foiled head.

LLANFIHANGEL-NANT-MELAN
MAP 3 REF I5
9 miles E of Llandrindod Wells off the A44

There is a pleasant walk to the top of the ravine through which the Water-Breaks-its-Neck falls run. For the ambitious, paths lead from here through Radnor Forest and on to Llanfihangel Rhydithon and Bleddfa.

NEW RADNOR
MAP 3 REF I5
10 miles E of Llandrindod Wells off the A44

Once the county town of Radnorshire, the village of New Radnor has a **motte and bailey castle** dating from the 11th century. Like many other castles here in the border region, it suffered under various hands. It was destroyed by King John, rebuilt by Henry III and again destroyed by Owain Glyndwr in 1401. The castle also claims to be the starting point of Archbishop Baldwin's travels through Wales to preach of the Third Crusade. In the 13th century the town was laid out in the then-popular style of square blocks, though little of this town planning is in evidence today.

OLD RADNOR
MAP 3 REF J5
11 miles E of Llandrindod Wells off the A44

Situated on a hill, Old Radnor was once home to King Harold. The motte by the church was the site of his castle, while the church itself contains interesting examples of 14th-century building design.

PRESTEIGNE
MAP 3 REF J5
15 miles E of Llandrindod Wells off the B4356

Presteigne was once the county town of Radnorshire. This border town has distinctive and handsome black-and-white half-timbered buildings, which grew around a Norman castle, long since gone, in place of which there is today a park.

Set on the south banks of the River Lugg, the castle which centuries ago was on the outskirts of Presteigne was an English stronghold until two of Wales' most loved patriots - Prince Llewellyn and, later, Owain Glyndwr - put an end to it. Famous for its annual Theatre and Music Festivals, including a popular Festival held every August, Presteigne also hosts a Science and Discovery Festival.

The **Radnorshire Arms Hotel** dates back to 1616 and is a fine example of Elizabethan 'Magpie' architecture. The **Judge's Lodging**, housed in the former Shire Hall on Broad Street, contains exhibitions of memorabilia, including the reconstruction of a courtroom and below-stairs servant quarters and lodgings of the judges themselves, all dating back to the Victorian era. Visitors can stand in the dock and sit in the Judge's chair, where many

Radnorshire Arms Hotel, Presteigne

a judgement was passed down in the past. The dark and sombre servants' quarters are lit with gas lamps, and all is as it would have been over a century ago. At one point decay beckoned as this once-grand building sank into obscurity. Then it was realised that this 'Victorian fossil' could and should be revived, thanks to a period interior hardly touched by time and the wealth of original furnishings discarded in the attics. After much research, repair and restoration, the old Shire Hall has reawakened as the Judge's Lodging, capturing the mid-Victorian heyday of a most unusual household - by gaslight, lamp and candle - for the present-day visitor to savour. From courtroom to kitchen, parlour to pantry, the trappings of over 120 years ago are all around - from the Judge's chair to his chamberpot. Visitors are accompanied by an 'eavesdropping' Audiotour of voices from the past as, room by room, the 'inside story' of this building and the people who lived here is told. This building is also the site of the town's Tourist Information Centre, with a permanent exhibition 'Neither Wales nor England' which tells the history of the Radnor Borders region.

The town also claims the oldest inn in Radnorshire, the **Duke's Arms**. An inn is recorded on the site dating back hundreds of years. Burned down in 1401 by Owain Glyndwr, the subsequent structure was the local headquarters for the Roundheads during the English Civil War, and in later centuries became an important coaching inn.

KNIGHTON

MAP 3 REF J4

15 miles NE of Llandrindod Wells off the A488

In the Teme Valley on the border of Powys and Shropshire lies **Offa's Dyke path**, a long-distance footpath built by the King of Mercia in the 8th century. The trail starts at Chepstow and winds itself northwards towards Monmouth, bypassing Abergavenny and on to the town of Hay-on-Wye. From Hay the trail takes you to the outskirts of Knighton and Presteigne. Knighton is filled with narrow streets offering an alternative route to explore some of the town's excellent shops.

The Welsh name for the town is Tref-y-Clawdd, which means the town of Dyke. Walkers come from the world over to visit the **Offa's Dyke Centre** (located off West Street) and to walk the long-distance footpath. The Centre gives the historic background to the dyke and the bloodshed of battle that continued along the borderlands for hundreds of years. the best example is here in Knighton, and reaches a height of up to 18 feet in places.

The town was granted a charter in 1230 to hold a weekly market and an annual fair. By the 17th century it had become an important centre for east Radnorshire. St Edward's Church, dedicated to Edward the Confessor, is Norman, dating from the 11th century. Only the original tower remains intact, the nave having been rebuilt in 1876 and the chancel in 1897.

Pinners Hole is a natural amphitheatre on the banks of the River Teme. It is strengthened on one side by a superb section of Offa's Dyke, which has a stone commemorating the opening of the footpath in 1971. Across the river from the town, **Kinsley Wood** is a sizeable area of native oak woodland, though much has been planted by the Forestry Commission. Sited on a hillside, trees of different species have been planted to form the letters 'ER' to commemorate the Coronation of HM Queen Elizabeth II. A railway runs through the town. Known as the Heart of Wales line, its station here is a shining example of Victorian Gothic railway architecture. The town is also home to the **Powys Observatory**.

Knighton and its near neighbour, the border town of Presteigne, have been in their time the scene of much bloodshed over the last millennium. Fierce pitched battles between Anglo-Saxons and Celts took place here, as the border line between England and Wales shifted. Turmoil began as far back as the 8th century, when the Saxon King Offa of Mercia built a tall bank on the English side, extended down into a deep ditch on the Welsh side, to prevent the Celts from invading his kingdom. 'It was customary for the English to cut off the ears of every Welshman, who was found to the east of the dyke, and for the Welsh to hang every Englishman fond to the west of it' wrote George Borrow in his 19th-century book, *Wild Wales*.

Glyndwr's Way follows the route taken by Owain Glyndwr, one of Wales' favourite sons of old, who was a thorn in the side of the English as he fought tooth and nail for independence for Wales back in the 1400s. This scenic and important route begins here in Knighton, travels south-west to Abbeycwmhir, passing the ruins of the ancient abbey - where Llwellyn the Great is buried. From there the route turns north towards the renowned market town of Llanidloes and the scenic Llyn Clywedog, before it continues on to Machynlleth in North Wales.

HOWEY   Map 3 ref I5
1½ miles S of Llandrindod Wells off the A483

Three Wells Farm Country House is in a uniquely beautiful location, situated in a tranquil valley overlooking its own idyllic fishing lake, with swans and ducks. It is so quiet here you can hear the birds sing ... Right in the heart of Wales, this is indeed a magic region of wooded hills and rocky crags, where wildlife abounds and peace and tranquillity reign supreme. Pauline Williams is your friendly and considerate host. The clientele of this superior establishment include fishermen, walkers, sightseers, tourers - anyone seeking a restful and peaceful break in this beautiful and secluded part of the county. The atmosphere is relaxed and convivial while also producing that sense of inner peace which being near so much natural beauty brings. Tastefully decorated throughout, it has 16 comfortable rooms, commanding magnificent views of the surrounding countryside. Four-poster beds are available - and some rooms have a private lounge. There is a comfortable lounge with adjoining sun lounge, TV room, large

Three Wells Farm Country House, Chapel Road, Howey, Llandrindod Wells, Powys LD1 5PB Tel: 01597 824427 Fax: 01597 822484.

lounge bar and an attractive dining room The extensive menu offers a range of superb dishes, many using fresh local ingredients where available. Located on the outskirts of the village of Howey, it makes an excellent base for exploring the glorious Elan Valley, Powis Castle, Offa's Dyke, Hergest Croft Gardens, Dan Yr Ogof Caves, Hay-on-Wye and the small market towns of Kington, Builth Wells and Rhayader. Commended by the Welsh Tourist Board, AA, RAC and many other tourism organisations. Cosy, comfortable, romantic and relaxing, this - the hidden gem in the heart of Wales - is well worth a prolonged visit.

Howey's position amid scenic countryside yet very close to a plethora of local sights and amenities makes it an ideal base for exploring this picturesque part of South Wales.

Holly Farm is a distinctive and impressive working farm offering traditional Welsh hospitality. Located close to the small village of Howey between Llandrindod Wells and Builth Wells, it's a fine stone-built 16th-century building extensively modernised to incorporate all the creature comforts, without sacrificing any of the period feel of the place. There are beamed ceilings, stone walls, a large stone fireplace in the guests' lounge, and all bedrooms afford lovely views out over the farm, well-kept gardens and surrounding woodland. Guests can enjoy a full cooked English breakfast, and also a four-course dinner if they wish. Packed lunches and filled flasks can also be prepared if required. Owner Ruth Jones is a hard-working, friendly and capable host. The farm attracts a wide range of clientele, particularly those wanting to explore the surrounding countryside and its wealth of spectacular scenery, and those interested in outdoor pursuits such as golf, tennis, fishing, bowls, swimming and pony-trekking.

Holly Farm, Howey, Llandrindod Wells, Powys LD1 5PP
Tel: 01597 822402
website: http://www.smoothhound.co.uk/hotels/hollyfm.html

DOLDOWLOD   MAP 3 REF H5
3 miles SW of Llandrindod Wells off the A470

Doldowlod House in the village was once the home of engineer James
Watt. **Pines Caravan Park** occupies a superb setting here in the heart of
Wales. Proprietors Ann and Ron Goulding care passionately about birds
and wildlife - and are proud to have achieved a silver David Bellamy Conservation Award for Environmental Standards. There are over 40 different
species on site. Visitors looking for peace and tranquillity amid truly magnificent scenery, in pine-clad hills near the lovely River Wye, need look no

The Pines Caravan Park, 'Pine Lodge', Doldowlod
Llandrindod Wells, Powys LD1 6NN Tel/Fax: 01597 810068.

further. This privately-run park within easy reach of the coast offers unspoilt rural beauty. The nearby Elan Valley with its reservoirs and dams is
renowned for its outstanding scenery. This is a select environment for
visitors with their own static holiday homes or those who would like to
hire one of the spacious fully-equipped six-berth caravans on site. The
wealth of local pursuits includes bowls, golf, trout and salmon fishing,
pony-trekking, hiking, climbing, biking and all the delights of nearby Brecon and its famous National Park, Llandrindod Wells, and Hay-on-Wye.
Whether visitors want relaxation in the form of quiet country walks,
birdwatching or touring, this park is ideally situated.

BUILTH WELLS

Lying by the River Wye, spanned by a six-arched bridge, Builth Wells is
another town which owes much of its character to once being a fashionable spa. The town is a maze of narrow streets crammed with interesting
shops. Much of its architecture dates back to Victorian and Edwardian
times.

In Welsh history Builth Wells has earned the nickname 'traitors of Bu-allt' because of the town's refusal to shelter Llewelyn the Last from the English in 1282. Perhaps they refused because, some 20 years earlier, Llewelyn had partly destroyed the town's castle. At the **Castle Mound** only the earthworks remain of the town's 13th-century castle, built by Edward I on the site of a motte and bailey castle built by Chieftain Elystan Gladrydd. The earthworks can be reached by a footpath from the town centre.

Since the 1963 opening of the **Royal Welsh Show Ground** at **Llanelwedd**, the annual Royal Welsh Show every July has gained a repu-tation as the premier agricultural show in the county. Builth Wells is regarded as the centre for farming and agriculture in Wales. The annual show, held on the third week in July, is when the farming communities of Wales converge and is considered one of the finest and most prestigious events of its kind. The showground also hosts a number of other interest-ing events and festivals, such as antiques fairs and youth festivals throughout the year.

The town first became a popular resort in the mid-1800s, when visitors came to *'take the waters'* of the town's spa. The spa treatments are no longer available, but Builth Wells remains a popular touring base. The **Wyeside Arts Centre** occupies a handsome building dating back to 1875. This cen-tre incorporates a theatre, cinema and exhibition area, and offers an interesting programme of arts and cultural events. Builth Wells also boasts an 18-hole golf course.

Cefn Carn Cafall is the nearby mountain with a cairn said to be built by King Arthur. The stone atop the cairn bears the imprint of a dog's paw. Legend has it that it was left by King Arthur's dog Cafall while they were out hunting one day. Arthur built the cairn, placing the stone on top and then naming the mountain. According to legend, even if the stone is re-moved it will always return to this spot.

Close to all the amenities and shops of this busy market town, **The Lion Hotel** is located in an impressive 18th-century stone-built building which has been recently refurbished and extensively renovated and mod-ernised. All renovations are in keeping with the age of the building, retaining the character and unique traditions of this stately building. There are 22 guest bedrooms, all tastefully appointed and including all the comforts that guests have come to expect. Director James Turner and his able staff are conscientious and friendly, maintaining highest standards of service. The hotel is popular with walkers, cyclists and all who have come to expe-rience the range of outdoor pursuits in the area. This haven of charm and elegance makes a good base from which to explore the delights of the town and environs. The atmosphere is always welcoming and lively. Lunch time and evening meals are available, and a range of dietary needs are catered for.

**The Lion Hotel, 2 Broad Street, Builth Wells, Powys LD2 3DT
Tel: 01982 550670.**

AROUND BUILTH WELLS

CILMERY
MAP 3 REF H5
3 miles W of Builth Wells off the A483

A rough-hewn stone memorial to **Llewelyn the Last** stands on the banks of the River Irfon. It was here, in 1282, that Llewelyn, escaping after the abortive Battle of Builth, was slain by the English. According to the legend, the place where Llewelyn fell and died was once covered in broom, which then ceased to grow on the site, mourning the death of the Welsh prince. Thirteen trees have been planted here to represent the 13 counties of Wales. There is also an English tablet by the monument which calls Llewelyn 'our prince'. Its Welsh counterpart describes him as 'ein llyw olaf' (our last leader). Following his death, Llewelyn's head was taken to London and paraded victoriously through the city's streets.

LLANGAMMARCH WELLS
MAP 3 REF H5
7 miles W of Builth Wells off the A483

Where the Rivers Irfon and Cammarch meet, Llangammarch Wells is the smallest of the Welsh spas, once renowned for its waters containing barium chloride, believed to be helpful for heart and rheumatic complaints. Birthplace of John Perry in 1559, a Puritan writer who was hanged in London in 1593 for treason. One of the town's former vicars was Theophilus Evans, grandson of the Reverend who discovered the waters at Llanwrtyd Wells. The vicar wrote a classic historical interpretation of the area entitled View of the Primitive Age.

LLANWRTYD WELLS   MAP 3 REF H5
8 miles W of Builth Wells off the A483

Close to this small town is **Mynydd Epynt**, a remote area of moorland, parts of which are used by the Ministry of Defence. Surrounded by rugged mountains and rolling hills, Llanwrtyd Wells became famous in the 19th century when visitors came in droves to the town's spas, with at their source the sulphur and chalybeate spring waters, discovered by the Reverend Theophilus Evans, who himself suffered from scurvy, in 1792.

Today claiming to be the smallest town in Britain, Llaynwrtyd boasts a popular pony-trekking centre and is used as a base for pursuits such as bird watching, fishing and walking. There are a number of unusual events held throughout the year, such as the Man v Horse v Mountain Bike Marathon, the World Bog Snorkelling Championships, Mid Wales Beer Festival and more.

On the outskirts of the town, the **Cambrian Woollen Mill** recalls a rich chapter of Wales' rural past. A state-of-the-art exposition takes visitors through 700 years of weaving history in 'The Wonderful World of Welsh Wool'. Ieuan, a friendly animatronic shepherd, introduces the tour with the aid of a film tracing the evolution of sheep farming and many changes to the woollen industry down through the centuries. The tour also visits the production floors where visitors learn about the processes which turn raw fleece into finished cloth. The shop stocks a range of exclusive garments for men and women, together with crafts and gift items.

William Williams, the poet, hymn writer and one of the leaders of the Methodist revival in Wales, lived at Llanwrtyd Wells in the 18th century. Another of the town's claims to fame is that the Welsh Rugby folksong Sosban Fach was written here in 1895 for an Eisteddfod. Llanwrtyd Wells is also home to one of the many Red Kite Visitor Centres.

ABERGWESYN   MAP 3 REF H5
8 miles W of Builth Wells off the A483/B4358

Situated in an isolated spot in the Irfon Valley, Abergwesyn lies on an old drovers' route which twists and climbs through the **Abergwesyn Pass**, known as the *'roof of Wales'*, is a beautiful pathway which follows the famous Drovers' Route. Centuries ago it consisted of nothing more than dirt tracks, along which the drovers would shepherd cattle and livestock from one market town to the next. Part of the route follows the River Irfon, and beside it are picnic sites and trails courtesy of the Forestry Commission.

There are actually a number of drovers' routes which can be followed - in parts by car. The roads are, however, very narrow. In the south one such route begins at Llandovery and travels across the Epynt mountain and crosses a ford over the River Wye at Erwood. Routes also travel east over the Cambrian Mountains to Abergwesyn. At the **Red Kite Centre** visitors can see birds feeding in the wild through the use of sophisticated audio-visual equipment. Above the village is **Camddwr Bleiddiaid**, or Wolf's Leap, a ravine where legend has it that young men would jump across to prove their love to their sweethearts.

Red Kite Centre, Abergwesyn

ERWOOD
MAP 3 REF I6

6 miles S of Builth Wells off the A470

Pronounced 'Errod', the village's name is actually a corruption of the Welsh 'Y Rhyd' (the ford), a name that harkens back to the days when the shallow river crossing here was much used by drovers.

PAINSCASTLE
MAP 3 REF I5

9 miles SE of Builth Wells off the B4594

Sometimes known as Castell Paen, this early Norman motte is associated with the notorious William de Breos. The castle was put under siege by Gwenwynwyn of Powys, unsuccessfully as it turned out, because he was seeking revenge for the capture of and murder of his cousin by de Breos.

The cruelty of de Breos has earned him a place in Welsh folklore. Sometimes named 'The Ogre of Abergavenny', his wife Maud is said to have lived on as a witch long after her death in the dungeons of King John's Corfe Castle in 1210. A stone in Llowes churchyard is said to have been thrown there by Maud from 3 miles away! The de Breos name lives on in the names of various breeds of cattle. Cruel though he may have been, de Breos was outdone in ruthlessness by King John. The King ensured de Breos' downfall by stripping him of his land. He died a pauper, while the routed Gwenwynwyn's dream of a united Wales did not come to pass.

GLASBURY   MAP 3 REF I6

12 miles SE of Builth Wells off the A4078/B4350

This was once the site of a Roman station and also of a Celtic monastery, from which the village takes its name (Clas-ar-Wy).

CLYRO   MAP 3 REF I6

13 miles SE of Builth Wells off the A438

The Romans had a station here and there are some remains of a motte and bailey castle built by de Breos. Diarist Francis Kilvert was curate here from 1865-72. He kept a diary recording village life and the changing face of the surrounding countryside.

HAY-ON-WYE   MAP 3 REF I6

14 miles SE of Builth Wells off the B4348

Right on the border of England and Wales, Hay also occupies the line of the Offa's Dyke National Trail running from Prestatyn in North Wales to Chepstow in South Wales. Offa's Dyke itself is a great earthwork constructed under the aegis of King Offa of Mercia in the 8th century.

Known the world over as the second-hand books capital of the world, Hay-on-Wye hosts an annual **Festival of Art and Literature** every May. Among the town's many characterful buildings can be found a plethora of book shops and antiques shops, print and craft shops. The first second-hand bookshop in the town opened in 1961; since then they have sprung up all over town - the old cinema, many houses, shops and even the old castle are now bookshops, the largest of which is said to have over half a million volumes.

There are traces of a Roman fort across the river, together with a Norman motte and bailey castle. The latter was replaced by a stone castle that was in the hands of the de Breos family but was destroyed by Glyndwr in the early 1400s. An Elizabethan/Jacobean manor house was been grafted on to part of the remaining walls. **St Mary's Church**, restored in 1834, incorporates part of a tower and porch which date back to Norman times.

The impressive **Hay-on-Wye Craft Centre** offers visitors the opportunity to see craftspeople at work, including glass-blowing, wood-turning, weaving, pot-making and jewellery-making, and to try out some craft making for themselves. Welsh speciality foods are available at the Bistro here. A livestock market is held every Monday, and a more general market every Thursday.

The church in this quiet and charming village boasts some interesting features, and the old tollbridge across the river is still in operation.

BRECON BEACONS NATIONAL PARK

Brecon Beacons National Park is situated in the south of the county of Powys and Brecknockshire. Brecknockshire is mostly rural in character; it is mountainous, made up of four mountain ranges: the Black Mountains to the east, Epynt Mountains in the north, Black mountain in the west, and the Brecon Beacons in the south. The highest of the Brecon Beacons is **Pen-y-Fan**, standing at almost 3,000 feet. From here can be had wonderful views across the rolling hillsides, encompassing numerous lakes, busy farms and countless sheep. Millions of people come from all over the world to enjoy the spectacular scenery and to experience a unique glimpse into Welsh life and culture.

From the solitude and remoteness of wild mountain ranges and rolling moorlands, the breathtaking beauty of hidden waterfalls and sheltered wooded river valleys, to the bustle of historic market towns, the National Park offers 519 square miles of unrivalled excitement and interest. It is a landscape that has evolved over thousands of years - mountains and valleys carved by the Ice Age, ancient monuments left by Stone Age peoples, Iron Age hillforts, Roman roads, ancestral trading routes and ancient churches - all have their part to tell of the history of the region. The greater part of the park lies above 1,000 feet and the whole area is popular with walkers. Straddling the county of Powys from west to east, the most remote areas are on the western side, where the vast, open terrain of Fforest Fawr and the Black Mountain form miles of tufted moorland and bleak peaks.

Fforest Fawr is located to the west of the National Park, and is renowned for being a former favourite hunting ground of royalty. The name means Great Forest, though it is actually an area of largely unforested hills. In days gone by, the word forest referred to land used as a hunting ground and not large woods as it is used today. This area, too, is popular with walkers and the small village of **Ystradfellte** is a recognised hiking centre. At the heart of a classic limestone landscape, the area around the village is one of the most impressive in the British Isles.

The two highest peaks in the Beacons, Pen y Fen (2,907 feet) and Corn Du (2,862 feet), lie to the north of Brecon itself. Offering dramatic terrain over old red sandstone country, this is probably the most popular part of the National Park. The 'Gap' route follows a pre-19th-century main road that winds its way north from the Neuadd reservoirs through the only natural break in the sandstone ridge of the central Beacons. Though no longer open to cars, this old road has car parks at both ends from which the ascent of both peaks can be made on foot.

The Brecon Beacons region has even more to offer apart from the beautiful and impressive scenery. The area abounds with historic and prehistoric sites including Roman remains at **Y Gaer** near Brecon and at **Y Pigwn** near Trecastle. One of the best remaining 13th-century castles in the country can be seen at **Carreg Cennen**, perched on a dramatic limestone crag near Trapp.**Ogof Ffynnon Ddu** is the longest cave system in the Park, with over 35 miles of discovered passageways.

The **Brecon Beacons National Park Visitor Centre** is located on **Mynydd Illtyd Common**, high above the village of Libanus on the southerly outskirts of Brecon. It offers unrivalled views of Pen-y-Fan and the highest Beacons, and also gives the visitor an excellent insight into the flora and fauna of the region.

The **Brecon Mountain Railway** is based at Merthyr Tydfil and runs a seven-mile scenic trip along the Taf Fechan Reservoir to Dol-y-Gaer. Generally in operation between April and October, it runs along almost the entire length of the Brecon and Merthyr railway which ran between 1859

Brecon Mountain Railway, Merthyr Tydfil

and 1962. The narrow gauge line, drawn by vintage steam locomotives, offers a seven-mile return journey through the forest and reservoir scenery of the southern part of the Park. Visitors can sample a ride on vintage locomotives as they puff and chug their way through the National Park. The 50-minute trip includes a 20-minute stop at Taf Fechan Reservoir.

East of Brecon, the interlocking peaks of the **Black Mountains** (not to be confused with Black Mountain) stretch all the way to the border with

England. Giving the impression of an area only partly tamed by human habitation, small villages and isolated churches can be discovered down quiet lanes in this undulating green landscape. Lying some 40 miles west of the Black Mountains, **Black Mountain** (Mynydd Ddu), though its name is singular, refers to an unpopulated range of barren, smooth-humped peaks that break suddenly into rocky escarpments.

BRECON

The market town of Brecon is famous for its ancient Cathedral, its Georgian architecture and its annual Jazz Festival held in August. Positioned on the banks of the River Usk and the confluence of the Rivers Honddu and Tarrell, Brecon evokes its historical past in many ways. Grand Georgian architecture lies around nearly every corner of its narrow winding streets. Lying at the foot of the Brecon Beacons, at the terminus of the Monmouth and Brecon Canal, it is a popular holiday base.

The **Monmouth and Brecon Canal** offers opportunities for scenic travel on a motor-powered or horse-drawn barge. This beautiful stretch of Welsh waterway was once used to bring coal and limestone into Brecon. Goytre and Govilion Wharf offer an enjoyable insight into the past. Visitors can also enjoy a gentle stroll along the towpath. The recently reconstructed canal basin in Brecon is becoming an attraction in its own right with canal boat trips during the summer months.

This town has very venerable origins. The remains of the Roman fort at Y Gaer, some three miles west of town, are tangible evidence of the area's early history. First built in around AD 75, it was rebuilt twice before being abandoned in about 290. In its time the fort garrisoned the 2nd Legion and the Vettonian Spanish cavalry. Parts were excavated by Sir Mortimer Wheeler in 1924 and some of the outer wall, in places as high as 10 feet tall, as well as traces of the gates can still be seen.

The River Usk flows through the town. There is a promenade along the Usk, just the place for a quiet stroll. Boating can be enjoyed on the river. A walk along this promenade will lead you to the medieval remains of **Brecon Castle**, found partly in the Bishop's Garden and the Castle Hotel. The town grew around this castle, built by Bernard of Newmarch in the late 11th century. Besieged by Llewelyn the Last and again during the Glyndwr rebellion, by the time of the Civil War the town considered its growing cloth trade of paramount importance and therefore remained neutral, the citizens going as far as pulling down parts of the town walls and castle.

To the rear of the Castle is the impressive Cathedral. The **Priory Church of St John the Evangelist**, originating from an 11th-century cell of the Benedictine monastery of Battle in Sussex, was elevated to **Cathedral** status in 1923. Inside there are many interesting examples of religious arte-facts and, by the aisles, once filled with chapels dedicated to craftspeople only that to the Corvisors (shoemakers) remains. Also known as Brecon Cathedral, it has its own heritage centre with an exhibition on the history of the Cathedral entitled 'From Priory to Cathedral'. Visitors can listen to voices of the past tell the story of this fascinating site. Enjoy a walk through a traditional hay meadow and, afterwards, visit the tea rooms located in the sensitively restored 16th-century Tithebarn. Brecon was the birthplace of several people of prominence, including Dr Hugh Price (1495-1574), founder of Jesus College, Oxford; Dr Thomas Coke (1747-1814), who established the American Methodist Episcopalian church; celebrated actress Sarah Siddons (1755-1831) and her brother Charles Kemble.

The **South Wales Borderers Museum** in Brecon features memorabilia of the Regiment's defence of Rorke's Drift. It records over 300 years of military history related to the town, including a Zulu war display featuring the heroic defence of Rorke's Drift, as immortalised in Sir Stanley Baker's film *Zulu*. Exhibits include armoury, uniforms, paintings and over 3,000 medals, including the largest collection of Victoria Crosses in the country. The gun collection traces the evolution of soldiers' weapons from the 18th century to the present day. Here among the treasures of the 'Old 24th' South Wales Borderers, the Monmouthshire Regiment and, more recently the Royal Regiment of Wales (24th/41st Foot), are pictures and paintings, dioramas and drums, assegais and ammunition, buttons, badges and uniforms. Few regiments of the British Army can boast the same varied and exciting history, from the time it served in Ireland as long ago as 1689, throughout Marlborough's campaigns until the present day. The Regiment has taken part in every major campaign and war, winning 29 Victoria Crosses and over 100 Battle Honours.

The **Brecknock Museum** is located in the town's elegant former Old Shire Hall, close to Captain's Walk (so-called because it was used to exercise captured French officers). Visitors can see the old assize court and catch a glimpse of Wales through the many artefacts on displays, including fine examples of Welsh love spoons. It is packed full of fascinating exhibits and artefacts from centuries past that have an association with the area. The museum also hosts regular art exhibitions.

Here in the centre of the busy market town of Brecon, close to all local attractions and amenities, the **George Hotel** is a large and impressive hotel. Extensive renovations and refurbishment have rendered this a truly magnificent hotel, though while underway they have in no way impinged on guests' enjoyment or comfort during their stay. There are 16 guest rooms, some with jacuzzi or sitting room and four-poster bed, many ensuite. There is a recent conservatory extension to the bar, a new wine bar called Mr Dickens, open five nights a week, a shopping arcade and new antiques centre, and a new ballroom. For guests' dining pleasure there are charcoal-

George Hotel, George Street, Brecon, Powys LD3 7LD
Tel: 01874 623421.

grilled snacks and dishes available in the Dickens bar, bar meals served in the conservatory extension, and a full à la carte menu on offer in the main (non-smoking) dining room. The floors, beamed ceilings and other original features have been retained throughout, to ensure that the George has not lost its traditional character and ambience.

The **Welsh Whisky Distillery and Visitor Centre** presents an excellent audio-visual presentation giving the history of whisky-making through the ages. Visitors can also view the copper vats producing whisky, and sample a complimentary tipple in the well-stocked giftshop. Brecon hosts a livestock market every Tuesday and Friday, and a craft market on the third Saturday of every month. Keen golfers will find the local 18-hole championship golf course at Cradoc, commanding splendid views of the Beacons just two miles north of Brecon itself. The **Taff Trail**, largely an off-road cycle and footpath, runs from Brecon to Cardiff.

AROUND BRECON

TALGARTH   MAP 3 REF I6
9 miles NE of Brecon off the A4078

Lying in the foothills of the Black Mountains, Talgarth is an attractive market town with attractive narrow streets and 19th-century architecture. The town boasts many historic associations and some fine buildings. The

15th-century parish **Church of St Gwendoline** has strong associations with Hywell Harris, an influential figure in the establishment of Welsh Methodism who established a religious community, The Connexion, at Trefecca House in 1752. Now a college, the house has a museum containing many rare books published by the community Talgarth also has historic associations with Sir William Vaughan, the first Sheriff of Breconshire.

The town once stood in the midst of the Norman drive into Wales, and still retains some defensive characteristics of those times. In particular, the 14th-century tower of the church and an earlier tower beside the river, dating from the 11th-13th century, which has served as a jail and is now incorporated into a house.

Talgarth is rapidly gaining a name for itself as a centre of walking, pony-trekking and gliding. The annual **Festival of the Black Mountains** offers visitors a glimpse of the food and craft producers in the area. Nearby **Langorse Lake** is a haven for water sports enthusiasts.

Flowing through the centre of the town, the River Ennig is crossed by the medieval **Tower Bridge**. Adjoining the bridge is the 13th-century tower, which has guarded this river crossing. On the outskirts of Talgarth, Bronllys Castle is a well-preserved centuries-old round keep built by the Norman baron Bernard de Neufmarche. Originally a motte and bailey castle, it was later replaced with a stone edifice. **Bronllys Castle** is now a lone tower standing on a steep mound to the north of the town.

Here in the quiet village of Talgarth, The **Strand Bookshop and Cafe** is a cosy and welcoming establishment attracting visitors from all round the region and beyond who want to sample the delights of a traditional book shop cum cafe. Covering three floors, it is a veritable Aladdin's cave of

**The Strand Bookshop and Cafe, Regent Street, Talgarth
Powys LD3 0DB Tel/Fax: 01874 711195.**

new and second-hand books, and also sells jewellery (much of it hand-made), love spoons and other unique and attractive gift items. The cafe offers a tempting range of snacks and meals, including a good variety of burgers, vegetarian meals, fish dishes and extras like garlic bread baguettes, salad and battered onion rings. There is also a take-away service specialising in Indian cuisine. Owners Ian and Kate Perry are an outgoing couple who make every effort throughout the year to maintain high standards of service and hospitality and to provide a cosy shop for all tastes. Open: Mon & Thurs-Sat 9-6; Sun 10-6; Tues 9-2. Closed Wednesdays. Fast food delivery service available; please ring for details.

BRONLLYS   Map 3 ref I6
8 miles NE of Brecon off the A438

Affording marvellous views out over the Brecon Beacons from its setting in two acres of grounds, **Beacons Edge** is an unusual 19th-century home offering bed and breakfast and self-catering accommodation. Within easy access of Brecon, Hay-on-Wye, Llangorse Lake, Abergavenny, Hereford and Builth Wells, it makes an ideal touring base for exploring the Black Mountains and pursuing trekking, riding, biking, gliding, fishing, canoeing, walking or just taking in the spectacular scenery. Events held nearby include the Brecon Jazz Festival, Royal Welsh Show, Hay Festival and regular markets in the surrounding towns. The bed and breakfast accommodation available comprises the chalet bungalow, two double rooms and 2 twin rooms, all ensuite with TV and hospitality tray. All guests are provided with a full breakfast; packed lunches can be provided, and evening meals can be taken in the candlelit restaurant with its panoramic views of the surrounding countryside. All meals are freshly cooked using fresh produce; special diets can be catered for. Guests are offered refreshments on

Beacons Edge, Pontithel, Bronllys, Brecon, Powys LD3 0RY
Tel: 01874 712164.

arrival, and there is always tea and cakes in the afternoons. The dining/lounge area is all on one level and suitable for people with disabilities. The lounge has beamed ceilings and is adorned with memorabilia, including an old butter churn, 1950s radiogram and an old spinning wheel. The self-catering accommodation comprises one double room, two twin rooms, lounge with a double and single bed settee, and two ensuite facilities, sleeping up to nine people. The lounge features a wood-burning stove; as this apartment is situated on the ground floor, it opens out onto the lovely garden with its lawn, pond, brick barbecue and garden furniture. The separate dining area opens onto a covered open area for wonderful views out over the countryside and open-air dining. There is also a fully equipped kitchen and a laundry room. Owner Margaret McClean is a welcoming and outgoing host. Well-behaved pets are welcome (though not in the bedrooms), as she herself is an animal lover with two German Shepherd dogs. Guests are also welcome to use the special lock-up area for boats, bikes, fishing tackle and the like.

FELINFACH   MAP 3 REF I6
4 miles NE of Brecon off the A470/A438

Caebetran Farm, 2½ miles from Felinfach village, is a comfortable and welcoming working farm offering bed and breakfast accommodation. Friendly owners Hazel and Gwyn Davies rear sheep and cattle, and open the farm to their guests, who are welcome to wander round and watch the animals being fed and cared for, observing the daily workings of a busy farm. Set amid beautiful surroundings, this traditional Welsh longhouse was built in the 17th century and stands high on a hillside looking out

Caebetran Farm, Felinfach, Brecon, Powys LD3 0UL
Tel/Fax: 01874 754460.

over a breathtaking panorama sweeping round from Hay Bluff in the Black Mountains to the Brecon Beacons. Just behind the farmhouse there is a 400-acre common, ideal for stretching your legs before breakfast. The three ensuite guest bedrooms are tastefully decorated and feature all the amenities guests have come to expect. Visitors can enjoy good home cooking using home-produced beef and lamb, and local produce. Vegetarians are also catered for. There are delightful walks in the surrounding countryside, where badgers, foxes, pheasants and rabbits are among the native wildlife. All this and a variety of pursuits in the area - including pony-trekking, hang-gliding and sailing - make this welcoming establishment ideal. Highly Commended/Three Crowns WTB. Non-smoking.

To get to Caebetran Farm, visitors need to travel along the A470/A438 east towards Builth Wells/Hereford. Four miles from Brecon, take the left turn signposted Felinfach. Go for 40 yards and turn right, signposted Llandefallo 2 miles. Go for 1 mile, and take the first left. Follow the signs for Caebetran B&B.

GROESFFORDD MAP 3 REF I6
3 miles E of Brecon off the A470

The Three Horseshoes is a charming and friendly public house set in a quiet countryside village amid spectacular views out over the nearby Brecon Beacons. Owners Ashley and Kim Haworth are a lively and gregarious young couple who have been welcoming customers to the pub since the spring of 1997. Built in the 18th century, it is one of the oldest pubs in the area, and has long been a centre of village life and a welcoming haven for

The Three Horseshoes, Groesffordd, Brecon, Powys LD3 7SN
Tel: 01874 665672.

travellers. Small, cosy and comfortable, with a lounge area that was originally the site of the village smithy, it offers fresh cooked meals served from
10 a.m.-3 p.m. and from 7-9 p.m. Special diets and vegetarians are catered
for, and there are children's meals on offer. The beer garden is just the
place to sit on fine days and drink in the atmosphere (and one of the range
of beers, ales, wines and spirits on offer!).

TALYLLYN   MAP 3 REF I6
3 miles E of Brecon off the A40

'**Dolycoed**' is a large Victorian-style semi-detached house offering bed and
breakfast accommodation. Set in its own extensive and beautifully kept
grounds, it is a welcoming and peaceful place to enjoy the warm hospitality and excellent service offered by owner Mary Cole. Located just 2 miles
from Llangorse Lake and all it has to offer in the way of water sports,
including fishing, canoeing and sailing, this pleasant and old-fashioned

'Dolycoed', Talyllyn, Brecon, Powys LD3 7SY Tel: 01874 658666.

B&B features two tastefully decorated and comfortable guest bedrooms.
The village of Talyllyn makes an excellent base for sampling the delights
of touring, walking, pony-trekking, hang-gliding and bird-watching, as
well, of course, as the nearby Brecon Beacons. The breakfasts in this traditional, homely establishment are home-cooked and hearty, and Mrs Cole
makes every effort to ensure that her guests have a relaxing and comfortable stay, and has created here a popular retreat for visitors from all over
the country.

LLANGORSE
MAP 3 REF I6
4 miles E of Brecon off the A40

Llangorse Lake (Llyn Syfaddan) follows its way round a low contour in the Brecon Beacons. In medieval times it was noted for its miraculous properties. About 4 miles in circumference and the largest natural lake in South Wales. Legend has it that the land beneath the lake belonged to a greedy and cruel princess. Though her lover was poor, she agreed to marry him on condition that he brought her great wealth. So, the lover set about his task and, in so doing, robbed and murdered a wealthy merchant, giving the riches to the princess. However, the merchant's ghost returned to warn the couple that their crime would be avenged upon the 9th generation of their family. The couple ignored the warning. One night a terrible flood burst from the hills, drowning the land and the inhabitants.

Today the lake is a mecca for fishing, horse-riding, sailing, wind-surfing and water-skiing. There's an all-weather activity centre based at the Llangorse Riding and Rope Centre, where an indoor climbing school has been founded. Here beginners can 'learn the ropes' and experienced climbers can brush up on their skills, under qualified supervision.

TALYBONT-ON-USK
MAP 3 REF I7
5 miles SE of Brecon off the A40

Just beyond this attractive village, the **Monmouthshire and Brecon Canal** passes through the 375 yards of the Ashford Tunnel. The **Talybont Reservoir** lies in an attractive narrow valley surrounded by forest on the southeast slope of the Brecons. From the carpark at the far end of the reservoir there are several forest trails and, for the energetic, a pleasant, if rugged walk, can be started from here. Passing by waterfalls a footpath follows the **Craig y Fan Ddu** ridge to some fine views across the Brecon Beacons. Continuing round on the footpath then, turning south, the route passes by a memorial to a Wellington bomber that crashed here in 1941 - some of its remains can be seen further along the path. From the 'Balcony', on a good day it is possible to see across to the Black Mountains and Sugar Loaf. The route drops down back towards the waterfalls and car park.

Here, Michael and Barbara Taylor have recently brought their many years of experience as hotelliers to bear on **The Usk Inn**. This old establishment was built in the last century at the time of the Brecon-to-Merthyr railway, but has been extended over the years. A traditional village inn with bar, restaurant and rooms is how the Taylors see it, where pine furnishings and country-style quilts enhance the cosiness and comfort of the guest bedrooms (there is a four-poster room, but you'll have to plan ahead

**The Usk Inn, Station Road, Talybont-on-Usk, Brecon, Powys LD3 7JE
Tel: 01874 676251 Fax: 01874 676392.**

to book it!). It is popular with walkers, cyclists and even canal boat residents, who stroll the hundred or so yards from the canal down Station Road to take lunch or dinner at what has quickly become a very popular dining venue. The fresh food and pleasant surroundings draw clients from a very wide area to this charming village inn.

LLANGYNIDR Map 3 ref I7
9 miles SE of Brecon off the B4558

There is a particularly attractive four-arched bridge over a pleasant stretch of the River Usk here. From the village, across the open moorland of Mynydd Llangynidr, a footpath leads to the Chartists' Cave, where members stored ammunition during their active years in the 19th century.

LIBANUS Map 3 ref H6
5 miles W of Brecon off the A470

The **Brecon Beacons Mountain Centre** lies to the west of this attractive hamlet, on Mynydd Illtyd Common. There are also some interesting remains to be seen in the area, including **Twyn y Gaer**, a Bronze Age burial chamber, and **Bedd Illtyd**, its modest stones belying the fact that tradition holds it to be the grave of St Illtyd, the founder of the monastery at Llanwit Major.

HEOL SENNI Map 3 ref H7
9 miles W of Brecon off the A4215

Here in a 17th-century stonebuilt former working farmhouse located in the picturesque valley of Heol Senni, **Maeswalter** offers superior bed and

**Maeswalter, Heol Senni, Nr Brecon, Powys LD3 8SU
Tel: 01874 636629.**

breakfast accommodation. The three guest bedrooms are handsome, spacious and comfortable, and offer superb views across the Senni Valley. Heol Senni itself is a farmers' hamlet of unalloyed natural beauty. There is excellent walking, pony-trekking, hang-gliding, touring and birdwatching in the area. This welcoming B&B makes a good base from which to explore Llangorse Lake, Henrhyd and Ystradfellte Falls, the caves at Dan-Yr-Ogof and the reservoirs of 'Neuadd', 'Pentwyn' and 'Pontsticill', Carreg Cennen Castle, the Towy Forest and Elan Valley, and the grounds at Graig-Y-Nos Country Park. Some of the finest views of the Beacons can be had by walking along the nearby Mynydd Illtyd Common from the national park's popular Mountain Centre. Owners Joy and Haydn Mayo are friendly and welcoming, and prepare good home-cookedbreakfasts. They can also cater for vegetarians.

DEFYNNOG   MAP 3 REF H6
12 miles W of Brecon off the A40

Beacons Pottery and Picture Gallery occupies two floors of the historic 16th-century Defynnog Old School. Owned and run by professional artists/potters Carole Longhurst and Colin Horsman, it features a range of distinctive and beautiful fine art ceramics and domestic pottery. The spacious picture gallery contains well-displayed, framed paintings and prints by qualified local artists.

SENNYBRIDGE   MAP 3 REF H6
12 miles W of Brecon off the A40

Along the southern edge of the Mynydd Epynt and on the northern border of the Brecon Beacons National Park, this village developed during the 19th century along with the railways as a centre for livestock trading in the area. The remains of **Castell Ddu**, just west of the village, date from the 14th century and are believed to stand on the site of an 11th-century manor house, home to Sir Reginald Aubrey.

Glynderi Pottery is a craft gallery and working pottery where stoneware pots are fashioned in a wide choice of glazes. The showroom has mugs, jugs, eggcups and casseroles, plantpots and hanging vases, and several sizes of bells. It also boasts a range of hand-modelled little animals and red dragons.

YSTRADFELLTE   MAP 3 REF H7
12 miles SW of Brecon off the A4059

The road north climbs sharply and squeezes its way along the narrow valley between **Fan Llia** (which rises to 2,071 feet on the east side) and **Fan Nedd** (2,200 feet, on the west side). The **Maen Madog** is a nine-foot-high standing stone with a Latin inscription proclaiming that Dervacus, son of Justus, lies there. The stone itself was probably erected around 2000 BC.

To the south around Ystradfellte is **Porth-yr-Ogof**, a delightful area with a collection of dramatic waterfalls as the River Mellte descends through woodland, linked together by woodland walks, with unusual limestone pockets beneath the hillside offering a challenge to the most daring potholer.

PEN-Y-CAE   MAP 3 REF H7
20 miles SW of Brecon off the A4067

Craig y Nos Country Park in Pen-y-Cae covers some 40 acres and provides the opportunity for a pleasant day out. The mansion in the grounds, known as **Craig y Nos Castle**, was once the home of world-famous 19th-century opera singer Madame Adelina Patti. Today the castle grounds are open to the public as landscaped country parkland.

YSTRADGYNLAIS   MAP 2 REF G7
22 miles SW of Brecon off the A4221

On the banks of the River Tawe, at the top end of the Tawe Valley and close to the boundary of the Brecon Beacons National Park, this is a former mining community. The Tawe Valley stretches from the city of Swansea to the Brecon Beacons.

Legend tells of three cauldrons filled with gold and buried beneath **Y Garn Goch**, the red cairn, on the summit of Mynydd y Drum just east of town. The story goes that one day a young girl will come to claim the treasure and that, until then, it is protected by fierce demons. To prevent booty-hunters even further, the legend tells of a wizard and his apprentice who attempted to overcome the demons with their magic. While the elements raged, a spirit on a wheel of fire swept the apprentice out of the protective circle he had made on the ground and gave him a lighted candle, saying his life would last only as long as the candle burned. As soon as the candle was spent he died, and the wizard, terrified, fled from the mountain.

Ystradgynlais is rich in industrial heritage. Iron was produced here as far back as the early 17th century; the legacy of this historical past can be seen at the **Ynyscedwyn Ironworks** recreation park. The **Ynyscedwyn Arms** is the oldest hostelry in the region, dating back to the 1800s. Friday is market day here in Ystradgynlais. The local area is known as *'waterfall country'*, making for lovely walks and rural pursuits. It attracts ramblers, walkers and caving enthusiasts.

Local attractions include **Dan Yr Ogof Showcaves** in **Abercrave**, which are some of the deepest and most impressive public showcaves in Europe. There are three separate caves to visit, discovered in 1912 and finally opened to the public in the 1960s: Dan-yr-Ogof itself is the longest show cave in Britain; the Cathedral cave is the largest in Britain; and in the Bone cave visitors can learn something of life in prehistoric times. Within the grounds there is also a Dinosaur Park, Shire Horse Centre and Ski Slope. The Iron Age village on site features an exhibition illustrating how early humans would have survived in the caves. All these attractions enhance the interest and appeal of this impressive site.

CRICKHOWELL

Crickhowell, in the beautiful Usk Valley, is a town brimming with charm and history. Sitting between the Table and Sugar Load Mountains, the town - birthplace of Sir George Everest in 1790 - gets its name from the hillfort on Table Mountain, **Crug Hywel**, an Iron Age stronghold overlooking the town.

The picturesque and famous 16th-century **stone bridge** over the River Usk - unique in having 13 arches on one side, and only 12 on the other - leads to avenues of elegant Georgian houses. At the north entrance of this small town is a picturesque 15th-century gateway that belonged to the long-since demolished Herbert's Mansion.

Two and a half miles west of Crickhowell off the A40, a quiet weekend away or a relaxing holiday base awaits at **Gliffaes Country House Hotel**, occupying a fine setting, spectacularly situated above the River Usk. The 33 acres of grounds and gardens are an absolute delight, with a beautiful collection of rare trees, shrubs and flowering plants plus lawned areas for putting, croquet and bowls. Guests can also enjoy fishing for wild brown

Gliffaes Country House Hotel, Crickhowell, Powys NP8 1RH
Tel: 0800 146719 Fax: 01874 730463
website: www.gliffaeshotel.com email: calls@gliffaeshotel.com

trout and salmon on 2½ private miles of the Usk. The hotel is beautifully furnished throughout, with antique furniture enhancing the country house atmosphere in the panelled sitting room and Regency-style drawing room. Accommodation is provided in 22 very comfortable ensuite guest rooms, all equipped to a high standard. The elegant dining room has French windows opening onto the terrace with fabulous views all round, and provides the perfect setting for the mouthwatering cuisine - the best of national dishes and Mediterranean specialities, using local produce. The accompanying wine list is equally impressive. The introductory words of Aristophanes provide additional incentive if any were needed, to sample some of the fine vintages offered:

'Tis when men drink they thrive, grow wealthy, speed their business, win their suits, make themselves happy, benefit their friends. Go fetch me out a stoup of wine, and let me moisten my wits, and utter something bright.'

The 14th-century parish **Church of St Edmund** has a shingle spire, unusual for Wales. The motte and two shattered towers remain of the 11th-century **Crickhowell Castle**, standing within a large park in the town. Stormed by Owain Glyndwr, it was abandoned in the 15th century. The gatehouse and portcullis remain. A market is held in the town every Thursday. The town is also quite near the **Monmouth and Brecon Canal**. Barge trips depart from the terminus in Brecon and from Llangrynach; cruisers can be hired for the more adventurous visitor.Crickhowell's close proximity to the Black Mountains makes it an ideal location for many outdoor activities including walking and hang-gliding. Just east of the town a minor road leads part way up Sugar Loaf Mountain and a footpath leads to the 1,955-foot summit - not quite Everest, but affording wonderful views of the Usk Valley, the Black Mountains and beyond.

AROUND CRICKHOWELL

LLANGATTOCK
Map 3 ref I7
1 mile W of Crickhowell off the B4558

Founded sometime during the early 6th century, the oldest part of **St Catwg's Church** is its tower, which dates back to the 12th century. St Catwg, one of Wales' most honoured saints, was born in around AD 497; at the end of his life, in about 577, he became a bishop and took the name Sophias.

Across the river, beyond Llangattock, a minor road leads to the **Craig-y-Cilau Nature Reserve**. This 157-acre reserve is one of the best in the Brecons, with over 250 plant species recorded and over 50 kinds of birds breeding within its grounds. A cave system of some 12 miles begins in the Reserve, but entrance is only allowed approved caving clubs.

TRETOWER
Map 3 ref I7
3 miles NW of Crickhowell off the A479

Tretower Court and Castle is an historic site where both a splendid 14th-century manor house and the remains of a 13th-century stone keep surmount a small mound, the remains of Tretower's original earthwork castle, built around 1100 to control a strategic route through the Black

Tretower Castle

Mountains. The stark round tower, clearly a military fortification of great antiquity, has as its companion piece A well-preserved, beautiful late medieval country stone manor house, which must have served as a very desirable domestic residence in its time. A fine example of a late medieval manor house, its oldest stonework dating from the 14th century. The wall-walk, originally built as a defensive structure, was given its roof and windows in the 17th century. The outstanding feature for today's visitor is the original woodwork, possibly dating from the 15th century. During the summer plays are performed here. Tretower Castle was built, as was Castell Dinas near Talgarth, in this valley to discourage Welsh rebellion. None the less, it was besieged by Llewelyn the Last and almost destroyed by Glyndwr in 1403. The 12th-century ruins lie across from the manor and are interesting in that the castle was unique in its design of a cylindrical tower within an older square keep.

CWMDU
MAP 3 REF I6

4 miles NE of Crickhowell off the A479

The Farmers Arms is a very friendly family-run public house. Susan and Andrew Lawrence have been running this welcoming establishment since 1997 - Sue looks after front of house while Andrew does the cooking. Located in a quiet country village at the foot of the Black Mountains, the surrounding area affords a wealth of opportunities for walking, pony-trekking, gliding and other outdoor pursuits. This handsome stone-built pub is full of traditional features, with its flagstone floors, large stone fireplace with wood-burning stove, exposed stone walls and horse brasses. The restaurant area has a wood-beamed ceiling. The extensive menu changes daily; bar snacks are also available. Andrew acquits himself well in the kitchen, making use of fresh local ingredients in a range of traditional favourites and innovative modern dishes. There are also two guest bedrooms should you wish to make this a base from which to explore this lovely part of South Wales.

**The Farmers Arms, Cwmdu, Nr Crickhowell, Powys NP8 1RU
Tel/Fax: 01874 730464.**

2 Ceredigion

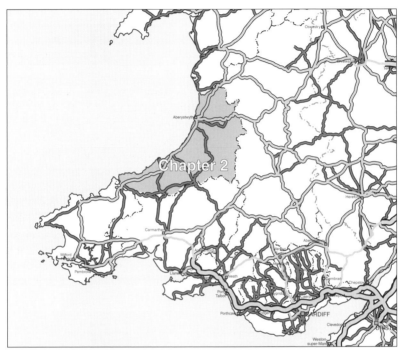

Ceredigion's countryside features some of Wales' most beautiful landscapes. The area is of special interest to those who love nature in all its profusion, with a multitude of lakes, mountains, forests and rivers. The area attracts many rare species of birds, wildlife and plants, and is home to the graceful Red Kite. Keen birdwatchers are well served by the reserves at Llangrannog, New Quay, Cors Caron and Teifi Marshes. Several unique habitats are protected by local and national wildlife organisations, including the RSPB reserve at Ynyshir, the Countryside Council for Wales' nature reserves along the Dyfi Estuary, and the Cors Fochno and Cors Caron, around Tregaron.

The spectacular waterfalls at Devil's Bridge can be reached by a trip on the Vale of Rheidol Narrow Gauge Railway, while the Cenarth Falls can be journeyed to along the Teifi Valley Railway. More natural beauties abound at the Welsh Wildlife Centre, Cilgerran, Cardigan Island Farm Park, and

Nant yr Arian Forest Centre near Goginan, as well as the peaceful lakes of Nant y Moch, Llyn Brianne and Teifi Pools.

'Ceredigion' means the land of Ceredig, son of the Celtic chieftain Cunedda. Dating from around 415 AD, the region is steeped in history and tradition. It is renowned for its unique brand of 'Welshness'. Within Wales, Ceredigion inhabitants are affectionately known as 'Cardis'. Welsh is the first language of three out of five Cardis, taught in every school and widely used both socially and in business. The Cardis proudly guard their heritage and identity over the centuries, always extending a warm and lasting welcome to visitors.

St David, patron saint of Wales, was born in Ceredigion, and many famous Welsh princes are buried in the monastic ruins of Strata Florida Abbey. Past battles and pageantry are recaptured in the dramatic castles of Aberystwyth and Cilgerran. Ceredigion has produced many national literary figures and musicians, having honed their art in local *eisteddfodau*.

Ceredigion also has over 50 miles of magnificent coastline with more than 30 spectacular beaches, ranging from small secluded coves to traditional seaside resorts. Twenty-two miles of Ceredigion's coastline have been designated Heritage Coast. Some sections are owned by the National Trust or are managed for their wildlife interest by the Dyfed Wildlife Trust, but most parts remain privately owned. Some sections are remote and inaccessible, providing havens for sensitive wildlife. A summer programme of guided walks along the coastal footpaths, together with specialist talks, are offered throughout the summer.

ABERYSTWYTH

Aberystwyth is the largest town in Cardigan Bay, seat of local government and home to University College of Wales and the National Library of Wales. Modern Aberystwyth (although settlement in the area was known to have existed before this time) can be traced to the castle, the ruins of which still remain. Built in 1277 by Edward I of Lancaster, this castle was one of a number constructed in Wales to subdue the Welsh. It withstood a siege by the Welsh in 1282 and Owain Glyndwr's revolt in 1404, whilst the surrounding town was destroyed. For four years it served as a Glyndwr base. During the Civil War **Aberystwyth Castle** was held for the royalist cause before surrendering to Cromwell's army in 1646; it was blown up in 1649. Finds from recent excavations can be seen in the Ceredigion Museum. Coins from the locally-mined silver were minted here from 1637 to 1646.

The original buildings of the University College were intended to be a hotel, but eventually housed the beginnings of the college, standing opposite the castle ruins. The majority of the college lies to the east of town along with the **Aberystwyth Arts Centre**, a well-used venue for concerts and theatre productions, and the **Catherine Lewis Gallery** with its permanent collection of art together with constantly changing exhibitions. This is Wales' largest Arts Centre with a wide programme of pantomime, top quality drama, light entertainment, music and dance, an annual festival and a summer season show. Its nationally renowned galleries show contemporary art paintings, sculpture, photography, ceramics and other crafts. The permanent ceramics gallery houses one of the best studio collections in the UK. The Centre also houses a popular cafe, craft shop and bookshop.

Close by, the **National Library of Wales** holds many treasures of early Welsh and Celtic manuscripts. Among the collection is the *Black Book of Carmarthen* dating from the 12th century, the oldest manuscript in Welsh. The library is also a mecca for amateur and professional genealogists alike.

The **Ceredigion Museum** in Terrace Road tells of the history of Cardigan with an interesting collection of materials to illustrate their exhibitions. The history of seafaring, agriculture and silver- and lead-mining is well chronicled here, housed in the carefully preserved Edwardian Coliseum Theatre. Displays show archaeology, local folk-life, a cottage of 1850, agriculture, dairying and various crafts, including carpentry, spinning and weaving, lead mining, clocks, seafaring and many more. Details of what is being held and when in the Museum and Aberystwyth's other attractions can be found at the Tourist Information Office close to the Museum.

The town itself is almost museum-like with the amount of well-preserved 18th and 19th century buildings, especially around **Laura Place**. The seafront offers magnificent views of the whole of Cardigan Bay. The **Aberystwyth Electric Cliff Railway** runs to the top of Constitution Hill, from the summit of which can be had even better views of the Bay reaching from the Lleyn Peninsula in the north to Pembrokeshire in the south. The **Great Aberystwyth Camera Obscura** on Constitution Hill is housed in an octagonal tower set on the 430-foot summit of the hill overlooking the town and Cardigan Bay. Opened in 1985, it is a faithful re-creation of a popular Victorian amusement. A massive 14-inch lens system focuses detailed views on a screen in a darkened viewing gallery.

For railway enthusiasts a trip from the main station in town on the **Vale of Rheidol Light Railway** is a must. Travelling 12 miles to Devil's Bridge, the line opened in 1902 to carry lead from the mines in the Rheidol Valley; it was soon taking passengers along this very attractive valley. British Rail operated the line until 1988, when Brecon Railway acquired the line.

Aberystwyth Harbour and Marina accommodates up to 104 vessels, with berths set aside for visiting yachtsmen. The **Town Quay** is the place to buy fresh lobster, mackerel and crabs in season. A number of deep-sea charter vessels also sail from the Town Quay, providing fishing and sight-

Aberystwyth Harbour and Marina

seeing excursions. Several charter boats operate out of Aberystwyth harbour, offering a wide range of deep-sea and inshore fishing trips - from 1-hour mackerel trips to 12-hour deep-sea trips. They also provide scenic tours along the Ceredigion Heritage Coast for wildlife and birdwatching enthusiasts.

The Aberystwyth Group of the Ramblers' Association meets at least fortnightly on Saturdays and Sundays, with walks that vary in length and grade. For details telephone Maldwyn Evans on 01970 828410. Aberystwyth Golf Club boasts an 18-hole course overlooking the town.

AROUND ABERYSTWYTH

EGLWYSFACH   MAP 4 REF G3
12 miles NE of Aberystwyth off the A487

Also known as Furnace, this was a place of silver refining and iron smelting. The River Einon plunges down a much-photographed waterfall providing the water power which drove the bellows of the charcoal-fired blast furnace where iron ore was once smelted. **Dyfi Furnace**, dating from the 18th century, is an industrial heritage site that has a fully operational waterwheel. This site was first used in the 17th century to refine silver by using the water power of the Einion; later it was used as a charcoal-burning blast furnace for iron.

The road opposite the site leads up the **Cwm Einion**, sometimes called the Artists Valley. Woodland trails and picnic spots combine to make this a lovely area to visit and spend the day.

Dyfi National Nature Reserve, where access is restricted because of dangerous tidal waters, is a corner of the Dyfi Estuary that is used by many waders and wildfowl. On the south side of the Dyfi Estuary, **RSPB Ynyshir Reserve** offers a wide range of habitats, salt- and freshwater marsh, reed bed, peat bog, woodland and open hillside. Sixty-seven species of bird breed here regularly, including wood warbler, pied flycatcher, garden warbler, blackcap, treecreeper and three species of woodpecker.

YNYSLAS   Map 2 ref F3
8 miles NE of Aberystwyth off the B4572

The sandy beach and spectacular sand dunes at the mouth of the River Dyfi, north of Borth, is part of the Dyfi National Nature Reserve run by the Countryside Council for Wales. Guided walks are arranged on Sundays for visitors to enjoy the scenic beauty and discover the wildlife that thrives in the area.

BORTH   Map 2 ref F3
6 miles N of Aberystwyth off the B4572

This popular seaside resort lies halfway along the Cardigan Bay coast, surrounded by fine scenery. The original settlement was located on the slopes of Rhiw Fawr, Upper Borth, and some of the older fishermens' and farmers' cottages remain. The growth of the village as a resort really took off in 1863 with the coming of the Aberystwyth and Welsh Coast Railway. A path, leading from the War Memorial, provides an exhilarating walk along cliff tops to Clarach and Aberystwyth.

Borth Animalarium is one of the top attractions of Mid Wales. Here, Capuchin monkeys, lemurs, wallabies, capybaras and more are on view. Indoors visitors can see reptiles, insects, bird aviaries and more. On site there is also a play area, picnic area, souvenir shop and cafe. The Borth and Ynyslas Golf Club was established in 1885. This championship links course has a modern clubhouse with bar and full catering facilities.

LLANBADARN FAWR   Map 2 ref F4
1½ miles E of Aberystwyth off the A44

At Llanbadarn Fawr, now a suburb of Aberystwyth but once an early pre-castle town in its own right, the **Church** was a 6th century bishopric founded by St Padarn; the bishopric later merged (in the 8th century) with St David. The present building is of 13th century origin and contains the tomb of St Padarn and two Celtic crosses that are associated with St Samson, the brother of Padarn. This is the oldest bishopric in Wales. Legend has it that St Padarn and his associate Cadfan sailed from Brittany with 847 monks in the 6th century and founded a religious order here. There is a fascinating exhibition placing the history of scholarship at Llanbadarn within the wider context of the history of Wales. The exhibition features an early chapel, a cell where St Padran might have lived, and a 13th century Celtic church.

LOVESGROVE   MAP 2 REF G4
3 miles E of Aberystwyth off the A44

In quiet countryside, three miles from the popular coastal town of Aberystwyth and just off the A44, visitors will find **Plas Dolau**, a unique holiday centre. Built around 1850 and set in 22 acres of unspoilt countryside, the centre includes a warm and welcoming country mansion offering very comfortable dormitory-style accommodation for up to 60 people. In the grounds, *Y Gelli*, a Wales Tourist Board 2-Star farm-guesthouse in Scandinavian style, offers bed and breakfast accommodation for up to 12 people in five bedrooms, including an ensuite family room with interlinked

**Plas Dolau, Y Gelli, Lovesgrove, Aberystwyth, Ceredigion SY23 3HP
Tel: 01970 617834.**

bunk room and an easy-access downstairs twin ensuite. Plas Dolau was recently renovated with WTB grand aid to include meeting rooms, dining rooms, games room, a small tuck-shop and adjacent sports areas. Meals can be provided by prior arrangement or partly self-catering. Owners Pat Twigg and Tony Wheeler are well-organised and conscientious hosts who are a mine of information about sites and attractions in the surrounding area. The location is perfect for groups or individuals wishing to explore the heartland of Wales. It is a haven of rural tranquillity with plenty of nearby opportunities for walking, cycling, birdwatching, riding, fishing, golf and much more. Evening attractions in Aberystwyth include a leisure centre, tenpin bowling and a year-round cultural programme in the University Arts Centre. Open all year round, Plas Dolau - recently awarded a Welcome Host Gold Business Award - is ideally suited for youth groups, field courses, retreats and house parties. Booking is recommended. The entire mansion can be hired for a set fee per night, while for individuals the price ranges from £10 to £20 per night.

LLANFARIAN   MAP 2 REF F4
3 miles S of Aberystwyth off the A487

The Royal Oak in Llanfarian is a handsome stonebuilt and whitewashed Free House. Owners Mike and Di Barr offer all their guests a warm welcome, and this friendly public house is popular with locals and holiday-makers alike. Traditionally a fishermen's pub, the owners are happy to arrange fishing holidays for their guests; other activities to take advantage of in the area include walking, pony-trekking and bird-watching. There are five comfortable and tastefully decorated rooms. Close to Aberystwyth on the main Aberystwyth-Cardigan road, as well as to the sea and spectacular countryside, this impressive establishment dates back to the early 18th century. The walls of the 'Elizabethan Lounge' feature the coats of arms of the Welsh counties. There is also a handsome Tudor-style carved fireplace and beamed ceilings, and many of the pub's original features are still intact. In the intimate candlelit dining room, guests choose from the

**The Royal Oak, Llanfarian, Aberystwyth SY23 4BS
Tel: 01970 615355.**

extensive menu of hearty favourites, home-cooked and home-prepared to order. The pub has a good range of beers, real ales and spirits, and an excellent wine list.

LLANRHYSTUD
MAP 2 REF F4
8 miles SW of Aberystwyth off the A487

Penrhos Golf and Country Club offers an exciting 18 hole championship length course, part parkland, part meadowland with spectacular views over Cardigan Bay. To the south of this village, the former hill-forts **Castell Bach** and **Castell Mawr** are separated by a vale known as *'the dell of slaughter'* in reference to an ancient battle. To the east are the remains of the castle **Caer Penrhos** overlooking the village. Built around 1148 by Cadwaladr Ap Gruffydd, the castle was razed to the ground about 50 years later to avoid it falling into a rival's hands.

LLANON
MAP 2 REF F4
9 miles SW of Aberystwyth off the A487

The **Old Cottage** in Llanon, is a small thatched cottage (now under a tin roof) with antique furnishings, near old ruins and a small public park. A booklet about the cottage, its history and surroundings is available in local shops.

A B&B with a difference, **The Barn House** offers 'stress-buster' breaks which include an individual therapy session comprising aromatherapy massage, reflexology or Indian head massage treatment. Owners Mary and Tony Rees are a very friendly, mature couple with a wealth of knowledge

The Barn House, Llanon, Aberystwyth, Ceredigion SY23 5LZ
Tel: 01974 202581

on the area and also on aromatherapy and reflexology. Mary is a fully qualified therapist who has many years of practical experience with a wide range of age groups. Situated in the heart of Red Kite country, off the main road between Aberystwyth and Cardigan, close to the sea, this picturesque B&B occupies a handsome stonebuilt building overlooking Cardigan Bay. Decorated with an eye towards comfort and quality throughout, the four guest rooms offer magnificent views over the surrounding countryside. For breakfast, guests have a choice of Full English or Continental, each expertly prepared and presented. There is a wealth of attractions nearby, including facilities for golfing, fishing, pony-trekking and more. The owners are also happy to arrange guided walks on request.

PONTERWYD   MAP 2 REF G4

10 miles E of Aberystwyth off the A4120

It was at a pub in this village that the linguist George Borrow, who once worked for the British and Foreign Bible Society and wrote a book on gypsies, dried out after staggering through a peat bog.

LLYWERNOG   MAP 2 REF G4

9 miles W of Aberystwyth off the A44

At **Llywernog Silver-Lead Mine Museum**, friendly guides kit visitors out with helmet and lamp to explore secret chambers where the lead and silver veins were worked in 1790. Welsh and Cornish miners once toiled by candlelight to blast out the rich ore. The award-winning exhibitions feature videos, splashing waterwheels, quaint machinery, a panning area, heritage trail and a unique narrow-gauge tramway ride. Mineral specimens and mining souvenirs are sold.

ABERAERON

At the mouth of the Aeron Valley, pleasant walks can be taken through woodland by the river. Returning to town by crossing Lovers' Bridge, the path passes by a pond where the waterwheel stands that helped to generate the power for the mill that now houses a crafts workshop.

Aberaeron is delightful, with brightly painted Georgian-style houses, especially around **Alban Square**. These are the result of astute town planning, which was initiated in the early 19th century by the Reverend Alban Gwynne, who was happy to spend his wife's inheritance on dredging the Aeron Estuary to create a new port for mid-Wales. This influence was instrumental in turning the place from a small fishing hamlet into a busy port. The town was also famed for its shipbuilding; the schooners and sloops constructed near the harbour were once highly sought after.

Owner Jim Dalton brought a wealth of experience to running **The Black Lion** public house in Aberaeron when he took over as owner early in 1998. Here in this small coastal village on the main road between Aberystwyth and Cardigan, this welcoming redbrick pub with attractive white trim is a focal point of local life, and an attraction for holidaymakers and, at weekends, local amateur football sides who play on the vast adjacent green.

The Black Lion, Alban Square, Aberaeron, Ceredigion SA46 0LT
Tel: 01545 571382.

This three-storey establishment has a relaxing and peaceful beer garden, where guests can enjoy a quiet drink and a meal. Meals are served all day, and the menu offers a range of hot and cold favourites, all home-cooked and home-prepared. The pub is furnished with an eye towards a high standard of comfort. There is a pool room, and plans are afoot to convert the first floor into an intimate restaurant with separate smoking and non-smoking areas. For quaffing your thirst, there's a good range of real ales, including a different guest ale each week, as well as lagers, spirits and a selection of wines.

On the quay there is a **Sea Aquarium and Animal Kingdom Centre** which makes for an interesting visit. Here visitors can see the creatures and fish that live in the waters of Cardigan Bay, and learn about life at sea, the fish we eat and the path towards a sustainable future for fishing. Upstairs there is a collection of photographs of old Aberaeron taken by Percy Lloyd on glass plates in the 19th century. Coastal voyages can be arranged at the aquarium, in open rigid inflatable jet boats taking in the Heritage Coastline. An on-board marine naturalist provides an informed commentary about guillemots, razorbills, cormorants, dolphins, seals and much more. Here visitors will also find the **Hive on the Quay**, which provides the opportunity to see bees as well as sample their products. The harbour itself can be crossed by the cable car **Aeron Express**, a bizarre 1980s recreation of a Victorian airborne hand-pulleyed carriage.

Clos Pengarreg is a craft centre hosting demonstrations of etching, pottery, furniture, jewellery and candle-making, quilting, knitting and pyrography. Traditional farm buildings have been carefully converted into 18 award-winning individual workshops and retail outlets offering a selection of locally-produced food and crafts. **Gwinllan Ffynnon Las Vineyard**, though north of the 52nd parallel, produces some excellent wines, with a refreshingly flowery 'nose' and a clean, crisp, gooseberry-apple tang. Free wine-tastings are on offer at this fascinating site.

Aberaeron Golf Club is an ideal course for beginners, with a 9-hole pitch and putt course. Hot air balloon flights are launched from the golf course throughout the season. The course is located on the A487 north of Aberaeron.

Close to Aberaeron, **Llys Aeron** is a welcoming guest house. Aberaeron is on the main coastal road from Aberystwyth to Cardigan, and the surrounding area offers numerous opportunities for river walks, cycling and just enjoying the unspoilt natural beauties all around. The River Aeron

Llys Aeron, Lampeter Road, Aberaeron, Ceredigion SA46 OED
Tel: 01545 570276.

(known for its fishing) winds its way down the valley to Llanerchaeron, one of the latest additions to the National Trust, only 2 miles away. This distinguished house is stonebuilt with an attached conservatory and a large walled garden in which guests are welcome to relax. Owners Diana and Simon Mace bought the guest house in April 1998 and have spent the last year refurbishing the whole house, always with an eye towards maintaining its ambience and traditional feel, while ensuring a high standard of comfort and taste. They make sure every guest receives a warm welcome and friendly service. With the wealth of sites and attractions in the area, this superior guest house makes a good base.

AROUND ABERAERON

CILIAU AERON   MAP 2 REF F5
5 miles SE of Aberaeron off the A482

Llanerchaeron is a rare survivor of the core of Welsh gentry estate. It was acquired by the National Trust in 1994 having received minimal maintenance in recent decades. Parts of this property are open to visitors to see restoration work in progress at this early stage. The house was designed by John Nash and built in 1794-96. Tours available. Check with Tourist Information Centres for the full programme of events.

Llanerchaeron Estate

ABERARTH   MAP 2 REF F5
1 mile NE of Aberaeron off the A487

Sometimes unjustly overlooked because of the charm of its more illustrious neighbour, it is worth taking the time to stop off at this small, picturesque village. On a hill overlooking the village stands **St David's Church**. Founded in the 6th century and originally hidden from the sea, the church was rebuilt in 1860. It contains three early Christian inscribed stones from the 9th and 10th centuries.

PENNANT   Map 2 ref F5
3½ miles NE of Aberaeron off the B4577

This village was the home, in the 19th century, of a recluse named Mari Berllan Piter (Mary of Peter's Orchard). Supposedly granted magical powers, her exploits were legendary: when a miller refused to grind her corn, she made his mill wheel turn in the wrong direction; a young girl who stole an apple from Mari's orchard was forced to walk home backwards and sometimes, it is said, she turned into a hare. The ruins of Mari's cottage, known as The Witch's Cottage, can still be seen, surrounded by the now-overgrown orchard.

NEW QUAY

This is a small, busy resort whose harbour now boasts more yachts than fishing boats. Like other harbour towns, New Quay's shipbuilding and coastal trading met with decline in the 19th century as road and rail links developed. Nevertheless, the town retains a maritime charm. The poet Evan Thomas Rees (1690-1762) of Llanarth referred to fishermen of 'y Cai Newydd' who lost their lives at Pwll y Ci, near Aberystwyth, suggesting that Penpolion was originally the 'new quay'. An Admiralty survey undertaken in 1748 by Lewis Morris refers to the herring industry in Cardigan Bay employing 97 small sloops, 38 of which were employed between Aberaeron and New Key (sic).

Hand in hand with the shipbuilding and fishing industry here, smuggling was also rife. In 1795, New Quay was described as a place of 'infamous notoriety' and the headland was reputedly riddled with a network of caves used for storing contraband goods. The natural advantages of New Quay as a port and harbour of refuge led to its being considered at one point as a suitable spot for direct communication with Wicklow and Dublin. The first vessel to built in the area was a 36-ton sloop; the subsequent shipping boom brought a great deal of employment to the area, and saw the population rise to 2,000.

The sands and boating facilities have long been an attraction for holidaymakers in search of a pleasant break. The town's **yacht club** welcomes all visitors in their activities. The north beach leads to the rocky headland, **New Quay Head**, where an invigorating path steers along the top of the sheer drops to **Bird Rock**, home to many sea birds.

New Quay is home to one of Wales' most bizarre annual rituals. Every New Year's Eve, the whole town dons fancy dress and spends most of the night locked into numerous pubs and dancing in the streets.

Along with Laugharne, Carmarthenshire, New Quay lays claim to being the original Llareggub in Dylan Thomas' *Under Milk Wood*. Thomas had an ambiguous relationship with New Quay: it is said he was disliked in the town, not least for his failure to pay his bills. It would seem he had his revenge, though: try spelling Llareggub backwards!

Several charter boats operate out of New Quay harbour, offering a wide range of deep-sea and inshore fishing trips - from 1-hour mackerel trips to 12-hour deep-sea trips. They also provide scenic tours along the Ceredigion Heritage Coast for wildlife and birdwatching enthusiasts. New Quay's **Bird Hospital** treats and returns to the wild any wild bird or mammal needing attention. It specialises in treating oiled seabirds. Visits by appointment only.

The coast to the south of New Quay is best described as rugged, suggestive of the towering cliffs of north Cornwall. There is a Heritage Coastal path which threads its way along the clifftops down through Cwmtudu to Llangrannog and beyond. In the mornings it is possible to see dolphins and Atlantic seals playing in the inaccessible coves. To the northeast of the village are the long sandy beaches of **Traeth Gwyn** (white beach) and **Cei Bach** (little quay). Once a hive of shipbuilding activity, they are now peaceful and secluded.

The Penrhiwllan Inn is located in this quiet seaside hamlet with its rugged coastline and a Heritage Coastal Path which wends its way along the cliff tops, passing two small Iron Age promontory forts. You can see dolphins and Atlantic seals splashing about in the secluded coves. From the village this coastal path winds up over the old cliff quarry to the headland by the former Coast Guard station. Originally built in 1750 as a series of cottages, this attractive inn boasts beamed ceilings, which are encrusted with horse brasses. Other original features include the exposed stone walls and flagstone floors. The extensive carvery, grill and bar menus offer such favourites as Welsh black steer and Welsh lamb, steak and scampi, accom-

Penrhiwllan Inn, New Quay, Ceredigion SA45 9RF
Tel: 01545 560471.

panied by a selection of mainly organically-grown vegetables. There are also vegetarian and children's menus. The spacious beer garden is just the place to relax and enjoy a quiet meal and drink. The three guest rooms (2 doubles and 1 twin) are very comfortable and welcoming.

AROUND NEW QUAY

LLANARTH   MAP 2 REF E5
3 miles SE of New Quay off the B4342

A local story goes that one night the Devil tried to steal the bell from Llanarth Church. He made such a noise that he woke the vicar who, armed with a bell, a book and a candle, climbed up into the belfry to investigate. By solemnly repeating the name of Christ, the vicar managed to drive the Devil to the top of the tower and forced him to jump off. In the graveyard there is a strangely scarred stone which is said to bear the marks made by the Devil when he fell.

Crochendy Llanarth Pottery is a thriving workshop where visitors can see pots being hand-thrown and hand-decorated. The range of pots is excellent, with a choice of sizes, glazes and styles to suit every taste.

LLANINA   MAP 2 REF E5
1 miles E of New Quay off the A486

The tiny village of Llanina has a long tradition of fishing. In the early 8th century, so a local story tells, among the villagers was a fisherman, his wife and daughter. One day, during a violent storm, a ship was wrecked on nearby rocks and the fisherman and his daughter rowed out several times to rescue the sailors. Once safe, the family, unable to understand the language spoken by the shipwrecked strangers, sent for a monk who told the fisherman and his family that they had saved King Ina of England. In thanksgiving, the King built a church from which the present church, Ina's Church, takes its name. **Cerrig Ina**, Ina's Stones, can be seen offshore and mark the spot where the original church stood.

TREGARON

The Tuesday market here brings together farmers, traders and livestock from the surrounding area. In the square there is a statue of Henry Richard, the liberal MP and son of Tregaron, a vociferous supporter of disarmament sometimes known as the 'Apostle of Peace'.

Celtic crafts are the speciality of **Canolfan Crefft Cymru**. Meanwhile, the **Welsh Gold Centre** (Canolfan Aur Cymru), established since 1971, has an international reputation as the premier Welsh Celtic craftshop. Here, Celtic art does not consist only of images from a distant past; it is a living and ever-developing tradition, created for today by today's Celts. Famous gold and silver jewellery is fashioned on the premises, and there is also a unique collection of fine and unusual gifts reflecting the wealth of Celtic tradition and heritage.

Cors Caron National Nature Reserve occupies an area originally covered by a glacier. At the end of the last Ice Age this glacier melted, creating a natural lake which filled with sediment and vegetation. The peat surface grew, creating three distinctive domes above the original lake bed level. Over 170 species of bird have been recorded here, including the rare Red Kite, Buzzards, Hen Harriers and Sparrow Hawks. The Old Railway Walk is accessible at all times.

Here in the lovely village of Tregaron, **Neuaddlas Guest House** has been welcoming visitors from far and wide for more than 20 years. Attracting walkers, birdwatchers, youth and school groups, and other visitors who come to sample the delights of this region in the heart of Red Kite country, this friendly and informal guest house boasts 11 rooms (six ensuite), all very comfortable and tastefully decorated. With facilities to accommodate people with disabilities, this attractive late 19th-century brickbuilt establishment - with its extensive paddock to the front - has been renovated and refurbished to offer the highest standard of comfort and quality. The full English breakfast is a hearty affair, to set you up for a day's sightseeing and exploring. Evening meals are available upon request. Owner Jacky Davies is happy to cater for her guests' special dietary needs, and is a cheerful and thoughtful hostess at all times.

**Neuaddlas Guest House, Tregaron, Ceredigion SY25 6LG
Tel: 01974 298905.**

AROUND TREGARON

CAPEL BETWS LLEUCU MAP 2 REF F5
5 miles W of Tregaron off the B4578

Set in the beautiful Aeron Valley, **Capel Betws Pony Centre and Farm Park** offers visitors fun, education and interest. You can explore the nature trail, featuring more than 50 plant species, butterflies and birds together with the farm animals and ponies.

PONTRHYDFENDIGAID MAP 2 REF G4
6 miles NE of Tregaron off the B4343

This village lies near the ford of the Blessed Virgin - where a mile and half to the southeast lie the ruins of **Strata Florida Abbey**. This Cistercian abbey in the *'Plain of Flowers'* was founded in 1164, only to have its lands overrun by Rhys ap Gruffyd two years later. In 1184, he refounded the Abbey and most of the ruins date from this period onwards. During the 12th and 13th centuries the Abbey acted as the political and religious centre for Wales; in 1238 Welsh princes swore their allegiance to Llewelyn the Great's son, Dafydd, in the Abbey. It also flourished in terms of wealth during this period, mainly through wool from the sheep that grazed on its vast lands which spread as far as Rhayader to the east. After the Dissolution, the lands passed through various hands; they are now in the hands of Cadw. The ruins consist mainly of the cloister and chapter house by the church which today serves the parish of Pontrhydfendigaid. Inside there are remains that have been integrated into the church and in the north transept stands a memorial to Dafydd ap Gwilym, considered by some to have been one of the greatest Welsh poets in the 14th century. His remains are thought to be buried either here or at Talley.

A pleasant walk can be made beyond the Abbey in a northeasterly direction to Llyn Teifi, small lakes that are the source of the River Teifi. **Cors Caron Nature Reserve**, an almost 2,000-acre reserve, containing the largest peat bog in Wales. With the River Teifi running through it, the reserve attracts the interest of botanists and ornithologists alike, for obvious reasons.

DEVIL'S BRIDGE MAP 2 REF G4
10 miles N of Tregaron off the A4120

This is the destination of the **Rheidol Railway** and the beauty spot attracts many who come to view the waterfalls, which drop 300 feet as the river changes direction from south to west. An iron bridge built in 1901 straddles the top of the falls and, just below it, there is a stone bridge from

1708. Further down still lies the original **Pont-y-gwr-Drwg** (Bridge of the Devil). The bridge is thought to have been built in the 11th century by monks from the Strata Florida Abbey eight miles south. Nature trails and footpaths descend the 94 steps of Jacob's Ladder to view the falls.

There are many footpaths to follow for different vantage points, the Forestry Commission have trails and picnic sites at **The Arch**. The arch was erected by Thomas Johnes in 1810 to honour the Golden Jubilee of George III. He also transformed the area with forestation, planting the area with over four million trees as if in anticipation of the Forestry Commission.

LAMPETER

Lampeter has long been the centre for this part of the Teifi Valley, but is perhaps best known for **St David's College**. This world-renowned ecclesiastical college; predominantly Welsh-speaking, is the oldest degree institution in Wales, having been founded in 1822 by Bishop Thomas Burgess of St David's. The main university buildings include C B Cockerell's original stuccoed quadrangle of buildings dating from 1827, which were designed to imitate an Oxbridge college. The town's long-vanished castle motte lies underneath these buildings and forms an incongruous mound amid such order. Since 1971 the college has been integrated with the University of Wales, though the campus retains its own unique atmosphere.

Y Pantri is a charming and welcoming restaurant located in the heart of Lampeter. Owner Delyth Jones offers a warm Welsh welcome to all guests, and runs this attractive and cosy restaurant with an eye towards maintaining a high standard of service and comfort. Catering for both children and adults, the restaurant is relaxed and informal. The menu offers a good variety of traditional favourites, freshly prepared by Mrs Jones. She bakes daily, and much of the produce used in making the delights on the menu comes from her husband's farm. A range of hearty Welsh fare is served here;

**Y Pantri, High Street, Lampeter
Ceredigion SA48 7BB
Tel: 01570 422304.**

hot and cold meals available include fresh sandwiches, salads, main courses such as Welsh black steak, grill specials, seafood and Welsh lamb, as well as an excellent range of scones, cakes, pies and puddings. Full breakfasts and children's meals are also available.

There is always something happening in this small, friendly market town. For those who enjoy shopping, the ladies and gents fashion shops sell superb designer labels. Most of them are old established family businesses drawing custom from as far afield as London. The town has a pleasant mixture of Georgian and Victorian buildings with many choices of places to eat or stay.

The Black Lion Royal Hotel, owned and run by Ednyfed and Janet Jones with the help of their children Emlyn and Rowena, is an old coaching inn dating as far back as the 16th century. The hotel is full of atmosphere, character and natural charm which endear it to everyone who comes here, whether to drink, eat or stay a while. There are two bars: The Stable Bar, much loved by locals, and The Residents Bar. Both are well stocked and an excellent menu is on offer in either one, with a good selec-

The Black Lion Royal Hotel, High Street, Lampeter
Ceredigian SA48 7BG Tel: 01570 422172 Fax: 01570 423630.

tion of vegetarian dishes. In the restaurant there is a delicious grill menu or one can choose from the exquisitely prepared table d'hote menu. There are 16 ensuite bedrooms, each individually furnished with pretty drapes and bed covers. The rooms all have colour television, radio alarms, direct dial telephones, central heating and generously supplied beverage trays. Lampeter lies in the valley of the River Teifi, a river noted for salmon and trout fishing. The hotel once again has its own stretch of private fishing on the River Teifi. Shooting - rough or driven shoots - can also be arranged. It is a convenient position to visit the coast, Cambrian Mountains, the Roman Gold Mines at Dolaucothi and many other places of beauty and interest. Open all year; children welcome. No pets. Credit cards accepted. No disabled access.

The Lampeter Group of the Ramblers' Association lead a series of country walks throughout the year - a wonderful way to view the beautiful countryside of Ceredigion and the Lampeter Group welcomes visitors and new members. Telephone 01570 480041 for more details.

AROUND LAMPETER

LLANWNNEN   MAP 2 REF F5
5 miles W of Lampeter off the A475/B4337

Pantycelyn Guest House is located in a peaceful valley about five miles west of the small market town of Lampeter. Convenient for Aberystwyth and Carmarthen, and the coastal resorts of Aberaeron and Newquay, this is a charming and traditional stonebuilt guest house. The three ensuite rooms (double, twin and single) are tastefully decorated throughout, and there are magnificent views over the peaceful and unspoilt natural beauty

**Pantycelyn Guest House, Llanwnnen, Lampeter
Ceredigion SA48 7LW Tel/Fax: 01570 434455.**

of the Teifi Valley. The sitting room is comfortable and has a television, good selection of books and leaflets full of information on local sites and attractions. All rooms are non-smoking. There's a full cooked breakfast every morning, and packed lunches and evening meals available if requested. Owners Huw and Ann Jenkins offer all their guests a warm welcome to this secluded and tranquil 10-acre Welsh Cob stud farm. Excellent for touring, walking, pony-trekking and birdwatching, this lovely guest house makes a good base from which to explore the delights of Ceredigion. Well-behaved dogs are welcome, and overnight grazing or stabling available for visitors with horses.

CRIBYN   MAP 2 REF F5
3 miles NW of Lampeter off the B4337

Noah's Ark is a working small-holding of rare-breed farm animals and poultry set amid peaceful countryside, with an attractive traditional farm house. On show are ducks, geese, fancy fowl, pigs, rabbits, guinea pigs, cows, chinchilla, horses, goats, pheasants, pea fowl, llamas and more.

LLANDDEWI-BREFI   MAP 2 REF G5
7 miles NE of Lampeter off the B4343

This town was host to a synod in 519 which St David attended. They were then debating the Pelagian heresy, a doctrine advocating freedom of thought rather than the biblical version of original sin that determined the morality of the time. **St David's Church**, in the village, stands on a mound which tradition says rose as St David preached during the synod. The church itself dates from the 13th century and inside contains some old inscribed stones: one is known as St David's Staff and another has an Ogham inscription that has been suggested commemorated a heretic of the sort that St David was denouncing.

Close by are the sites of several hill-forts including **Llanfair Clydogau**, where the Romans mined for silver, which sits by the Sarn Helen - a military road. The road once connected a gold mine in the south at Dolaucothi with a fort at Bremia in the north.

CARDIGAN

The demise of Cardigan as a maritime port has not diminished the town's charm, which is enhanced by the six-arched **Teifi Bridge** spanning the river. Of ancient origin, this bridge was rebuilt in 1726. In fact it is the River Teifi which gives Cardigan its Welsh name, Aberteifi. The silting of the estuary along with the arrival of the railway were the main causes of Cardigan's decline from a once-busy port that had over 300 ships registered here. The town is, however, an ancient borough, having received its first charter in 1199. The few remains of the castle, which fell to Parliament forces in 1645 and conceal a turbulent history, stand close by the river. Before then, Cardigan Castle had changed hands probably some 16 times during its use as the Welsh and English fought for supremacy in the area. The castle is also thought to be the site of the first Eisteddfod, in 1176.

The river is still fished for trout, and some still use the traditional coracle boat. Dating from the pre-Christian era, coracles were once common on many of Britain's rivers and they have changed little over the centuries.

In the town, the Victorian **Guildhall** is a noteworthy building where markets are often held that are sure to attract the interested visitor. The tiny **Museum** has displays of fishing memorabilia, while the well-known **Theatr Mwldan** hosts an innovative programme of art, theatre, cinema and music events. The **Custom House Shop and Gallery** boasts three large exhibition spaces filled with changing exhibits of arts, crafts and contemporary design, many produced by local artists and craftspeople. Hand-made furniture, sculpture, architectural stained glass, greetings cards, exclusive designer gifts combined with home and gardening accessories, all set in Cardigan's original 18th-century Custom House.

The **Welsh Wildlife Centre** is a superb 260-acre nature reserve owned and managed by The Wildlife Trust (West Wales) offers a picturesque and extensive footpath network (most are suitable for all abilities) leading into woodland, reed beds, meadows and to the River Teifi. The award-winning Visitor Centre includes a restaurant with panoramic views of the reserve, a gift shop and an exhibition area. Visitors can also enquire about educational programmes, wildlife events and guided walks. Cardigan Ramblers meets fortnightly for walks of various lengths. For information telephone 01239 711057. The surrounding coastline has many places of beauty and interest to visit.

AROUND CARDIGAN

LLANGRANNOG   MAP 2 REF E5
9 miles NE of Cardigan off the B4334

This is one of the most popular resorts in the area and one of the most attractive villages along the Ceredigion coast. It lies in a narrow valley and is reminiscent of a Cornish fishing village. The surrounding headland and cliffs are National Trust property and offer excellent walks and some rather dramatic scenery. As well as sustaining a thriving shipbuilding industry the sheltered coves around Llangrannog provided perfect hiding places for smuggling activities. Along with tobacco, tea, wine and spirits, salt was a valuable booty as it was necessary for food preservation. On the beach here, so the story goes, the Devil, having a toothache, pulled and then threw the tooth to land at the rocky crop known as **Carreg Bica**.

The **Walled Garden of Pigeonsford** is a 1-acre Georgian walled garden replanted with botanical collections of herbaceous plants and shrubs, vegetables and fruits, all maintained as a working garden. The outdoor contemporary sculpture exhibition dots the 14-acre landscape of shrubbery, woodland and rolling countryside. There is also an interesting maize maze. Plants, fruits and vegetables are for sale in season.

PENBRYN   MAP 2 REF E5
8½ miles NE of Cardigan off the B4334

Penbryn's **Church of St Michael** overlooks a valley of woodland stretching down towards a large beach and the sea. The shallow beach is ideal for days out by the sea, and the footpaths around offer pleasant walks. The church contains artefacts such as a weeping chancel; nearby, remains have been uncovered of an Iron Age settlement. At **Dyffryn Bern** a short distance inland, a standing stone bears the inscription 'Corbalengi lacit Ordovs'. This is thought to refer to a battle in the vicinity involving the Ordovices tribe of mid-Wales.

TRESAITH   MAP 2 REF E5
8 miles NE of Cardigan off the B4333

The River Saith becomes a waterfall to the east of this village and the safe, shallow beach that reveal golden sands and rock pools at low tide combine to attract families here. The village's name literally means *'seven beaches'*, but tradition has it that the name comes from seven princesses landing here after being cast away by their father.

ABERPORTH   MAP 2 REF E5
7½ miles NE of Cardigan off the B4333

The original village consisted of small, single-storied cottages with thick mud walls and thatched roofs. Leading a simple and hard life, the villagers relied on farming and fishing to survive. At one time Aberporth became famous for its herring industry; the fish came to feed and spawn in the shallow waters of this sheltered coast. Today the village is a thriving resort, particularly popular with sailing boats.

Felinwynt Rainforest and Butterfly Centre here in Aberporth has a tropical house where visitors can wander amidst exotic plants and butterflies. The Rainforest Exhibition is home to many fascinating displays and information.

RHYDLEWIS   MAP 2 REF E5
10 miles E of Cardigan off the B4334

Rhydlewis Fishery provides good trout fishing: Tourist Information Centres have all the necessary information.

Nestling here in the quiet Teifi Valley among the gently rolling hills of west Wales, **Llwyn-Yr-Eos** is a charming early 19th-century farmhouse offering bed and breakfast accommodation. Tastefully decorated throughout, the two ensuite guest rooms are comfortable and pleasant, both facing south and overlooking the farmhouse garden, with views across to the Preseli Hills. Just four miles from the lovely National Trust beach at Penbryn and the safe beaches at Tresaith, Llangrannog and Aberporth, there are a wealth of secluded coves and 'secret' beaches nearby which can be discovered while walking the cliff paths. The farmland slopes gently down to the pretty River Ceri. The surrounding countryside is among the most beautiful and unspoilt in Britain. Keen walkers will be glad of the proximity of the Preseli Hills and the Pembrokeshire Coast Path. Fresh local produce and home-grown lamb and vegetables are used whenever possible in the preparation of the excellent meals available.

**Llwyn-Yr-Eos, Rhydlewis, Llandysul, Ceredigion SA44 5QU
Tel: 01239 851268.**

MWNT   MAP 2 REF D5
4 miles N of Cardigan off the A487

This beauty spot was on the Pilgrims' Route to Bardsey Island in the north
- the saints' burial ground. The tiny **Church of the Holy Cross** dates from
around 1400 and stands on the site of a much earlier Celtic church, originally built in a hollow to hide it from view and protect it from possible
raids from the sea. The church was once a strategic point on the pilgrims'
route to Bardsey Island off the Llyn Peninsula, where 20,000 Celtic Saints
are said to be buried. Owned by the National Trust, the cliffs, rocky headland and beach attract many visitors.

GWBERT-ON-SEA   MAP 2 REF D5
4 miles NW of Cardigan off the B4548

This small resort on the east side of the River Teifi is an excellent place for
cliff walks and surveying the estuary and its wildlife. Boat trips can be
taken to **Cardigan Island**, home of seabirds such as terns, seals and wild
Soay sheep. **Cardigan Island Coastal Farm Park** occupies a superb location on scenic headland overlooking the nature reserve of Cardigan Island
(200 metres offshore). Grey seals breed in the caves below the Farm Park
cliffs (safely fenced) and can be seen most days. The waters are regularly
visited by Cardigan Bay's bottle-nosed dolphins. Rare chuffs nest on the
cliffs. Visitors can also feed friendly farm animals - goats, sheep, llama,
ducks, geese and more. Meet the Shetland ponies, pigs and rare breed cattle, and say 'G'day' to Bruce, the wallaby. Refreshments available in summer.

The hamlet is named after St Gwbert, who is thought to have landed
here. One of the nearby caves is still known as Ogof Eglwys, or **Church
Cave.** Cardigan Golf Club in Gwbert is an 18-hole meadowland/links course.
Founded in 1895, in 1996 it was the venue for the Welsh Team Championships.

ST DOGMAELS   MAP 2 REF D5
1 mile W of Cardigan off the A487

Monks of the French order of Tiron founded St Dogmaels Abbey in the
12th century. At **St Dogmaels Abbey and Water Mill** the church adjacent
to the abbey ruins features an inscribed Sagranus stone. The stone's inscribed markings and the Latin inscription on its face provided the key to
deciphering the ancient Goidelic language. Near the abbey is Y Felin - the
mill - a water-powered flour mill still producing and selling flour ground
in the traditional way.

CILGERRAN
MAP 2 REF D6
2 miles SE of Cardigan off the A478

The remains of **Cilgerran Castle** can still be seen sitting on a rocky promontory overlooking the River Teifi. The ruins have inspired artists such as Turner in the past and still continue to do so for today's painters. The castle is thought to have been begun around 1093, but was strengthened by Gerald de Windsor who was granted it by Henry I. Thereafter it changed hands many times, being partially sacked by Rhys ap Gruffyd in 1164, retaken by the Earl of Pembroke in 1204 before Llewelyn the Great captured it in 1233. Its final rebuild happened then but 100 years later the castle was regarded as a ruin. However, the remains are inspiring and a

Cilgerran Castle

visit is highly recommended. The castle is also the legendary site of the abduction of Nest, the Welsh Helen of Troy, by a lovestruck Prince Owain of Powys in 1109. Her husband, Gerald of Pembroke, escaped by slithering down a chute through the castle walls.

North of the village is **Cardigan Wildlife Park**, a 50 acre area of riverbank and woodland with nature trails, hides for observation and a picnic spot.

LLECHRYD
MAP 2 REF D6
2 miles W of Cardigan off the A484

Set in the beautiful valley of the River Teifi, there is an old five-arched bridge in the village; the church is known as the **Coracle Church**.

LLANDYSUL
MAP 2 REF E6
15 miles E of Cardigan off the A486

On the main Cardigan-Aberystwyth road, just a few miles from the sea, Llandysul is a peaceful and picturesque village which attracts holidaymakers to its scenic rural delights. Here, the **Brynhoffnant Inn** is housed in an impressive early-Victorian stone-built building. This attractive inn boasts

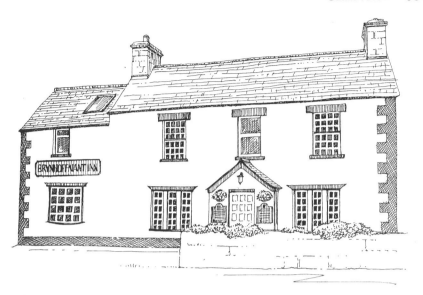

**Brynhoffnant Inn, Brynhoffnant, Llandysul, Ceredigion SA44 6DU
Tel: 01239 654413.**

many original features including the large open fireplace and beamed ceilings. The walls are adorned with an extensive bottle collection and a smaller grouping of cups, jugs and brass plates. The atmosphere is relaxed and friendly. There is an intimate dining area where a good variety of meals are served, and a secluded beer garden affording wonderful views of the coastline. There is a good range of ales, beers, lagers, wines and spirits on offer. Owners Mark and Jenny Hartwell have only recently taken over this distinctive public house, and are welcoming and vivacious hosts. They have plans for future development with an eye towards enhancing the existing pub while retaining its many traditional features.

Llandysul is another centre for the wool industry, and Maesllyn is a working museum that is well worth a visit. Llandysul was also the birthplace, in the early 19th century, of Christmas Evans, a Baptist minister who was famed for his fiery, emotional sermons. Becoming a Baptist because his ideal choice, the Presbyterians, demanded academic standards he hadn't achieved; he preached mainly in the Lleyn and Anglesey.

CAPEL DEWI
MAP 2 REF F6
17 miles E of Cardigan on the B4459

Rock Mills Woollen and Water Mill was established in 1890 by John Morgan, whose descendants still weave here. The machinery is powered by a water wheel which also drives a small alternator providing the lighting. The mill once provided power to the neighbouring church. From pure new wool the mill produces bedspreads, blankets, rugs, table mats and fabrics. This is one of the last traditional mills where the entire process from fleece to fabric may be viewed.

3 Pembrokeshire

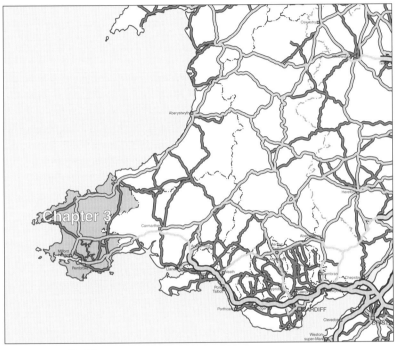

Known as Sir Benfro in Welsh, Pembrokeshire is home to Britain's only Coastal National Park. The spectacular grandeur and tranquil beauty of one of Europe's leading holiday destinations are truly impressive. Visitors to this region can take a walk along 200 miles of coast path, visit the island bird sanctuaries, and enjoy the area's castles together with Victorian Tenby and Britain's smallest city, St David's.

The north Pembrokeshire coastline between Cardigan and St David's is quieter than the more popular and populous southern coastline. The places to stay here are small, while the rugged, rocky coastline consists of a succession of headlands, little bays and occasional sandy beaches. One feature, above all else, dominates this part of Wales: the magnificent Pembrokeshire Coast National Park, one of the most spectacular stretches of coastal natural beauty in Europe. The Pembrokeshire Coast National Park is 180 miles long. Its starting point on the south-facing shoreline is Amroth, near Tenby. The park then runs right the way around to the ruggedly beautiful southwestern tip of Wales and up along the north-facing coast almost to Cardigan. From Amroth in the south to Poppit Sands in the north visitors can follow this most stunning coastline, varying from the huge wave-washed cliffs at Castlemartin to sweeping golden beaches such as Whitesand Bay, Marloes and Newport. In between there are the small bustling harbours of Little Haven, Solva and Lower Fishguard, the buzzing holiday resorts of Saundersfoot and Tenby, and hidden smugglers' coves. Offshore the horizon is dotted with islands - Skokholm, Skomer, Grassholm and Ramsey are wildlife havens, while Caldey has a modern Cistercian monastery and 12th-century priory.

Walking enthusiasts sing the praises of Pembrokeshire, for there's a long-distance footpath which travels almost the entire length of the National Park. The most popular sections of the coast path and, indeed, the most ruggedly inspiring, are those around St David's Head and the Marloes Peninsula, either side of Bride's Bay and the stretch from Manorbier castle to the tiny cliff chapel at Borsherson. Most visitors are content to walk short stretches of it and, whether undertaking the full length or shorter stages, walkers spot a great variety of seabirds including guillemots, cormorants and oystercatchers. Pembrokeshire really is a birdwatcher's paradise.

Although essentially centred around coastal areas, the Park does include the Preseli Hills which lie to the south between Fishguard and Cardigan. An open, brown moorland dotted with forest and rocky outcrops, the range is reminiscent of Dartmoor. Flocks of mountain sheep graze here, as do mountain ponies. The wealth of prehistoric archaeology also draws people to the area. The hills are dotted with cairns, burial chambers and standing stones, and they are also famous for providing the bluestones used to create Stonehenge. Local traditions are important in this corner of Wales. South Pembrokeshire, for example, still has a reputation for being the 'little England beyond Wales' because of its English-speaking population and Anglicised place names, while north Pembrokeshire fosters the Welsh language and customs.

TENBY

Retaining its charming medieval character together with its crooked lanes leading down to a picturesque harbour, it is easy to see why Tenby is such a popular resort. Tenby has lovely sheltered beaches and rock coves. The 13th-century town wall is beautifully preserved, and retains many of its original towers and its superb 14th-century arched gateway. A moat once ran the length of what is today a tree-lined street. There are a great many antique treasures in Tenby, including the Five Arches, a fortified gate which is part of the medieval wall enclosing the old town.

On the way down to the quay is the **Tudor Merchant's House**, a relic of Tenby's prosperous seafaring days and a fine example of a comfortable townhouse of about 500 years ago. It features gabled 15th-century architecture, with a Flemish chimney. Three walls boast the remains of handsome frescoes.

St Mary's Church displays the building styles of several periods, the oldest being a 13th-century rebuilding of an earlier church. The church boasts a huge steeple. A plaque here commemorates the equals sign, a mathematical symbol invented locally. Much of the structure extant today dates from the 15th century, with extensive 19th-century modifications which reflect the two great periods of prosperity in the town.

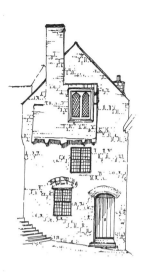

Tudor Merchant's House

The Evergreen in St Johns Hill is a welcoming public house. Originally a railway worker's cottage built in the 18th century, this large stone-built establishment stands opposite the attractive village green right on the outskirts of the busy seaside town of Tenby. Leanne and Dom Brodie have been at the Evergreen only since late 1998, bringing a wealth of enthusi-

The Evergreen, St Johns Hill, Tenby, Pembrokeshire SA70 8EY
Tel: 01834 843364.

asm to their task. They plan always to maintain a respect for the original features and character of the pub, including the exposed stone walls and beamed ceilings. The clientele is made up mostly of locals, but visitors are always made most welcome, as this pub boasts a lively and friendly atmosphere. This traditional pub, one of only two in Tenby, favours traditional pastimes such as pub card games and dominoes, with occasional live music, to the hub-bub of more modern establishments. There is a good selection of wines, spirits, lagers and ales on offer, to accompany the relaxed and sociable ambience.

Hallsville Hotel in Tenby is only a short walk from the centre of the old walled town, and just a few hundred yards from the Esplanade on South Beach. This spacious family-run hotel offers 10 very comfortable and well-appointed guest bedrooms, eight of which are ensuite. Owners Ann and Ron Davison have been at Hallsville Hotel for five years. They are friendly and welcoming hosts. Their clientele is varied, as the hotel attracts holiday-makers and those attracted to the area's excellent walking, birdwatching, cycling, boating and other water sports, and freshwater fishing.

Guests in this attractive establishment can choose between B&B or half-board accommodation. Vegetarian and other special diets are accommodated for. There is a licensed Cellar Bar with a variety of wines, spirits, liqueurs, bottled and draught beers, and a good

Hallsville Hotel, 28 Victoria Street, Tenby Pembrokeshire SA70 7DY Tel: 01834 842410.

selection of bar meals in the evenings. The first-floor guests' lounge is light and airy, with facilities for playing pool, watching television, playing a board game or browsing through the selection of books on hand.

The few remains of **Tenby Castle** stand on a small green promontory to the east of the harbour, where there is also a statue to Prince Albert. Within the castle site is a local history and geology museum. **Tenby Museum** began life as early as 1878 and, as well as having archaeological and historical material relating to the area and in particular a fascinating maritime section, the museum is also home to an impressive art gallery. The artist Augustus John was born at Belgrave House in the town in 1878, and a collection of his works and those of his sister Gwen can be found here.

Over the past 50 years and three generations of ownership by the Osborne family, the **Fourcroft Hotel** has garnered a reputation as one of Tenby's most luxurious hotels. This justly renowned establishment provides a high standard of service and comfort to its guests. With 46 ensuite rooms, this extensive and superior hotel occupies the cliffs above Tenby's sheltered North Beach. Commanding views over the old fishing harbour and across Carmarthen Bay, this impressive building forms part of a listed late-Georgian terrace built as individual summer homes. Private paths from the hotel lead down to the beach through several levels of beautiful landscaped gardens. Among this fine hotel's many amenities are a heated open-air swimming pool, giant chess board and figures, children's playground, large beach garden, spa, sauna and games room. There are also well-appointed function and conference rooms, and the attractive and comfortable Hollywood Bar. The traditional cooked breakfasts, bar meals at lunchtime and an extensive evening menu are all freshly prepared, making use of the best local produce. AA/RAC/WTB 3 Stars.

Fourcroft Hotel, North Beach, Tenby, Pembrokeshire SA70 8AP
Tel: 01834 842886 Fax: 01834 842888
email: tenby@walledtowns.com.

Heywood Mount Hotel, Heywood Lane, Tenby
Pembrokeshire SA70 8DD Tel/Fax: 01834 842087.

The Heywood Mount Hotel is a well-established and justly renowned establishment built in 1747 as an exclusive gentlemen's residence. Guests cannot fail to be impressed by the spaciousness, warmth and character of this 18th-century manor house. Owners Dennis and Jennifer Andrews are welcoming and friendly hosts who believe in providing value for money. They have retained the period elegance of this gracious hotel while providing every modern convenience. Standing in one acre of private grounds in an attractive and tree-lined lane, it provides true peace and tranquillity yet is just a 15-minute stroll from the centre of Tenby. The extensive gardens are immaculate, and the large and inviting guests' lounge opens out onto the south-facing rear lawns. The restaurant maintains a well-deserved reputation for quality and service. The 21 ensuite rooms are tastefully decorated and furnished. Golfers can enjoy discount rates at two local courses as well as an opportunity to play at Tenby's championship links. AA/RAC 2 Stars, highly acclaimed. WTB 4 Crowns/Highly Acclaimed rating. Mentioned in Ashley Courtenay's Guide to Highly Recommended Hotels.

AROUND TENBY

ST FLORENCE
MAP 1 REF D8
4 miles W of Tenby off the B4318/A4139

St Florence is a small and quiet village with three public houses, a post office, gift shop and a village shop. Located on the border of the National Park, the village is noted for its Flemish chimneys and Norman church. It has been awarded the Best Kept Village and Floral Village of Wales titles on several occasions, and was recently voted Floral Village of Britain. Just 4 miles from Tenby, it is ideally situated for exploring south Pembrokeshire with its interesting sights and golden beaches. **Heatherton Country Sports Park** offers an exciting range of outdoor pursuits, including a laser clay pigeon shoot, air pistol range, 18-hole pitch and putt golf course, indoor green bowls stadium, karting centre and bumper boat racing.

In the centre of the picturesque village of St Florence, **West Hall** is a three-storey stonebuilt farmhouse offering self-catering accommodation. This attractive establishment boasts a large walled front garden, palm-lined drive, and lawn with a Koi pond. Owners Alan and Dorothy Lesser are a

West Hall, St Florence, Nr Tenby, Dyfed SA70 8LW
Tel: 01834 871336.

friendly, mature couple who offer their guests a warm welcome and are always on hand, in the separate, annexed area to the rear of the house, should guests need assistance with anything. This very pleasant and comfortable self-catering facility boasts six spacious bedrooms in the main house, sleeping up to 15 people. The large kitchen features every modern amenity, including electric cooker, fridge/freezer and microwave oven. The first floor comprises a 36-foot long open-plan lounge/dining room with colour television, log fire and comfortable seating at one end, and a dining area at the other. Guests include walkers, cyclists, birdwatchers, and anyone wishing to sample West Hall's peaceful, relaxing atmosphere.

MANORBIER
MAP 1 REF D8

5 miles SW of Tenby off the A4139

The cliffs, beaches and bays of the south Pembrokeshire coast are magnificent. As early as the 12th century the small village of Manorbier, just around the headland from Tenby, was being described as the most pleasant spot in Wales. **Manorbier Castle** belonged to Giraldus Cambrensis, Gerald of Wales, the person responsible for that flattering description. Giraldus, a monk and chronicler, wrote the first account of life in medieval Wales, in which he proved to be a keen and accurate observer of the Welsh character. The castle is still in the hands of the family who have owned it since the 17th century. The well-preserved medieval fortress with its 13th-century chapel and other buildings that form part of this impressive site stand above the sandy beach. From the village church, across the valley, it can be viewed in all its glory.

CALDEY ISLAND
MAP 1 REF D8

3 miles SE of Tenby off the A4139

Short boat trips of two miles from Tenby harbour take visitors across to Caldey Island to the working monastery here. Apart from the modern abbey the island is also home to a 13th-century church and several ancient priory buildings. The Cistercian monks grow flowers from which they distil scent and, as well as purchasing samples of the famous ranges of creams and honeys, visitors can see an Ogham stone and also marvel at the variety and number of sea birds.

AMROTH
MAP 1 REF D7

5 miles NE of Tenby off the A477

Lying at the start of the **Pembrokeshire Coastal National Park** and **Wildfowl Centre**, this quiet village has a lovely beach. Amroth is also home to the delightful **Colby Woodland Garden**, with 8 acres of garden with unusual specimen trees, shrubs and fine collections of rhododendrons, azaleas and camellias; there are superb estate walks with views across Carmarthen Bay. The garden tea rooms serve a sampling of local delights: Prince's Gate water, Upton Farmhouse ice cream, Welsh cheeses and butter - everything home-made.

SAUNDERSFOOT
MAP 1 REF D7

3 miles NE of Tenby off the A478

Everything in this small but busy seaside resort revolves around its harbour, which is packed with colourful sailing craft in summer. The resort, which has an attractive sandy beach, is probably the busiest watersports centre in South Wales. The **Stepaside Heritage Project**, just up from the shore, offers an insight into the industrial history of the area.

BEGELLY   MAP 1 REF D7
4 miles NE of Tenby off the A478

Folly Farm features a pets' corner, museum, education centre and farm trail, milking parlour, adventure playground and restaurant, making for a fun and informative day out for all the family.

PEMBROKE

This historic town has well-preserved medieval town walls, but the structure that dominates everything else here is the mighty castle, a truly monumental piece of military architecture which stands on a rocky crag above the river. The Great Keep of **Pembroke Castle**, a towering building nearly 80 foot high, with walls 19 foot thick, is one of the most impressive of its kind in Europe. The castle was the birthplace of Harri Tudor, better known perhaps as Henry Tudor, a Welshman who defeated Richard III at the Battle of Bosworth to become Henry VII and founder of the Tudor dynasty. Close to the Castle are **The Museum of the Home**, with its collection of household utensils and appliances which span three centuries, and the Sea Historic Gallery, which also has a sea aquarium.

Across Monkton Pill, just half a mile from the castle, is **Monkton Priory**. Founded in 1098 by Arnulf de Montgomery for Benedictine monks, the priory was given to St Albans in 1473. The priory church, with its long, narrow barrel-vaulted nave and monastic chancel, was rearranged in the 14th century and, after lying in ruins for many years, restored in 1878-87.

Here in the busy county town of Pembroke with its castle and varied shops, **The Watermans Arms** is a welcoming retreat. Occupying a 17th-century building with later extensions, it is attractively set on the edge of a mill pond. This attractive pub is popular with locals and holiday-makers alike, many of whom come to enjoy the excellent birdwatching - an outdoor balcony makes an ideal vantage point for birdwatching. The exterior walls are brimming with lovely floral decorations which are varied twice a year. Owners John and Jan have only been at the Watermans Arms for a short time, but they have already made a great many improvements to this welcoming public house, all the while retaining the charm and elegance of its original ambience, with traditional features which include beamed ceilings. After extensive research, Jan and John have discovered that this is one of only six original pubs named the Watermans Arms in

**The Watermans Arms, 2 The Green, Mill Bridge
Pembrokeshire SA71 4NU Tel: 01646 682718.**

Britain. There is good-quality pub food on offer, such as steak and ale pie; meals can be taken in the bar or in the separate restaurant area.

AROUND PEMBROKE

PEMBROKE DOCK
2 miles NW of Pembroke off the A477

MAP 1 REF C8

Once an important naval dockyard, Pembroke Dock stands on the dividing line between the developed and undeveloped shores of the Milford Haven. Downstream there are large petro-chemical plants and oil terminals, built to take advantage of the Haven's deepwater channels that can accommodate today's giant supertankers.

Admiral Lord Nelson regarded the Milford Haven waterway as one of the world's best safe and sheltered anchorages. Regular trains run along the South Pembrokeshire line from Pembroke Dock to Whitland, stopping at Lamphey, Manorbier, Penally, Saundersfoot, Kilgetty and Narberth.

ST GOVAN'S HEAD
5 miles S of Pembroke off the B4319

MAP 1 REF C8

The cliff scenery is at its most spectacular around **Stack Rocks** and St Govan's Head, where the tiny religious site of **St Govan's Chapel** huddles amongst the rocks almost at sea level. This minute chapel, accessible by 52 stone steps, was built on the site of a holy well (which reputedly had miraculous healing powers) that once attracted pilgrims from far and wide.

Inside the chapel there is a vertical cleft in the rock which, according to legend, first miraculously opened to conceal St Govan from his enemies. Closing behind him, the rock did not reopen until the danger had passed. Apparently, a wish made while standing in the cleft and facing the rock will come true provided the person does not change his or her mind before turning around.

CAREW   MAP 1 REF D8
5 miles E of Pembroke off the A477

Carew Castle is one of the few that displays the development from Norman fortification to Elizabethan country manor. Here visitors can also see archaeological evidence of a much earlier settlement, dating back perhaps 2,000 years. Exploring the winding stairways, massive towers, lofty halls and many intricate rooms and passages of the castle is like stepping back

Carew Castle

into the past. Set in lovely countryside overlooking the 23 acre Mill Pond, the site also features one of only three restored tidal mills in Britain, with all its original machinery. The Story of Milling exhibition traces milling through the ages.

MILFORD HAVEN

As well as being the name of the town, Milford Haven is of course also the name of the huge natural harbour here. Described by Nelson as the best in the world for offering shelter to large ships, the harbour is some 10 miles long by up to 2 miles broad. Shipping has dominated life around the harbour for centuries, though during the past 100 years there have been periods of decline. During both World Wars, the Haven was busy with Atlantic convoys, but after 1945 there was a decline and trawling also begin to disappear. However, since the 1960s the Haven has developed as a major oil port and today is used by leading oil companies.

The town itself was the creation of R R Greville who, in the late 18th century, imported a group of Quaker whalers and contracted a Frenchman, J-L Barrallier, to lay out the town and dockyard in the squared pattern still seen today. The **Kaleidoscope Discovery Centre** offers the opportunity to experience puzzles and illusions created by electronic and computer gadgetry while, also at the Marina, the **Milford Haven Museum** is housed in a former whale oil warehouse dating from 1797, and follows the fortunes of the town and dockyard, with hands-on exhibits tracing the town's history from whaling port to premier oil port. In the graveyard at **St Katherine's Church** is the tomb of Sir William Hamilton, while within the church itself is a bible and prayer book presented by Nelson.

Occupying an enviable position right on the waterfront in Milford Haven, **Martha's Vineyard** is a superior restaurant - the perfect place for anyone who enjoys good food, especially seafood, in a friendly, relaxed and informal atmosphere. With a first-floor terrace bar and à la carte restaurant commanding spectacular views over the marina and Cleddau estuary, the restaurant is intimate and tastefully decorated, with the ac-

Martha's Vineyard, Milford Marina, Milford Haven
Pembrokeshire SA73 3AA Tel: 01646 697083.

cent firmly on comfort. Margaret Roblin is the polite and conscientious owner. She and her friendly, efficient staff contribute a great deal to making a visit to this wonderful restaurant a very enjoyable experience. The menu, as might be expected in a restaurant so near to the waterfront, specialises in locally caught fish, as well as deep-sea fish. Among the many choice favourites, the menu boasts unusual varieties not usually found in the UK, including Orange Roughy, Cardinal and Sabre fish. This fine establishment is open seven days a week.

One claim to fame which Milford Haven did not ask for was the 1996 grounding of the oil tanker *The Sea Empress*. Happily, since that time the beaches and surrounding area have been thoroughly cleaned and, thanks to the efforts of both man and nature, the region has recovered.

AROUND MILFORD HAVEN

MARLOES
MAP 1 REF B7

9 miles W of Milford Haven off the B4327

This inland village, near **Wooltrack Point**, has a sandy bay about a mile to the southwest. At the western extremity of the bay is **Gateholm Island**, its name coming from the Norse for Goat Island, which is actually only an island at high tide. The pagan custom of hunting the wren, a bird that is meant to embody the evils of winter, was strongly followed in Wales until the end of the 19th century. In Pembrokeshire the hunting took place on Twelfth Night, when the captured bird would be placed in a carved, be-ribboned 'wren-house'. The wren-house would then be carried around the town by four men singing songs about the hunt. A wren-house from Marloes can be seen in the Welsh Folk Museum in Cardiff.

DALE
MAP 1 REF B7

8 miles W of Milford Haven off the B4327

This delightful little sailing and watersports centre stands at the approach to the Dale Peninsula on the mouth of Milford Haven. At **St Ann's Head**, the southern tip of the peninsula, a coastguard and lighthouse station keeps a close watch over dangerous, rocky shores at the entrance to the Haven. This is also one of the windiest places in Britain where gusts have been known to exceed 100 miles an hour. But the other side of the climatic coin is Dale's sunshine record, for it is also one of the sunniest places in the country with an annual average of 1800 hours of sunshine a year - that's 5 hours a day, on average. This part of Pembrokeshire is dotted with little coastal centres, too small to be called resorts in the usual sense of the word, which are perfect for lovers of the quieter style of seaside holidays.

ST ISHMAELS

MAP 1 REF C7

6 miles W of Milford Haven off the B4327

This small village on the **Marloes and Dale Peninsula** is named after a 6th-century colleague of St Teilo. There is a local tale attached to Mullock Bridge, north of the village in the direction of Marloes. Sir Rhys ap Thomas of Carew Castle is said to have promised Richard III that if Henry Tudor passed through Pembroke it would be by riding over his body. When Henry landed at Mill Bay, to salve his conscious Sir Rhys lay under the bridge as Henry rode across it. Thomas then switched allegiances and rode swiftly to Carew Castle to welcome Henry. **St Ishmael's Nurseries and Garden Centre** is the largest in southwest Wales, offering a superb afternoon's browsing amid the wide range of trees, shrubs, conifers, alpines, heathers and herbaceous plants, many grown in the on-site nurseries.

SANDY HAVEN

MAP 1 REF C7

5 miles W of Milford Haven off the B4327

A path from Sandy Haven overlooks the entrance to Milford Haven harbour. A sheltered creek here in this lovely village has been described as truly idyllic. Many species of birds can be seen here, particularly when the stream is at low tide in the spring and autumn. The picturesque banks are heavily clad in trees reaching the water's edge. Visitors will pass a lime kiln on the approach to Sandy Haven, once supplied with lime from sailing ships on their way to Bristol and other ports.

Skerryback is an 18th-century stonebuilt farmhouse offering bed and breakfast accommodation. Very much still a working farm, it is set in an

Skerryback, Sandy Haven, St Ishmaels, Haverfordwest SA62 3DN
Tel: 01646 636598 Fax: 01646 636595.

attractive garden and surrounded by tranquil countryside and the coastal footpath. The region boasts many sandy beaches and coves to explore, and is only a short drive from picturesque Martins Haven, where boats leave for Skomer Island. The two guest rooms - one double, one ensuite family - are tastefully decorated and offer magnificent views. A good base for walking, pony-trekking, birdwatching or just taking in the unspoilt natural beauty of the area, this welcoming B&B is well worth a short or long stay. Owner Margaret Williams is well-known for her excellent home-cooked food; breakfasts are a real treat, hearty and delicious, the perfect start to a day of taking in the sights, sounds and attractions of this lovely part of South Wales. Welsh Tourist Board Farmhouse Award, Highly Commended.

Six of the forts built in the 1850s to repel the French can be seen from **Little Castle Head lighthouse**.

HAVERFORDWEST

This old county town with its pleasant rural surroundings is located more or less in the centre of Pembrokeshire. With steep streets and several Georgian buildings, much of the town centre is now a conservation area. The fine buildings date back to the time when Haverfordwest was a prosperous port, trading largely with Bristol and Ireland.

The town, however, is much older than this. Its unusual name is a legacy of Viking raids and it was around the Norman castle, built around 1120 by Gilbert de Clare, that the town grew. Thanks to a major conservation programme, the shell of the essentially 13th century inner wards of **Haverfordwest Castle** remain in use. Built as a gaol in 1820, it is home to the town's **Museum and Art Gallery**.

The remains of a **Priory Church**, founded for Augustinian Canons in the early 13th century, can be found by the Western Cleddau. Close by a strange, ghostly border exists which cannot be found on any map. Known locally as the **Landsker** (or land scar), it divides the English-speaking 'little England beyond Wales' of south Pembrokeshire from the Welsh-speaking north. This abrupt division of Pembrokeshire into two can be traced to early medieval times, when Norman invasions into these parts paved the way for Anglo-Saxon and Flemish immigrants. A line of castles was built from Amroth right across country to Roch in the far west, separating the south from the Welshry in the north. Although the Landsker is an invisible border, its significance has been profound for much of the past, it was unthinkable that marriage should take place between a man and woman from different sides of the line, even though they may have lived within a short distance of each other. The Landsker Borderlands feature delightful countryside, fascinating villages and hamlets with a rich heritage and many stories to tell.

Picton Castle is located 3 miles east of Haverfordwest, 2 miles south of the A40. The historic home of the Philipps family, the castle was built in the 13th century, and retains many of its original medieval features. The Woodland Gardens around the castle extend to nearly 40 acres, and are home to a feast of wildflowers, ancient oaks, beeches and many other mature trees along with a unique collection of rhododendrons, azaleas, camellias, magnolia, myrtle, embothrium and eucriphia bred over 40 years. There is also a maze (planted in 1992) and a picnic area. The Walled Garden area has a large collection of culinary and medical herbs together with herbaceous borders, rose beds, fish pond and fernery.

AROUND HAVERFORDWEST

THE RHOS   MAP 1 REF C7
3 miles E of Haverfordwest off the A40

East of the Cleddau toll bridge a delicate silvery ribbon winds a trail through the rural landscape to scenes of true rural tranquillity. This is the **Daugleddau**, a tidal estuary formed by the confluence of the Western and Eastern Cleddau rivers, and into which flow the Rivers Cresswell and Carew. Along its mysterious banks nestle many of the most beautiful and select treasures of the Pembrokeshire Coast National Park. Yet it is so often overlooked by visitors that is has become known as the Secret Waterway. The Rhos is the only village in the ancient parish of Slebach. Millin Cross and Bethesda are two other villages within this peaceful and beautiful region.

SIMPSON CROSS   MAP 1 REF C7
4 miles W of Haverfordwest off the A487

The **Pembrokeshire Motor Museum** features more than 50 veteran, vintage and classic cars and motorcycles, together with a collection of over 1,500 toy cars (Dinky, Matchbox and Corgi varieties), turn-of-the-century bicycles and more.

NOLTON HAVEN   MAP 1 REF C7
6 miles W of Haverfordwest off the A487

The **Mariners' Inn**, built in 1749, was originally a smugglers' inn and has been used by generations of seafarers. This distinguished hotel and restaurant is located in an area of outstanding natural beauty, with sandy coves and bays and large surfing beaches. Situated between high cliffs, Nolton

The Mariners' Inn, Nolton Haven, Pembrokeshire SA62 3NH
Tel: 01437 710469.

Haven is a quiet, small and intimate hamlet lying at the centre of the beautiful St Brides Bay coastline. The comfortable and attractive guest rooms are ensuite and have many modern amenities. The restaurant's table d'hote menu incorporates fresh vegetables, home-made soups and tempting sweets. There is a good selection of wines. Bar meals are available in the Family Room, every day from noon-3 p.m. and 6.30-10 p.m. The Bridge Bar and Residents' Lounge are two more attractive and very comfortable enticements offered by this superior privately owned and run inn.

The St Brides Bay coastline here has steep, undulating cliffs and sandy beaches, completely unspoilt but within easy reach of Haverfordwest and many nearby coastal villages. As part of the Pembrokeshire Coast National Park, the coastline here is rich in outstanding natural beauty with a wide variety of natural amenities available to the holidaymaker including the Coast Path (over 160 miles) that passes through the Haven, an abundance of wildlife, sea birds, wildflowers and beaches safe for swimming, surfing, boating and fishing. The area is also a mecca for walking, birdwatching, surfing and swimming, boating, wind surfing, pony-trekking, golf and guided walks.

Half a mile from Nolton Haven beach, **East Nolton Riding Stables** is part of a working farm and offers visitors the chance to explore and enjoy the lovely surrounding countryside on horseback.

BROAD HAVEN   MAP 1 REF C7
8 miles SW of Haverfordwest off the B4341

This is an enchanting place to visit, a small and welcoming holiday resort with a soft sandy beach which is very safe and ideal for families with small children.

WOLFSCASTLE   MAP 1 REF C6
6 miles N of Haverfordwest off the A40

Wolfscastle is ideally situated for trips to every part of Pembrokeshire. The county is encompassed on three sides by 200 miles of cliff walks - mostly under the auspices of the National Parks. These walks take visitors through small fishing villages, harbours, creeks and estuaries and along miles and miles of golden sands. Exciting boat trips allow you to watch nesting puffins, guillemots skimming the waves and seals lounging on rocks. To the east, the magnificent Preseli Hills dominate a rural landscape rich in history and myth. Skomer Island, just one of Pembrokeshire's many beautiful picturesque locations, lies to the west.

The Wolfe is an impressive and very picturesque restaurant located in the tranquil and scenic village of Wolfscastle, just 10 minutes from both the market town of Haverfordwest and the port of Fishguard. This distinguished and very attractive establishment has a charming stone-built exterior adorned with handing baskets and creeping ivy. The restaurant boasts three different themed rooms. All feature beamed ceilings and accoutrements reflecting the room's theme. All are pristine and comfortable. The menu offers haute cuisine for the discerning diner. Chef Mike Lewis is one of the most experienced in his field. Owners Gianni and Jackie Di Lorenzo have been here since June of 1998, and are an experienced man-

**The Wolfe, Wolfscastle, Nr Haverfordwest, Pembrokeshire SA62 5LS
Tel: 01437 741662.**

agement team offering all their guests a high standard of service and hospitality. Lunch is served from noon-2 p.m.; dinner from 7-9 p.m. Specialities include Welsh lamb, Normandy pork casserole, Thai chicken, Welsh beef, and a fish of the day and vegetarian option, all home-cooked and home-prepared. The home-made desserts are a real treat.

Wolfscastle Pottery offers a fine selection of functional ceramics and unusual one-off pieces in both decorated and plain traditional glazes. Visitors can try their hand at making their own pot, and can take away what they make. Everything is designed and tested in owners Madeleine and Phillip Cunningham's kitchen before it is put into production, and all is guaranteed dishwasher-, freezer-, oven- and microwave-proof.

Good old-fashioned hospitality awaits guests to the **Wolfscastle Country Hotel**. Located just off the A40 in this attractive village, 10 minutes from both Haverfordwest and Fishguard, this distinguished hotel and restaurant is run by welcoming and friendly managers and owners Andrew and Pauline Stirling. Once a vicarage, this imposing building is known as Allt Yr Afon (wood by the river) and is stone-built under a slate roof. Exquisitely decorated and furnished throughout, it maintains a period theme. The intimate and relaxing restaurant has earned a reputation far and wide for its tempting menus, which feature both haute cuisine and good home cooking. The residents bar has a welcoming atmosphere; orders are taken for the a la carte restaurant and bar meals are served. All dishes make the

Wolfscastle Country Hotel, Wolfscastle, Nr Haverfordwest, Pembrokeshire SA62 5LZ Tel: 01437 741225/688 Fax: 01437 741383.

most of fresh, local produce and are expertly prepared by the four chefs. The 20 guest bedrooms offer every modern convenience in a setting of traditional comfort.

CANASTON BRIDGE   MAP 1 REF D7
6 miles E of Haverfordwest off the A40

Oakwood Park is an award-winning attraction with 80 acres of amusements and rides, including 8 miles of rollercoasters, water coasters and more. Nearby, **CC2000** is billed as *'an interactive experience for all the family'*, an indoor centre based on the Crystal Maze television series. Visitors race against the clock as they are guided through the four 'zones' - Aztec, Medieval, Ocean and Futuristic - and meet a series of enjoyable and informative challenges.

NARBERTH   MAP 1 REF D7
7 miles E of Haverfordwest off the A40

For those who like their diversions a bit more low-key, **Heron's Brook Country Park and Wildfowl Centre** offers a very enjoyable day out. The Park features a pitch and putt and approach golf course, animal and bird park, Punch and Judy shows, landscaped gardens, otter area, pony rides, farming demonstrations and more.

LLANDDEWI VELFREY   MAP 1 REF D7
10 miles E of Haverfordwest off the A40

Mrs Mair Evans has run the friendly and informal **Preseli Country Cafe** since 1994. The cafe is adjacent to a petrol station (also run by Mrs Evans) and attracts a varied clientele including coach parties, tourists and day-trippers as well as loyal regular customers. Overlooking the Preseli mountains and close to the south Pembrokeshire seaside resorts of Saundersfoot and Tenby, this welcoming establishment is comfortably fur-

Preseli Country Cafe, Llanddewi Velfrey, Narberth
Pembrokeshire SA67 7PD Tel: 01834 861425.

nished and has a lively atmosphere. A single-storey block-built structure festooned with hanging baskets, the cafe features an extensive menu which boasts hearty all-day breakfasts and brunches, and a range of traditional favourites such as mouth-watering sandwiches, soups, burgers and jacket potatoes, as well as tempting hot and cold meals including fish, Grimsby pie (a cod and prawn crumble), chicken curry, lasagna, beanburgers and salads. The Sunday roast beef, pork, lamb and turkey roasts are a speciality. There are also vegetarian and children's menus. And, if you've still got room, there is a variety of puddings on offer, including home-made apple pie, cheesecake, home-made trifle, spotted dick and hot chocolate fudge cake. Open daily from 7 a.m. to 6 p.m. (8 p.m. in summer).

MARTLETWY   MAP 1 REF C7
6 miles SE of Haverfordwest off the A4075

Cwm Deri Vineyard is the place to see Pembrokeshire wine growing on the vines from spring to the autumn harvest, to sample estate-grown vintages and buy from the selection of wines, liqueurs and meads available from the 'Wine Seller' vineyard shop.

ST DAVID'S

Britain's smallest city is named after the patron saint of Wales. **St David's Cathedral**, which gives it city status, is situated in a deep hollow below the streets, so that not even its square tower can be seen above the rooftops. Founded on the site of St David's 6th-century monastic settlement, the cathedral dates from the 12th century and contains many treasures. the highlight of the interior is the oak roof, which displayed wonderfully ornate carvings by 15th-century craftsmen. St David's Cathedral has been an important Christian shrine since medieval times, when two pilgrimages to St David's equalled one to Rome. Successive monarchs from William the Conqueror to Queen Elizabeth II have worshipped here. The Queen has a special seat reserved for her in the Cathedral, and not too long ago distributed Maundy Money, for the first time in Wales, from here. The cathedral stands next door to another impressive religious site, the **Bishop's Palace**. Although now a roofless ruin, this 14th-century palace would once have been the opulent residence of the influential leaders of the medieval church.

Quite apart from these religious sites, there are pretty craft shops and attractions such as the **Marine Life Centre**, where visitors can come face to face with sea scorpions, suckerfish, octopus, members of the shark family and many other examples of marine life. Displays, information boards, models, weather charts and more give vital facts about all aspects of sea life.

The Oceanarium in New Street is the largest aquarium in St David's, with a purpose-built large-scale seawater setting housed on two floors. The ground floor boasts a spectacular 30-foot long panoramic tank and an 11-sided shark and ray tank, which can be viewed from the upstairs gallery. The first floor has a 20-foot diameter rock pool, where visitors can handle a variety of marine species under the supervision of the resident aquarists.

The City Inn on New Street in St David's is an attractive and convivial public house offering bed and breakfast accommodation. Mother and son Pauline and Howard Bush have owned and run the Inn since 1995; they offer a warm and genuine welcome to all guests. The atmosphere in this large and distinguished establishment is quiet and relaxed. This stone-built pub was built around 1850 as a commercial hotel. It was originally called the Aleric, as the main roof beam was a bulk head taken from a shipwreck of the same name. There are a number of original features in-cluding the exposed stone wall in the bar area. Bar meals are served all day, and there is also a large and comfortable dining room. There are five guest bedrooms, two ensuite, all decorated and furnished to a high standard of comfort and homeliness. Located near several fine beaches, including White Sands Bay, as well as a wealth of walks, sites of historic interest and many amenities, it makes an ideal base from which to explore this part of south-western Wales.

The City Inn, New Street, St David's, Pembrokeshire SA62 6SU
Tel: 01437 720829.

Just along the road in a stunningly beautiful spot overlooking the sea is **St Non's Well**, next to the ruins of **St Non's Chapel**. Legend has it that David was born here during a great storm in around AD500. The waters of

St Non's Well are said to have magical powers for healing eye diseases; the well was much visited by pilgrims to St David's.

Another beautiful coastal spot close by is **St Justinian's**, also steeped in legend. Justinian was a 6th-century hermit who retreated across to **Ramsey Island**, a short distance offshore, to devote himself to God. A strict disciplinarian, he must have been too severe with his followers, for they eventually rebelled and cut off his head! Justinian is then said to have walked across the waters of Ramsey Sound, back to the mainland, carrying his head in his arms. The tiny little rockbound harbour named after him is now the location for the **St David's Lifeboat Station** and also the place from which boat trips depart for Ramsey Island. Ramsey is a Norse name, a legacy of the Dark Ages when this part of the coast was terrorised by Viking invaders. **Ramsey Island Cruises** (boat booking office in the St David's High Street) offer a guided 1½ hour cruise around the RSPB reserve, where countless rare and common species can be seen. The cruises also allow visitors to observe at close hand the largest breeding colony of Atlantic Grey Seals on the Welsh coastline. Porpoises and the occasional tropical visitor such as Leatherback turtles and Sunfish sometimes also make an appearance. **Thousand Islands Expeditions** in Cross Square also offer voyages in and around the area.

The Grove Hotel in St David's is a Regency home built in 1816 of stone from nearby Caerbwdi Bay. This handsome hotel boasts 10 cosy and comfortable guest bedrooms, all with private facilities. There is also a lovely guests' lounge and attractive beamed bar. This haven of peace and rural splendour has a large walled garden to the rear, just the place to relax and

Grove Hotel, High Street, St David's, Pembrokeshire SA62 6SB
Tel: 01437 720341 Fax: 01437 720770.

enjoy the changing colours and scents of the surrounding countryside.

Diane and Grahame Pengelly are the excellent and friendly hosts, and have been at the hotel since 1989. Just a few miles from several beautiful beaches and the boating harbour of Solva, the locality is wonderful for walking, birdwatching, surfing, swimming, boating, wind-surfing, pony-trekking, golf and guided walks. This fine hotel is also three-quarters of a mile from the coastal path and the delightful bay of Caerfai, and just a few minutes' walk from the Cathedral and historic Bishop's Palace. The full English breakfast, light lunches, evening bar meals or a la carte dinners offer a high standard of imaginative and delicious home cooking, making use of the freshest local produce wherever possible.

AROUND ST DAVID'S

SOLVA   MAP 1 REF B6
3 miles SE of St David's off the A487

Solva Harbour is among the most sheltered in Wales. It is located at the end of a long inlet, well protected from the sometimes stormy waters of St Bride's Bay. Green hills roll down to the quayside, creating a picturesque scene. This was the last view of Wales for many 19th-century emigrants sailing from Solva to America for 10 shillings, the price of a one-way ticket. In addition to its high-quality craft shops, Solva is also the home of **The Nectarium**, a tropical butterfly farm, where colourful species from all over the world can be seen flying in a specially-designed glasshouse.

Solva also boasts two outstanding craftshops. The **Open Studio and Gallery** exhibits the paintings, photographs, handmade cards, crafts, gifts, music and art materials, while **The Woollen Mill**, one of the original Welsh woollen mills (opened in 1907), produces a range of carpets and floor rugs in traditional and contemporary Welsh designs.

FISHGUARD

Fishguard's geography can be a bit confusing: the town's name means 'mouth of the River Gwaun'. The picturesque old harbour, a pretty little quayside lined with fishermen's cottages, is in Lower Fishguard. This harbour was used to depict Dylan Thomas' fictional seaside town of Llareggub, when his play Under Milk Wood was made into a 1970's film starring Richard Burton. The new harbour, built at the turn of the century, lies across the bay at Goodwick. It is from here that ferries cross the Irish Sea to Rosslare. The main town of Upper Fishguard lies on high ground between the two harbours.

The last invasion of Britain, a farcical episode in 1797 when a poorly-equipped band of Frenchmen landed at nearby **Carregwastad Point** and were seen off by the locals, is remembered at the Royal Oak Inn. The French retreated to the beach below Goodwick, where an inscribed stone now marks the spot where they surrendered to Lord Cawdor some two days after they landed. **St Mary's Church** contains the headstone of the formidable Jemima Nicholas, who reputedly captured 14 of the French invaders armed with only a pitchfork.

The port of Fishguard is the setting for the welcoming **Cartref Hotel**. Fishguard is an ideal base from which to explore (both by car and on foot) the stunning beauty and variety of the countryside. The Pembrokeshire coastal path alone attracts many walkers and birdwatchers. Owners Kristina and Eric Bjorkqvist have been running this attractive and friendly hotel

The Cartref Hotel, 15-19 High Street, Fishguard Pembrokeshire SA65 9AW Tel: 01348 872430.

since 1995; they are congenial hosts who offer their guests genuine hospitality. There are 10 ensuite guest bedrooms, tastefully decorated and furnished and with a relaxing and supremely comfortable ambience. The hotel restaurant is intimate and tranquil, and has a licensed bar. Meals are served all day; all the dishes on offer are home-cooked and home-prepared, and make best use of fresh local produce when in season. This RAC and AA 2-Star-rated hotel provides a high standard of quality and comfort, with an accent on traditional style and service. Open 24 hours; garage available.

AROUND FISHGUARD

GOODWICK   MAP 1 REF C6
1 mile NW of Fishguard off the A40

Once a fishing village, Goodwick is now, effectively, the base for Fishguard Harbour which was built between 1894 and 1906 by the specially created Fishguard and Rosslare Railway and Harbours Company. James Wade, who died in 1887, was one of Pembrokeshire's best-known storytellers; many of his tall tales are recounted to this day. On one occasion he told how a carrion crow swooped down as he was fishing, grabbed him in its beak and carried him to Ireland. The crow eventually dropped him and he spent the night where he landed, in a cannon. The next morning, before he got up, the cannon was fired and he was propelled back across to St George's Channel and landed, unharmed, next to his fishing tackle on Goodwick Beach!

Ivybridge is a distinguished and luxurious B&B located amidst the spectacular scenery of the Pembrokeshire coastline, the perfect setting for a relaxing break. Colin, Jan and Sara offer the best in personal attention to each guest. This comfortable and handsome establishment boasts a range of wonderful amenities including an indoor heated swimming pool, whirlpool and solarium, games room and a licensed bar with a large and welcoming open fire. All rooms are ensuite with all the facilities guests have come to expect. A full home-cooked English or Continental breakfast (vegetarians catered for) will get the day off to a good start. Snacks and

Ivybridge, Drim Mill, Dyffryn, Goodwick, Pembrokeshire SA64 0FT
Tel: 01348 875366/872623 Fax: 01348 872338.

packed lunches are available upon request. Guests are certain to enjoy a relaxing and pleasurable stay at this superior establishment, which makes a good base from which to explore the historic towns, picturesque villages and magnificent scenery of the region.

The ancients knew Pembrokeshire as Gwlad hud a Lledrith - the land of mystery and enchantment - and Goodwick and its environs certainly live up to this epithet. Also nearby is the fascinating Gwaun Valley. Salmon, seatrout and brown trout, bird species such as buzzards, peregrine falcons, choughs, puffins and razorbills abound in the region. Golf, horse-riding, boating, surfing, canoeing, cycling, flying and walking opportunities are also plentiful.

Glendower Hotel is a handsome and impressive hotel located in the charming village of Goodwick, in the heart of north Pembrokeshire coastal National Park, less than 400 metres from the entrance of the ferry port at Fishguard Harbour. Owner Bernard Jackman was a seafarer for many years before taking over at the hotel. He runs it with great efficiency and offers all guests a high standard of service and comfort. There are 11 guest bedrooms, all ensuite. Each room is tastefully furnished and decorated, and contains all the modern facilities guests have come to expect, while retaining a traditional and luxurious ambience. The full English breakfast is served in the large and handsome restaurant. Evening meals are also available from the extensive a la carte menus. The bar serves a wide range of draught beers, stouts, lagers and spirits. A complimentary mini-bus service is avail-

**Glendower Hotel, Goodwick, Pembrokeshire SA64 0DH
Tel: 01348 872873 Fax: 01348 874252.**

able from the port and local railway station. Rated Three Crowns by the Welsh Tourist Board.

STRUMBLE HEAD   MAP 1 REF C6
4 miles NW of Fishguard off the A487

This is a huge headland with a lighthouse built to warn ships of the cliffs on the approach to Fishguard harbour. **Carregwastad Point**, a remote headland near Strumble Head, was as mentioned earlier the scene of the last 'invasion' of Britain. The ill-fated 1,400 French troops were led by an American colonel. At a roadside stand along the winding road from Goodwick to Strumble Head Lighthouse, **Miranda's Preserves** offer homemade jellies, marmalades and chutneys, made from wild berries and plants such as elderflowers, rosehips, damsons, sloes, rowan, elderberries and blackberries.

CASTLE MORRIS   MAP 1 REF C6
5 miles SW of Fishguard off the B4331

Llangloffan Farmhouse Cheese Centre is the place to see the cheesemaking process in action, from milk to the final product, delicious Llangloffan cheese. Daily demonstrations and access to the farmland are just part of a day out here, where visitors can also sample and buy cheeses and home-made bread in the farm shop, and enjoy a picnic in the grounds.

PORTHGAIN   MAP 1 REF B6
8 miles SW of Fishguard off the A487

Porthgain has a sheltered harbour with a unique personality. The uniqueness comes from Porthgain's combination of natural beauty and industrial heritage. Dominating the harbourside is the shell of a 19th-century brickworks, which stands close to remnants from Porthgain's heyday as a slate and granite exporting port. In fact, many buildings in places as far afield as London and Liverpool are made from Porthgain granite. Nowadays it is difficult to imagine the hectic scenes of 100 years ago when the harbour would have been packed with boats queueing for their cargoes of stone and brick needed for the building of the booming industrial towns of Britain. Porthgain's strange beauty has attracted many film-makers.

CROES GOCH   MAP 1 REF C6
8 miles SW of Fishguard off the A487

Croes Goch is an attractive and tranquil community located midway between St David's and Fishguard.

The Artramont Arms, Croes Goch, Pembrokeshire SA62 5J
Tel: 01348 831309.

Owners Margaret and Ray Nadollek took over at the attractive
Artramont Arms in Croes Goch late in 1998; Ray has experience as an
advanced diver and Margaret is a boat handler. These interesting and welcoming hosts make every guest to this comfortable public house feel
welcome. The atmosphere is quiet, relaxed and friendly. Lying within the
very picturesque Pembrokeshire National Park, and close to the sea, the
area offers a wealth of attractions and amenities. The handsome exterior is
stone-built and half-rendered. Just over 200 years old, it was built for Irish
quarry workers - and is said to have been a resting place for pilgrims on
their way to nearby St David's. It is tastefully decorated and incorporates a
cosy and intimate restaurant. Meals are available both at lunch and in the
evenings; the menu specialises in roasts and vegetarian dishes. To quaff
your thirst, there's a good variety of at least three real ales plus a guest ale,
and a range of lagers, wines and spirits.

PONTFAEN   MAP 1 REF C6
4 miles SE of Fishguard off the B4313

Gerddi Penlan-Uchaf Gardens in the heart of the Gwaun Valley is the
place to see an abundant display of miniature flowering plants, dwarf conifers and alpines. Set in landscaped surroundings with a fast flowing stream
running through it, it is the ideal location to relax and admire the natural
beauty of the plants.

TRECWN   MAP 1 REF C6
3 miles S of Fishguard off the A40/B4313

Knox Valley Llanstinan Quad Trail is set, as its name suggests, in the
Llanstinan estate in Knox Valley. Here a *'quad assault course'* for buggies
has been laid out over four miles. With experienced instructors to help
visitors manoeuvre the scenic and exciting course, the terrain takes in the
ruins of Llanstinan Mansion and the old walled garden. Safety helmets
and wet weather gear are provided, and participants must be over 14 years
of age.

ROSEBUSH   MAP 1 REF D6
9 miles SE of Fishguard off the B431

The village of Rosebush is full of memories of the old slate quarries and
the now closed railway line to Fishguard. It is a peaceful rural community
set amid some lovely natural scenery. **Pant Mawr Farm** in Rosebush offers
three varieties of hand-made cheeses: a plain cow's cheese and its smoked
counterpart, and a delicious soft goat's cheese.

   Tucked away in a fold of the Preseli hills, situated in the heart of
Pembrokeshire equidistant between Fishguard and Haverfordwest, **The Old
Post Office** is a delightful stonebuilt structure run by Dot and Dave Thomas, who have been running it for over 20 years. This former post office
now incorporates a craft shop, visitors' centre, bistro, bar, a la carte restaurant and bed and breakfast accommodation. In short, it is the centre of

**The Old Post Office, Rosebush, Pembrokeshire SA66 7QU
Tel: 01437 532205.**

village life. The bar area is adorned with wagon wheels and other historic memorabilia such as farm implements, milk churns and other items collected by the Thomases over the years. The three guest bedrooms are cosy and comfortable. There are family meals served in the Bistro and an extensive a la carte menu in the intimate restaurant. All food is freshly prepared from local produce, and a wide range of diets are catered for. Welsh teas and traditional Sunday lunches are a speciality — and no one ever leaves feeling hungry! Dot and Dave can offer guidance, maps and information on walks in the Preselis. Open Monday-Saturday 10-late; Sunday 10-6.

GWAUN VALLEY   Map 1 ref D6
8 miles SE of Fishguard off the B4329

The Pembrokeshire Coast National Park hugs the seashore for most of its length, venturing inland only to encompass the **Mynydd Preseli** (the **Preseli Hills**). Although the highest point of the Preselis is Foel Cwmcerwyn at only 536 metres, there are views that stretch as far as Snowdonia and the Gower Peninsula. This was home to the ancient Celts, and Bronze Age burial cairns and standing stones dot the 'Golden Road', an ancient bridleway across the hills. In the foothills of the Preselis is Gwaun Valley, a place that truly is hidden away. The locals here still celebrate New Year on 13th January, in keeping with the customs of the pre-1752 calendar. Anyone interested in history will be fascinated by this haunting, treeless area of moor and mountain. The Preselis are scattered with prehistoric sites ranging from mysterious burial chambers to Iron Age hill forts.

LLANGOLMAN   Map 1 ref D6
10 miles SE of Fishguard off the B4313

The **Slate Workshop** is located in a converted 18th-century corn mill within this beautiful, tranquil valley. Here are designed and crafted unique, high-quality plaques, sundials, housenames and numbers, clocks, objets d'art and more, made from Pembrokeshire and other Welsh slate. While in Llangolman, **Karen Jones** is a gallery featuring lively colourful watercolours painted by Ms Jones herself, a member of the Society of Equestrian Artists.

CROSSWELL   Map 1 ref D6
9 miles E of Fishguard off the A487/B4329

Pentre Ifan Cromlech is an ancient burial chamber with a huge 16-foot capstone. It is made of the same Preseli bluestones that somehow found their way - no one has yet come up with a fully convincing explanation - to Stonehenge on Salisbury Plain.

NEVERN
MAP 1 REF D6

7 miles E of Fishguard off the A487/B4582

The village of Nevern's most interesting feature is the **Church of St Brynach**, dedicated to a 5th-century Irish saint whose cell was nearby on **Carn Ingli** (the Hill of the Angels). Inside the church are two carved stones: the Maglocunus Stone (dating from around the 5th century) bears both Latin and Ogham inscriptions and commemorates Maglocunus, the son of Clutor; the other stone, the Cross Stone, is younger, dating from the 10th century and bears a cross of entwined Viking pattern. Outside the church, the Great Cross is one of the most perfect Celtic crosses in Wales. Some 13 feet high and dating from the 10th century, it has an elaborate pattern and, according to tradition, the first cuckoo to be heard each year in Pembrokeshire sings from the top of the cross.

On a hill northwest of the village lie the remains of **Nevern Castle**. Originally a fortress of the local chieftains of Cemaes, the site was rebuilt in around 1100 as a motte and bailey by the Norman Robert Martyn. Though now overgrown, the motte can still be seen along with some fragments of the stone castle.

NEWPORT
MAP 1 REF D6

6 miles E of Fishguard off the A487

This pretty little seaside centre has a fine beach. As its name suggests, it was once an important port in the area. In particular, the wool trade was brisk here until Tudor times, when the plague diverted trade to Fishguard. The town was also once the capital of the Marcher Lords of Cemaes, the only one not to have been abolished during Henry VIII's reign. The remains of the 13th century Norman castle that was built for the Lords of Cemaes are now part of a modern mansion.

CILGWYN
MAP 1 REF D6

6 miles E of Fishguard off the A487

Pembrokeshire Candle Centre is the only place in Wales where visitors can see hand-dipped candles made just as they were centuries ago. Here is one of Pembrokeshire's most beautiful secret valleys, as the hamlet of Cilgwyn lies in a sheltered hollow at the entrance to Cwm Gwaun, beneath the rocky peak of Carn Ingli - right at the heart of bluestone coutnry. The workshop is packed with candles of all shapes and sizes, together with candlesticks, snuffers, lanterns, oil-burners, candle-making kits and more. Alongside the workshop is Britain's smallest museum, with fascinating displays telling the history and traditions of candle-making dating back to Roman times.

DINAS CROSS
MAP 1 REF C6
4 miles E of Fishguard off the A487

The village of Dinas Cross is located close to **Dinas Head** and island. No longer a true island, it was given the name because it was, at the end of the Ice Age, separated from the mainland.

BONCATH
MAP 1 REF D6
12 miles E of Fishguard off the A478

Wendy Brandon is a leading authority on preserve-making and her products are sold worldwide. Here in Boncath, a very pretty and secluded spot at the bottom of a picturesque valley just outside Pembrokeshire National Park with the Preseli Hills close by, county records show that there has been a mill on this site for hundreds of years. It took on its current name, **Felin Wen** (White Mill) when a new corn mill was built in 1748. The 18th-century farmhouse is available for weekly holiday lettings - early booking is recommended. Here in this striking stonebuilt mill, damaged by fire in the 1970s but restored and one of the best preserved in the area, Wendy Brandon manufactures an impressive range of over 100 handmade preserves. Voted Best Jam and Preserve Maker by the Good Food Lover's Guide to Britain, the varieties on offer include 24 chutneys, plus fruit sauces, marmalades, jams, jellies, vinegars, pickles and, as an extra treat, three types of fudge. These tempting delights feature traditional favourites such as strawberry and blackcurrant as well as more innovative and creative flavours such as apple ginger, plum with plum brandy, and blueberry and apple.

Wendy Brandon Handmade Preserves, Felin Wen, Boncath
Pembrokeshire SA37 0JR Tel: 01239 841568 Fax: 01239 841746

4 Carmarthenshire

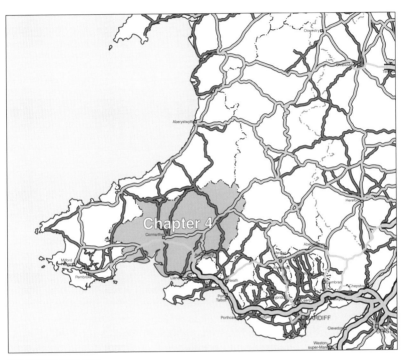

Carmarthenshire is a county of contrasts. From the Black Mountain to the tranquil Towy Valley; from the picturesque coastal villages to the golden sands of Carmarthen Bay. The county comprises 1,000 square miles of the most beautiful coastal and inland areas of South Wales.

The 50-mile coastline includes award-winning Pembrey Country Park and beach, together with Pendine, world famous for the land speed record attempts held there. Seaside villages such as Laugharne, renowned for its associations with Dylan Thomas, offer tranquil havens. The River Loughor is a favourite haunt of migratory birds on the local wetlands. The estuary is famous for its cockle-gatherers, who have combed the shoreline for this local delicacy for centuries. Here too visitors will find Wales' only Wildfowl and Wetlands Centre, at Penclacwydd.

The area has a number of Sites of Scientific Interest. Landscape, wildlife, archaeology and ancient woodlands are actively preserved. Carmarthenshire is a haven for amateur and dedicated geologists, zoologists, botanists and bird-lovers.

The moorlands of Llanllwni and the Llanybydder mountains are breathtaking. South the scenery changes yet again, as the road travel through the Brechfa Forest, Abergorlech and Talley. To the extreme west of the county, on the border with Pembrokeshire, there is open, rolling countryside and attractive towns and villages such as Whitland and St Clears.

The county's 40,000-year-old history is visible everywhere. Llandovery was an important Roman outpost; Norman influences in the 11th century resulted in numerous castles built throughout the region. By the 19th century towns such as Llanelli had become prominent maritime bases, and tinplate, copper and, of course, coal - particularly that from the Amman Valley - were important industries.

LLANDOVERY

Llandovery is a traditional 18th- and 19th-century town with an attractive square and covered market place. The town's Welsh name, Llanymddyfri, means 'the church amid the waters'; Llandovery stands at the confluence of the rivers Bran, Gwydderig and Twyi. Evidence suggests that the area has been of some importance since Roman times and the church has Roman tiles within its fabric. Rhys Pritchard, known for his preaching and as the author of *The Welshman's Candle*, a collection of verses, lived here in the 17th century. So, too, did William Williams, who in the 18th century was a renowned revivalist and hymn-writer.

A castle once occupied the mound by the cattle market; remnants of this medieval structure remain, overlooking the cattle market. The town is dotted with pleasant and attractive architecture, such as the 19th-century **Market Hall**. Llandovery is the ideal place for those looking for a true taste of traditional Wales.

Llandovery Heritage Centre examines the life and times of Twm Sion Cati, the Welsh Robin Hood, in this educational exhibition exploring the social and industrial heritage of Wales. Learn about the journey of the drovers who took stock to market. The centre also provides tourist information.

Llandovery's **Royal Society for the Protection of Birds Visitor Centre** offers an opportunity to observe birdlife, including the Red Kite, at close quarters.

AROUND LLANDOVERY

CILYCWM
MAP 2 REF G6
4 miles N of Llandovery off the A483

The attractive **Dolauhirion Bridge**, a single-arched construction spanning the River Twyi, was built in 1173 by William Edwards. In the village the 15th-century church contains old wall paintings, and the chapel is said to have been the first meeting place of Methodists in Wales. Nearby, **Twm Sion Cati's Cave** was the hideout of the 16th-century 'Robin Hood of Wales'.

PUMSAINT
MAP 2 REF G6
8 miles NW of Llandovery off the A482

Sometimes spelled Pumpsaint, this hamlet's name means 'five saints' in Welsh. The **Dolaucothi Gold Mines** nearby date back some 2,000 years when the open-cast gold workings were secured by the Roman army. Still in a remarkable state of preservation despite mining activity in the last 100 years or so, the Roman workings include at least five open-cast sites and a number of adits (horizontal tunnels dug into the hillside for drainage and access). Owned by the National Trust, there is also a trail through the woodland with views over the valley leading to the main features of the Roman and modern workings. There is also a collection of 1930s mining equipment onsite.

TALLEY
MAP 2 REF G6
8 miles W of Llandovery off the B4302

Along the B4302, **Talley Abbey** was founded in the 12th century by Rhys ap Gruffyd for Premonstratensian canons who, ejected by the Cistercians, had appealed to the Archbishop of Canterbury and were granted their religious rights. Parts of the abbey tower, naves and cloisters survive and there is an air of peace and tranquillity hanging over the ruins. There are also pleasant walks by the lakes, after which the Abbey is named.

ABERGORLECH
MAP 2 REF F6
11 miles W of Llandovery off the B4310

Located in the picturesque village of Abergorlech, close to the Brechfa Forest and the River Cothi, **The Black Lion** is a distinctive rural public house. Popular with locals and visiting walkers and tourers alike, this handsome, welcoming pub boasts an attractive whitewashed stone-built exterior, case-

**The Black Lion, Abergorlech, Nr Carmarthen
Carmarthenshire SA32 7SN   Tel: 01558 685271.**

ment windows and other original 16th-century features. The interior is very comfortable, with a well-worn flagstone floor, original fireplace and beamed ceilings. The natural stone walls are adorned with traditional horse brasses and coach lanterns. Reputedly home to two ghosts, this evocative pub serves a range of fine ales, spirits and wines. The lush beer garden overlooks an attractive stone bridge spanning the River Cothi. Standing next to the village church, it is a centre of community life here in Abergorlech. The owner, Mrs Entwistle, is a friendly and charming host.

LLANGADOG   MAP 2 REF G6
5 miles SW of Llandovery off the A4069

This small town in the Vale of Towy once boasted a castle, though all that remains now is a mound. The castle was destroyed by its owners in 1277, preferring this to the alternative of having the castle fall into English hands. Carn Goch, the largest hillfort in Wales, lies about 3 miles to the south of Llangadog, its stone ramparts and earthworks covering roughly 15 acres.

The Castle Hotel, set in this small country village not far from the Black Mountains, offers guests a warm welcome in peaceful and supremely comfortable surroundings. Built in 1756 on what was the old drovers' road to London, it is a large stone-built building which retains some of its original features, including the impressive polished oak staircase and open log fires. A focal point for the community, the hotel's three guest bedrooms are cosy and comfortable, with every amenity guests have come to expect.

**The Castle Hotel, Queen Square, Llangadog
Carmarthenshire SA19 9BW Tel: 01550 777377.**

Owners Mary and Steve Bevan are conscientious about making sure guests have a relaxing and enjoyable stay. Mary does all the cooking, using some of the 30 or so herbs in her garden and fresh local produce, to make delicious home-made meals which can be enjoyed in the separate restaurant or sheltered beer garden. To complement a meal, a choice of real ales is available, as Steve is a CAMRA member - in fact, a small beer festival is held during the summer.

LLANDEILO

Former ancient capital of west Wales, Llandeilo retains its old-world atmosphere with its narrow streets and attractive historic buildings. Pastel-coloured Georgian houses line the main road which curves elegantly up from the **Towy bridge** (the longest single-span stone bridge in Wales) to the **church of St Teilo**, the 6th-century Celtic saint who gave his name to the town.

Fanny's of Llandeilo is a friendly and cosy restaurant with a well-deserved reputation for good quality food. Mother-and-son partnership Sue and Rick Toller bring their individual skills and talents to bear on their shared commitment to the use of home-grown, organic and local produce as central to their varied and creative menu - Rick is a fully qualified chef who gained invaluable experience at large manor house hotels, Sue has many years' practical catering experience. The chalkboard lists some 20 daily choices, including specials such as asparagus crepes and the popular

Fanny's Restaurant, 3 King Street, Llandeilo
Carmarthenshire SA19 6AA Tel: 01558 822908.

Red Dragon pie, made with kidney beans with lentil bolognese under a potato crust. Afternoon tea is a real treat, with both traditional tea-time favourites and Rick's own creations: Divine Caramel Meringue filled with melting toffee cream, light lemon cheesecake, and scones to die for: wholemeal or plain, sweet or savoury, to be accompanied by their range of speciality teas and freshly brewed coffee. Listed in both Egon Ronay's Guide and Gilli Davies' Red Book guide to dining out in Wales. Open Tues-Sat from 10-5 (closed for 3 weeks in January); Fri & Sat April-October until 8.

Located in its own tranquil grounds in an historic stone-built hunting lodge near Llandeilo, off the A40 and half a mile after the Nag's Head public house, **King's Lodge Pottery** is a treasure trove of unique and interesting stoneware, earthenware and ceramics. Owners Roger and Jean Leyshon have been living at the lodge for 12 years, and started the Pottery 9 years ago. Both of them are gifted artists; together they create their distinctive collection of hand-thrown domestic studio ceramics in softly coloured stoneware. The colours they use come from nature, in particular the colours found in quails' eggs. They also fashion hand-painted commemorative pieces in blue and white 'Delft'-style earthenware. They are happy to create either production range or individual commissions to order and to the specifications of their clientele. Each piece is unique, and individually crafted; throughout the Lodge visitors will find fine examples of their range of plates, cups, mugs, jugs, vases, honey jars, herb jars,

King's Lodge Pottery, King's Lodge, Old Carmarthen Road
Llandeilo, Carmarthenshire SA19 6RY Tel: 01558 823532.

mortars and pestles, candelabra, crockery, oil dispensers, condiment dispensers and much more. The pieces range from delicate to sturdy, for
occasional or everyday use, in muted colours and patterns that will make
an attractive and useful addition to any home. Their pottery also, of course,
makes for excellent one-of-a-kind gifts. Both Roger and Jean are former
teachers, and welcome the opportunity to encourage children and adults
to learn the art of potting. They are warm and friendly, and only too pleased
to involve visitors in their art. They hold regular demonstrations and workshops, and are always happy to answer any questions about the process
and techniques involved in their art. Open daily 10 am - 5 pm. Jan-Feb
early closing.

This small market town in the centre of Carmarthenshire serves the
rich farmland surrounding it, and is close to several places of interest that
make worthwhile diversions whilst in the area.

AROUND LLANDEILO

DINEFWR CASTLE   MAP 2 REF F7
1 mile W of Llandeilo off the A40

Now part of a National Trust-owned **Dinefwr Park**, but with a long tradition and history, **Dinefwr Old Castle** stands on the site of an Iron Age
fort. The princedom of Deheubarth was ruled from here. Legend has it
that Merlin's grave is in the area. Rhys ap Gruffydd is thought to have

Dinefwr Park

built the first stone castle here in the 12th century. Seen as an important target, the castle was under constant siege until the arrival of Edward I. The Park has extensive areas of parkland open to the public and is being restored to something of the glory it once knew when landscaped in 1775 by Capability Brown, at which time the medieval castle, house, gardens, woods and deer park were integrated into one vast and breathtaking panorama. Footpaths through the park lead to the castle, bog wood and beech clumps, and offer outstanding views of the Towy Valley. Special events are held in the park throughout the year.

Nearby **Newton House**, privately owned, dates from the 17th century, an earlier 15th-century manor having replaced the Old Castle as a place of residence for the Rhys family. The ground floor and basement of Newton House are open to the public.

GOLDEN GROVE   Map 2 ref F7
3 miles SW of Llandeilo off the A476

Golden Grove mansion, now part of a college, was originally built to replace a building burned down in 1769. In that mansion Jeremy Taylor, a writer and Royalist, took refuge during the Civil War; while there he wrote many works including *Golden Grove*.

TRAPP   Map 2 ref G7
4½ miles SE of Llandeilo off the A483

The spectacularly evocative **Carreg Cennen Castle** crowns a remote limestone crag 300 feet above the River Cennen. This dramatic and romantic setting befits the impressiveness of this medieval fortress. The path up is

Carreg Cennen Castle

fairly rigorous but the reward of the remains and the views of Brecon Beacon National Park and Black Mountains worth the effort. The present remains date from around 1300, when it was built as an English outpost by one of Edward I's barons, but this naturally defensible site may even have been a prehistoric hillfort and was certainly a stronghold of the Welsh princes. Tradition has it that the castle was once occupied by Urien, a knight of Arthur's Round Table. Despite its strengths, Carreg Cennan fell to Owain Glyndwr's Welsh insurgents and, during the Wars of the Roses, became a base for bandit Lancastrians. It was taken and ruined by the Yorkists in 1462, when it was laboriously dismantled by 500 men with picks and crowbars. In spite of this the remains are fairly substantial, and moved Dylan Thomas to refer to it in some of his work as 'Carreg Cennen, King of Time'.

Trapp Art and Crafts Centre features an art gallery, craft shop, tea room, exhibitions, demonstrations, videos and workshops, covering a range of artistic pursuits such as pottery, stained glass, lovespoon carving, embroidery, quilting, jewellery, prints and rugs, to name but a few.

DRYSLWYN   MAP 2 REF F7
5 miles W of Llandeilo off the A40

By the side of the River Tywi lie the remains of the Welsh **Dryslwyn Castle**, the victim of undermining when besieged in the 13th century, an attack which indirectly contributed to its present condition. Built on the site of an Iron Age hillfort, traces of the chapel, a hall and a round keep can still be seen.

LLANARTHNEY
MAP 2 REF F7

7 miles W of Llandeilo off the B4300

Middleton Hall here in Llanarthey is currently being developed as the National Botanic Garden of Wales, as part of a Millennium Project for Carmarthenshire. **Paxton Tower** was built in 1811 by Sir William Paxton in honour of Nelson. Its location offers some fine views.

LLANDYBIE
MAP 2 REF F7

4½ miles S of Llandeilo off the A483

Set in the delightful, sleepy village of Llandybie, just 4 miles from Ammanford, **The Red Lion Hotel** is a friendly and pleasant public house (formerly a hotel, hence its name) offering good food, a selection of ales, wines and spirits, and a warm welcome. Owners and co-partners Antony Richards and Paul Hinder took over in June of 1998. Antony is the licensee, and is a lively, gregarious and welcoming host. Though new to the trade, they have brought a real enthusiasm and zest to this venture, and it shows. The pub is a centre for walkers and sports-orientated people as well as visitors from further afield, and has a lively atmosphere and occasional

**The Red Lion Hotel, 6 Llandeilo Road, Llandybie
Carmarthenshire SA18 3JA Tel: 01269 851202.**

evening entertainment. Built in 1786 of stone construction, the attractive cream-coloured paintwork and red trim make a welcoming sight to visitors to this part of Carmarthenshire. The interior is redolent with old world atmosphere, with its natural stone walls and exposed beamed ceilings. The main restaurant has an American theme, with lots of memorabilia and photographs adorning the walls. There are separate smoking and non-smoking dining rooms. The chef cooks up home-made and freshly prepared dishes. There are large beautifully maintained gardens at the rear - the perfect place to enjoy a drink, snack or meal in lovely and peaceful surroundings. Antony, having a young family himself, is happy to cater for children's parties upon request.

AMMANFORD   MAP 2 REF F7
6 miles S of Llandeilo off the A483

The Brynamman Walk from Ammanford takes in wooded gorges, peaceful rivers and a nature reserve.

BRYNAMMAN   MAP 3 REF G7
7 miles SE of Llandeilo off the A4069

Brynamman means 'hill by the River Amman'. Situated on the southeast edge of the Brecon Beacons, in the foothills of the Black Mountains, 200 years ago there was no village here. There were instead some two dozen farms, scattered within easy reach of water. It was the working of coal, as early as the 17th century, that led to the creation of a man-made brook, called Y Gwter Fawr. This is the true name of the village, borne proudly on the shirts of Brynamman rugby football club - organised rugby arrived in the village about 100 years ago.

The first shop opened in 1831. Cottage industries produced wooden kitchen utensils and woollen goods, and the first school started up in one of the farms. In 1840 a contract was drawn up between the Llanelly Railway and Dock Company and John Jones (said to be the architect of Brynamman, and born in 1795). John Jones was responsible for building the mountain road to enable the mined coal to reach the market place and the limekilns. Jones also built the Cwmgarw road and all the bridges in Brynamman. The house he built for himself on in 1837, in what is now Station Road, he named Brynamman House; when the railway reached the village in 1864, the name given to the station was Brynamman.

Commercial mining came with the opening of the first coalmine here in 1810. In 1800 the village population was 120; by 1860 it had risen to 1,060. On the opposite bank of the Amman the Amman Iron Company employed most of the population. By 1889, however, the ironworks had gone, and the Amman tinplate works had started. By then, coalmining had become the main source of employment in the village.

The coal strikes of the 1920s did not miss the village, and marked the beginning of the end for Brynamman as an industrial village. During the Second World War, St Catherine's Church was hit by two bombs and the local school was destroyed by a fire. Twenty-nine villagers lost their lives during the war.

Today, a few shops and businesses survive, though the railway has gone. One craft that has survived is that of the blacksmith, who still plies his trade at Cwmgarw Road.

Here in Brynamman, close to some spectacular scenery, the **Derlwyn Arms** is a comfortable and welcoming pub and restaurant of the highest quality, also offering bed and breakfast accommodation. Blair Fisher and Bonnie Heavens bought the Derlwyn Arms in 1997, and have been very successful in making it a thriving concern. This family-orientated establishment boasts an extensive a la carte and bar menu. Childrens' portions are half price, and children under two eat free. The interior features a large stone fireplace, beamed ceilings, and a floor fitted with imported Italian slate tiles. The attractive bar is made of rough-hewn stone and polished wood. The large and masterly mural behind the bar depicts a bit of the town's history, portraying a scene that harkens back to Brynamman's heritage as a centre for coal-mining, iron work and blacksmithing. The atmosphere is always warm, friendly and lively. There is an extensive beer garden with barbecue, and a big children's play area. The B&B accommodation consists of seven large and very comfortable guest bedrooms, suitable for both couples and families. Apart from the charms of the town itself, Brynamman makes an ideal base for exploring local places of interest such

Derlwyn Arms, 118 Mountain Road, Brynamman, Ammanford Carmarthenshire SA18 1AN Tel: 01269 826380.

as the Pentre Riding Centre (offering trekking and lessons), hang-gliding and paragliding centres, Kidwelly Castle, Carreg Cennen Castle and Tretower Court. There is also fishing, canoeing and sailing available on Llangorse Lake (the largest natural lake in South Wales), and the town also makes an excellent place from which to set out on any one of the 1,250 miles of walks in the region.

FOELGASTELL
Map 2 ref F7

6½ miles SW of Llandeilo off the A48

Near Cefneithin and Cross Hands, **Y Goeden Fach Bonsai** is the place to discover the Oriental world of these wonderful plants, with an extensive selection of indoor and outdoor trees, together with tools and accessories. In a tranquil Japanese garden setting, this attractive bonsai centre has experts on hand to offer advice, instructions, repotting and a holiday service.

GORSLAS
Map 2 ref F7

6 miles SW of Llandeilo off the A476

Llyn Llech Owain Country Park has 158 acres of woodland and a 10-acre lake. This development is sensitive to conservig the natural flora and fauna of the site. Video links make it possible to view the native birdlife at close quarters.

NEWCASTLE EMLYN

Newcastle Emlyn is an unprepossessing and attractive place, home to the first printing press in Wales, set up by Isaac Carter in 1718. **The castle** remains here are now little more than a gateway. Like other castles in Wales, Newcastle Emlyn's turbulent history is in some ways confirmed by its present condition. Changing hands several times until it was destroyed during the Glyndwr rebellion in the early 1400s, the castle fell into disrepair until given to Sir Rhys ap Thomas by Henry VII in the 16th century. The castle was destroyed after the Civil War for harbouring Royalist sympathisers.

Close to the centre of this quiet rural town, near both hills and the sea, **The Bunch of Grapes** is an attractive public house occupying an early 17th-century listed building. Built using stone from the Castle and oak reputedly stolen from Kent, it retains a traditional feel in both its ambience and tasteful decor. The interior boasts a wealth of old oak beams; two of the walls are natural stone, one covered in photographs of yesteryear in the town. Landlord Billy Brewer was once in the second-hand timber business, and has restored when necessary with timber from all over the country.

**The Bunch of Grapes, Bridge Street, Newcastle Emlyn
Carmarthenshire SA38 9DU Tel: 01239 711185.**

The big wooden bar is made of timber from Welsh pews. A woollen mill in Lancashire, manor house in Yorkshire and army barracks in Wiltshire have all contributed to the pub as it stands today. The pool room has a huge inglenook fireplace. There is a covered interior garden area with pot plants, vines and cacti. Outdoors, guests can sit at the front tables or in the beer garden to the rear. This welcoming pub attracts a range of different people. Guest ales are a speciality, in addition to the two regular real ales, Courage Directors and Theakstons Best. The menu is extensive and makes the most of fresh local produce. Sunday lunch is one of landlady Pam Brewer's specialities, as are vegetarian dishes (husband Billy has been a vegetarian for over 20 years). Fresh salmon in season is another highlight. Word of her culinary skills has spread far and wide, so it is advisable to book in advance. Live music every Thursday, of all sorts including traditional Welsh and Irish music. Billy and Pam have been running this characterful pub for 10 years, and bring a wealth of experience to offering good service and keeping the atmosphere friendly and relaxed.

AROUND NEWCASTLE EMLYN

CENARTH   MAP 2 REF E6
1 mile W of Newcastle Emlyn off the A484

The Old Smith is a craft shop and restored 18th-century blacksmith's forge located within the sound of Cenarth's famous Salmon Leap Falls. The smithy - last in operation in 1953 - contains an interesting collection of equipment together with many rural and cottage bygones. The craft shop is well stocked with local pottery, Celtic jewellery, wood carvings, Welsh woollens, books, basketware and much more. The site of Cenarth Castle or 'Motte' can be seen from the garden at the rear of the smithy.

The **National Coracle Centre** houses a unique collection of coracles from Wales and many other parts of the world, including Iraq, Vietnam, India and North America. Coracles date from the Ice Age in this country and are still made and used on the rivers of West Wales. The 17th-century flour mill also forms part of the Centre, together with superb views of the Cenarth salmon leap falls. Coracles can be seen often on the river during the summer months.

DREFACH FELINDRE   MAP 2 REF E6
4 miles SE of Newcastle Emlyn off the A484

Many of the water-driven mills of southern Ceredigion continue to produce flour and distinctive woollen goods. This important part of the region's industrial heritage is explored in the **Museum of the Welsh Woollen Industry**. Here is told the story of one of the most traditional and rural industries, with demonstrations of the cloth-making and dyeing processes carried out on 19th-century machines. Visitors can try their hand at spinning and stroll around the sites of the old woollen mills in the village, which still produce flannel cloth, tweeds, traditional clothing and blankets. A 24-mile Woollen Mill Trail here in the Teifi Valley concentrates on the industrial heritage of the villages around Drefach.

CARMARTHEN

Carmarthen is one of the oldest Roman towns in Wales, now the county town and a thriving centre for crafts and traditional market activity. The administrative and market centre for the region, Carmarthen is especially busy on Wednesdays when its huge livestock market is in full swing. This historic old town grew up around a medieval **Castle** overlooking the River

Towy. Unfortunately, there's not much left of the castle today, though its gatehouse still stands close to the shops and busy streets.

The **Guildhall**, in the town centre, was rebuilt in 1767, replacing a hall of 1583. Nott Sqaure, where the hall stands, is named after a victor of the First Afghan War in the 1840s, while a monument recalls the martyrdom of Bishop Ferrar in 1555.

If legend is to be believed, Carmarthen was Merlin's City. One legend associated with the town has thankfully turned out to be untrue. Carmarthen's inhabitants are eternally grateful that the prophesy concerning Merlin's Oak proved to be incorrect. The wizened old tree stump was removed during a road widening scheme, despite the threat: When Merlin's Oak shall tumble down, then shall fall Carmarthen town.

On the eastern outskirts of Carmarthen, in a grassy knoll below a row of houses, is a Roman amphitheatre, one of only seven known in Britain. The Romans pushed no further west than Carmarthen, establishing an important base here, most of which lies buried beneath the modern town.

AROUND CARMARTHEN

ABERGWILI   Map 2 ref F7
1 mile E of Carmarthen off the A40

Carmarthenshire County Museum occupies a lovely old house which was previously a **Palace of the Bishop of St David's**. The museum of Carmarthenshire's past, it features a wide range of exhibits including Roman gold and other finds, items from anceint Egypt, domestic exhibits from rural Wales, Welsh furniture, costumes, a school room and even a penny-farthing, to name but a few.

Just to the north of the village, **Caws Ffermdy Nantybwla Cheesemaking & Museum** has viewing windows onto the cheesemaking room, where visitors can see the award-winning Nantybwla Cheese in the making. Onsite there is also a shop.

BRONWYDD   Map 2 ref E7
3 miles NE of Carmarthen off the A484

The **Gwili Railway**, a private venture staffed by volunteers, lies to the north of Carmarthen at Bronwydd Arms Station and offers a short ride by steam or diesel on a stretch of the old Great Western Line. Full-sized reminders of the age of steam take visitors past fields and the meandering River Gwili. The railway through Bronwydd Arms opened in 1860, becoming the property of British Railways in 1948. The line closed in 1973, but in 1975 the Gwili Railway Company was formed. Volunteers opened the first section of the line for visitors in 1978. The line runs for 1.6 miles to Llwyfan Cerrig, the perfect rural spot for a picnic.

PONTARGOTHI   MAP 2 REF F7
9 miles E of Carmarthen off the A40

Swyn Yr Afon is a charming Austrian-style wooden chalet with a slate roof and 'gingerbread' trim along the eaves offering totally self-contained self-catering accommodation in an area of outstanding natural beauty. Excellently located for tranquil walks through the nearby woods, strolls along the river - or, alternatively, salmon fishing (licence required) - it is a haven of peace and bucolic beauty just 15 miles from the coast. The chalet sleeps four, and has beamed ceilings, pine furnishings and a well-equipped kitchen. There are views of the river and woods from the window and an attractive first-floor gallery. Guests can also make use of the barbecue and picnic table outdoors. Owner Anne Lesley is a gifted artist who fashions pressed flower pictures, cards, birth pictures made to order, and embroidered pieces - all of which make unique and captivating presents. For a truly relaxing break in pastoral surroundings, this lovely establishment makes a good choice. Guests should provide their own bedding. No pets. No smoking.

**Swyn Yr Afon, Bwthyn Clwtau, Pontargothi, Carmarthen
Carmarthenshire SA32 7NR Tel: 01267 290555.**

PONTARSAIS   MAP 2 REF F6
5 miles N of Carmarthen off the A485

Gwili Pottery offers finely made hand-thrown and hand-decorated domestic ware, in a beautiful range of colours and designs.

ST CLEARS   MAP 2 REF E7
6 miles SW of Carmarthen off the A40

St Clears has some claim to fame in that Owain Glyndwr suffered defeat here in 1406 at the hands of Pembrokeshire's army. The village also featured in the Rebecca Riots of the 1840s, when rioters, with grievances similar to those of the Chartists, destroyed tollgates. Reform was eventually introduced in 1884 and no tollgates were left in South Wales. This small market town has a Norman castle and a fine example of motte and bailey.

On the A40 between St Clears and Whitland at Pwll-Trap, **Glyn-Coch Studios** is a Welsh craft centre featuring bone china and porcelain collectors' pieces, hand-painted china gifts, period dolls, candles, hand-weaved basketware and more.

LLANGYNIN   MAP 2 REF E7
9 miles W of Carmarthen off the B4299

Coed Llys Uchaf is the ideal bed and breakfast establishment for anyone who appreciates luxury and being pampered. Located in a peaceful rural village, it has a quiet, restful atmosphere. There are two guest bedrooms, one ensuite and one with a private bathroom, each decorated to a high

**Coed Llys Uchaf, Llangynin, St Clears, Carmarthenshire SA33 4JY
Tel: 01994 231455 Fax: 01994 231441.**

standard of taste and comfort. In addition there is a welcoming and cosy guests' lounge, and the kitchen/dining area with stone walls, beamed ceilings and a large 'walk-in' fireplace. Breakfast and, if required, candle-lit dinner (the latter complete with complementary wine from crystal glasses) are served in the dining room. The views from the windows are panoramic across lush open countryside. For that extra special touch there are towelling dressing gowns, slippers, a complementary Body Shop basket, fruit basket and chocolates in the rooms, all inclusive in the modest price. Friendly owners Valerie and Keith Harber go out of their way to ensure guests' every comfort and convenience.

WHITLAND
MAP 2 REF D7
12 miles W of Carmarthen off the A40

This small market town and centre of the dairy industry is historically important as the meeting place of the assembly convened by Hywel Dda in 930 to establish a unified legal system for Wales. The success of the code, which survived, in parts, until the Act of Union in 1536, is remembered in a Memoral complex, with Visitor Centre. The six small memorial gardens at the Hywel Dda visitor centre each take one of the main legal themes, namely Society and Status, Crime and Tort, Women, Contract, the King, and Property.

Just north of town lie the remains of the once-great **Whitland Abbey**. Founded in 1143 by Bernard, the first Norman bishop of St David's, this Cistercian House became the mother-house to Cwmhir in the same year, and to Strata Florida in 1164.

LAUGHARNE
MAP 2 REF E7
8 miles SW of Carmarthen off the A4066

Laugharne is a coastal town on the Taf Estuary. The rich farmlands in these parts inspired some of Dylan Thomas' most evocative writing. It was here, in The Boat House, that Thomas wrote some of his greatest works. He discovered the obscure little seaside town in the 1940s, spending one of the happiest periods of his life here beside the shore, heavily colonised by herons. This timeless, mild, beguiling island of a town provided much of the inspiration for his best-known work, *Under Milk Wood*, a day in the life of his imaginary village of Llareggub (spell it backwards!). Thomas, no stranger to destructive drinking sprees, died in The White Horse bar in New York City in 1953, when he was only 39. A plain white cross in Laugharne's churchyard marks his final resting place, and **The Boat House** is now a museum dedicated to his life and work.

Located in the square behind the Town Hall and clocktower, **Laugharne Glass** is a distinguished centre selling handmade hallmarked silver orna-

Laugharne Castle

mental glass. In the glass-blowing studio, demonstrations are held and visitors can watch these exquisite creations in the making. Laugharne has waymarked and interpreted scenic walks well worth experiencing.

LLANSTEFFAN   MAP 2 REF E7
7 miles SW of Carmarthen off the B4312

This village near the mouth of the River Towy has a magnificent ruined Norman **Castle** situated on a headland above the village and the estuary. Built during the 11th to 13th centuries, and successor to an earlier defensive earthwork, the castle's main feature is a fine gatehouse of 1280. **St Anthony's Well**, a wishing well to the southwest of the castle, is said to have medicinal properties.

Llansteffan, along with its neighbour across the estuary, Ferryside, is a paradise for walkers and boat owners. There are waymarked walks taking in some truly breathtaking coastal scenery.

PENDINE   MAP 2 REF E7
12 miles SW of Carmarthen off the AA4066

With endless stretches of sand, Pendine was used for land speed records in the 1920s by Sir Malcolm Campbell and others. In 1924, Sir Malcolm broke the World Motor Flying Kilometre Record by averaging 146 mph. But soon afterwards tragedy struck. While attempting to beat Sir Malcolm's record, Welshman J G Parry Thomas was killed in an accident on the beach. His car, Babs, was buried in the sands for 42 years before being dug up for restoration in 1969. As a tribute to the history of motorsport, there is a **Museum of Speed** featuring the history of these men and other land speed record breakers, with seasonal visits by historic motor cars. Pendine also offers good bathing. The **Carmarthen Bay Coastal Walk** links Pendine and Amroth to the west, taking in some spectacular scenery along the way.

LLANNON   MAP 2 REF F7
11 miles SE of Carmarthen off the B4306/A476

Llywyn-teg is a small and picturesque hamlet close to Llannon. To the north lies a large area of wet heath and bog known as **Gwenwydd Cochion**. This expanse of rushes, cotton grass, heather and large spreads of *Malinia caerulea* (Purple Moor grass) attracts a great many birds (including curlews, stone chats, winchats, snipe and wild ducks) and butterflies. Within Llwyn-teg itself, the wet bog covers a large surrounding area, and here a more diverse bogland flora can be seen. The area is also rich in dragon flies and damsel flies, dormice, Pgymy shrews and other rare fauna. The whole of the area is very rich in diverse habitats, making it unique in Carmarthenshire. This is due in part to the land being suitable for small holding rather than the more intensive large-scale farming, thus providing an oasis for naturalists.

A 200-year-old stone-built farmhouse amid the tranquil beauty of the Carmarthenshire countryside, **Ffynnon Rhosfa Farm** is an attractive and comfortable bed and breakfast which makes an ideal base for touring and sightseeing in the region, or as a stop-over on the way to Ireland. The quiet hamlet of Llwyn-teg is only 5 minutes off the M4 - Carmarthen, Swansea, Mumbles, the Gower and the Black Mountains are all within easy distance. The two double rooms and two-bedroom family unit, all en-suite, are lovely and cosy, and plans are afoot to extend the accommodation available by converting the existing stable block - please ring, fax or e-mail

**Ffynnon Rhosfa Farm, Llwyn-teg, Llannon, Carmarthenshire CA14 8JN
Tel: 01269 845874 Fax: 831500 email: ffynnon.rhosfa@virgin.net
Internet address: http://freespace.virgin/ffynnon.rhosfa**

for details. The homely guests' lounge has a large open fireplace. The full English or Continental breakfast is home-made, and evening meals, snacks and packed lunches are available upon request. Special diets also catered for. Owner Mrs Aloisia Barker personally presides over this tasteful establishment. Of Austrian descent, she speaks fluent German and basic French as well as English. Fishing, golfing and riding, as well as painting lessons under the tutelage of a local artist, can all be arranged. WTB 2 Crowns Commended.

KIDWELLY
8 miles S of Carmarthen off the A484

MAP 2 REF E7

Kidwelly is an historic town whose Charter was granted by Henry I. The town boasts an ancient church and 14th-century bridge. Another of those little known Welsh fortresses that merit much greater public acclaim, the Norman **Kidwelly Castle** has a formidable twin-towered gatehouse that still sends shivers down the spine. On a steep bluff overlooking the River Gwendraeth, this remarkably well-preserved castle offers a glimpse into medieval times. The castle was founded by the Normans as an earth and timber stronghold in 1106. In the 1270s it was rebuilt in stone as the fortress visitors see today. The castle's most arresting feature is the Great Gatehouse, completed in 1422. A new hall, kitchen and lodgings were added during Tudor times.

Kidwelly Castle

On the outskirts of town, the **Kidwelly Industrial Museum** pays tribute to the once-important tinplate manufacturing industry and has preserved the old works along with the furnaces, steam engines and metal cutters that resemble giant tin openers.

PEMBREY   MAP 2 REF E8
11 miles S of Carmarthen off the A484

Pembrey Country Park is set in 500 acres of landscaped woods and parkland. It is a most unusual and fascinating place, a mixture of pine forest, sand dune and huge beach. The beach, no fewer than 8 miles long, is known as **Cefn Sidan**. Pembrey's strange forest beside the sea, which was planted to help stabilise the dunes, can be explored by following a waymarked footpath or from the saddle of a pony. The park also has a narrow gauge railway, dry ski slope, the longest toboggan run in Wales, 9-hole pitch and putt course, children's play areas and picnic sites.

The 30 mile circular walk from Pembrey to the Swiss Valley reservoir provides a wonderful journey through some spectacular natural beauty. The 64 mile St Illtyd's Walk links Pembrey Country Park and Margam Park, east of Swansea.

BURRY PORT   MAP 2 REF F8
12 miles SE of Carmarthen off the A484

Burry Port Harbour commemorates an event in aeronautical history. On 18th June 1928, the first aircraft to cross the Atlantic non-stop splashed into the harbour after a 23 hour flight!

PWLL   MAP 2 REF F8
13 miles SE of Carmarthen off the A484

Tafarn Y Sospan is a very attractive restaurant on the outskirts of Llanelli. Situated close to the famous Strady Park Llanelli rugby ground and Pembroke Park, it attracts a wide variety of customers and always has a convivial, lively atmosphere. The interior of this handsome establishment boasts exposed beamed ceilings, brass fittings and a part-wood block floor, and is spacious and light, the sun pouring in through the large front win-

**Tafarn Y Sospan, 8 Bassett Terrace, Pwll, Llanelli
Carmarthenshire SA15 4DY Tel: 01554 771052.**

dows on fine days. The seating is comfortable and the ambience relaxed and friendly. The menu offers a range of snacks and meals, created by chef Nathan. Owner Ivor Jones and his staff take great pride in maintaining a strong reputation for service and quality. Lunch is served from 11 a.m.-3 p.m., dinner from 6-9 p.m. The Sunday carvery is a popular favourite, and there is also a special children's menu.

LLANELLI   MAP 2 REF F8
15 miles SE of Carmarthen off the A484

Essentially an industrial town based around its steel, chemical and engineering works, the town was named after the Celt St Elli, to whom the parish church is dedicated. The town is also famous for the 'Scarlets', one of Wales' most famous rugby teams.

Rick Leech on James Street creates hand-engraved glassware in custom-made designs and specifications. Llanelli pottery enjoyed fame in the mid-19th century, and a marvellous exhibition can be seen in the **Parc Howard Museum and Art Gallery**. Displays also include collections of paintings by local artists. Parc Howard mansion is an historic building set in a delightful park. **Sandy Water Park** west of Llanelli features a 16-acre lake and landscaped walks. **Penclacwydd Wildfowl and Wetlands Centre** offers visitors a perfect opportunity to get close to nature.

5 Gower Peninsula & The Heritage Coast

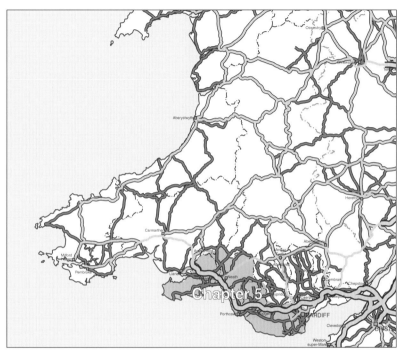

The charming and exciting city of Swansea marks the gateway to the lovely Gower Peninsula, quite rightly designated an Area of Outstanding Natural Beauty. Gower's southern coast is made up of a succession of sandy, sheltered bays. The Peninsula is a slip of land some 8 miles wide at its widest point and stretching some 15 miles west of Swansea. It is surrounded by the waters of the River Loughour to the north, Rhossili Bay to the west, and Port Eynon, Oxwich and Swansea Bays to the south. Punctuated with charming and relaxed seaside resorts, this is an area rich in natural beauty, with magnificent beaches with miles of golden sand and delightful waterside communities, both at the coast and inland where small rivers and other waterways ply their way across the Peninsula.

The Vale of Glamorgan is characterised by gentle rolling hills, genteel towns, pretty villages and a splendid natural coastline. The rich farmlands of the Vale of Glamorgan, standing at the foot of the stunning and spectacular Valleys of South Wales, offer an enticing green alternative to the pleasures of the Glamorgan Heritage Coast to the south. The Vale is rich in history. Many castles were constructed here by Norman warlords. The best way to explore the beauties of the Vale is to get into a car and follow one of the leafy country lanes which criss-cross this lush green swathe of hills and wooded valleys. It won't be long before a visitor comes across one of the many pretty villages dotted around the Vale. The unspoilt Glamorgan Heritage Coast is the name given the coastal part of this region.

The Ogmore, Garw and Llynfi Valleys of this part of Wales are world famous for coal-mining and heavy industry. Their names may conjure up images of collieries, rows of miners' cottages clinging to the hillsides and spoil from the pits piled high in smouldering pinnacles above the villages - yet today's visitor will find a very different landscape here. Nature has reclaimed the hills and vales once scarred and blackened by the mining industry. The legacy of pride in industry remains, however, in the shape of heritage centres, country parks and nature trails.

This area also includes the capital city of Wales, Cardiff. It has everything a city can offer: culture, fine architecture, superb entertainments, shopping, historical sites and acres of beautiful parks.

SWANSEA

Swansea is an appealing blend of traditional and modern. Wales' second city is a very attractive and welcoming place. Dylan Thomas, who was born and raised in the Uplands area of the city described his home as an 'ugly, lovely town' as part of his evocative depictions of Swansea. Having said this, much of the Swansea of Thomas' youth was destroyed by German bombs during the Second World War.

The city centre is modern and pleasant, though arguably the most impressive part of town is the **Maritime Quarter**. The centrepiece of this modern development is the old dock, which has been transformed into a marina and surrounded by stylish waterfront buildings. Look out for the modern sculptures on the walls and by the walkways, which add to the charm of this well-thought-out, architecturally adventurous development.

A former warehouse on the waterfront has been converted into a **Maritime and Industrial Museum**, tracing the development of Swansea as a port. Upstairs there's a complete woollen mill in working order which still produces traditional Welsh weaves.

Unlike Cardiff, Welsh is occasionally spoken as a first language in the Swansea streets. 'Old' Swansea also lives on in the city's covered market, which is probably the best fresh foods market in Wales. A jar of cockles, freshly picked from the nearby Penclawdd cockle beds on the Gower Peninsula, can be purchased together with laverbread - a uniquely Welsh delicacy which may look like a strange black paste but is made from health-giving seaweed and makes a most tasty accompaniment to bacon and eggs.

Swansea's setting is impressive. Dylan Thomas described the Swansea he could see by gazing down over the rooftops from his hillside home as 'by the side of a long and splendidly curving shore'. He also wrote that 'you've got to be a Sherpa' to be able to negotiate the route to his home, at 5 Cwmdonkin Drive. Cwmdonkin Drive is in fact a very steep street, and No 5 not far from the top! An ordinary looking semi-detached house, it is still in private ownership though marked with a blue plaque with the simple inscription, 'Dylan Thomas, Poet, 1914-53. Born in this house.'

Swansea Castle will once again take its place as the centrepiece of the redeveloped city centre. A former motte and bailey castle was rebuilt in stone in the late 13th century. The northern block gained notoriety as a debtors' prison in the 18th century.

AROUND SWANSEA

THE MUMBLES
MAP 2 REF F8
5 miles SW of Swansea off the A4067

The Coffee Bean is a small and very popular coffee shop/cafe in Castleton Walk, a small shopping mall in The Mumbles area of Swansea. Owner Kathy Davies bought the premises in 1994, and has refurbished it to a high standard of taste and comfort. The decor is bright and attractive; paintings by local artists adorn the walls. With the able assistance of Sue and Geraldine, she offers a warm welcome, friendly service and an excellent choice of home-cooked meals and snacks, including all-day breakfasts, hot and cold sandwiches, jacket potatoes and

The Coffee Bean, Castleton Walk, Newton Rd The Mumbles SA3 4AX Tel: 01792 361734.

tempting desserts. In addition to the menu there are always daily specials and vegetarian options. To wash down these delicious meals there are a good range of coffees, teas and soft drinks. The homely atmosphere of this charming cafe will appeal to guests just as much as the menu. Open Monday-Saturday 9-5 (slightly later in summer). Separate smoking and non-smoking areas.

The Mumbles is a small and unspoilt sailing and watersports centre along Swansea Bay. The village's unusual name is actually derived from the French 'mamelles', meaning 'breasts' - a reference to the two islets off the promontory beyond Oystermouth.

Overlooking picturesque Swansea Bay, **Patricks** is one of the best restaurants for miles around, open Monday-Saturday for morning coffee from 10.30 a.m., lunches (noon-2.30) and evening meals from 6.30-10 p.m., as well as Sundays from noon-2.30. Patricks has a seating capacity of 62 with baby changing and disabled facilities and an atmosphere created by the four partners, Catherine and Sally on the front of house and Patrick and Dean behind the scenes in the kitchen. All the food is home-made, including the freshly baked breads, and some of the tempting specialities from

Patricks, 636-638 Mumbles Road, The Mumbles, Swansea SA3 4EA
Tel: 01792 360199.

the extensive menu and blackboard include game casserole with mustard and wild herb dumplings, sword fish steak with Indonesian butter sauce, and field mushrooms in pastry with mashed potato and a red wine sauce. The desserts are also truly marvellous creations, guaranteed to tempt you into leaving extra room for. The Patricks philosophy is always to offer seriously good food, wine and service! Booking is advisable in the evenings.

The ruins of **Oystermouth Castle** lie in a small park overlooking the bay. Family home of the de Breos lineage, the gatehouse, chapel and great hall date from the 13th-14th century. The resort boasts a fine collection of Welsh love spoons and a surprisingly active nightlife.

Situated in the main street in The Mumbles, **Vincent's** restaurant and bar is a popular destination for locals and visitors alike. The premises date back to the 1850s; up until 1991 it was a public house. Gregarious owner Vincent Moreno then bought the place, and has undertaken major refurbishments to transform it into a spacious, comfortable and relaxed restaurant. The menu boasts a good range of Spanish-influenced dishes, such as gambas salsa verde (small prawns with a garlic/parsley vinaigrette) and lomo de cerdo (loin of pork fried with apples and seasonings). There's also an unrivalled selection of fresh fish and sea food.

Vincent's hosts nightly events, including candlelight evenings, a sports night on Wednesdays, specials offers on beers on Tuesdays, and other lively and memorable entertainments. The range of ales come from near and far, and the restaurant has featured in the *Good Beer Guide*. For great food and drink in a lively and welcoming atmosphere, this excellent establishment is well worth a visit.

Vincent's, 580 Mumbles Road, The Mumbles, Swansea SA34DL
Tel: 01792 368308 Fax: 01792 367947
email: elpatron@btinteret.com

Beyond The Mumbles lies the lovely **Gower Peninsula**, quite rightly designated an Area of Outstanding Natural Beauty. Gower's southern coast is made up of a succession of sandy, sheltered bays. The first of these, **Langland Bay**, is just around the headland from The Mumbles, a short distance from Newton.

UPPER KILLAY   MAP 2 REF F8
6 miles W of Swansea off the A4118

The **Railway Inn** is a rustic and traditional tavern standing alongside the now disused L.M. & S.R. Swansea-Shrewsbury railway line, closed since the early 1960s. Hidden away off the road, this distinctive public house dates back to 1864. It has a great deal of character, style and charm. The

**The Railway Inn, 553 Gower Road, Upper Killay, Swansea SA2 7DS
Tel: 01792 203946.**

interior boasts many old photographs and prints of the engines and carriages which used to ply their way past the inn. The beamed ceilings and lovely roaring fire enhance the pub's warm and cosy ambience. It is renowned for its atmosphere and fine array of ales, which includes three ales brewed locally at Bishopston. A centre of the local community, owners Willie and Chris and their conscientious, friendly staff also offer a warm Welsh welcome to all their guests. Whether you choose to sit in the front bar, snug or lounge bar, you are sure to enjoy the surroundings, company and excellent range of ales, lagers, spirits and wines here. Open all day every day.

PARKMILL
MAP 2 REF F8
8 miles SW of Swansea off the A4118

Parc Le Breos Burial Chamber is a neolithic tomb in a hidden valley close to the Gower Heritage Centre. The chamber once held the 6,000 year old remains of up to 40 people. Nearby **Cathole Cave** is still older, and held Ice Age remains of mammoth and woolly rhino.

PENMAEN
MAP 2 REF F8
9 miles SW of Swansea off the A4118

Here in Penmaen, **North Hills Farm Cottages** and **Three Cliffs Bay Caravan Park** offer guests two different kinds of accommodation. North Hills Farm Cottages are self-catering homes contained within the old refurbished stables and outbuildings of this 147-acre working farm. Honoured with a

Three Cliffs Bay Caravan Park, North Hills Farm, Penmaen, Gower Swansea SA3 2HB Tel: 01792 371218.

5-Star rating by the Welsh Tourist Board, these three single-storey cottages are well appointed and comfortably furnished. Two have one bedroom, while the third has two. They are available all year round, for weekly lets in summer and shorter stays (minimum of three days) out of season. Three Cliffs Bay sits high up overlooking Oxwich Bay, with tremendous views in every direction. The caravan park covers 5 acres, taking up to 20 caravans and an unlimited amount of campers. Open 1st April-end October, the park boasts excellent facilities such as 20 electric hook-ups, toilets, hand basins, showers and laundry and kitchen area. There is also a farm shop on-site.

LLANRHIDIAN
MAP 2 REF F8
11 miles SW of Swansea off the B4271

Llanrhidian is a small, quiet village in the heart of the Gower Peninsula

Weobley Castle, Llanrhidian

region, near some of Britain's finest beaches. There are long glistening cockle sands below Llanrhidian, perfect for wandering. Weobley Castle is the ruin of a larger 13th and 14th century fortified manor house. It is a fine illustration of the era when comfort was becoming as important as security. Within the castle is an exhibition on the Gower Peninsula.

Co-partners Robert, Sheila and Tim Allen took over the **Welcome to Town Country Bistro and Bar** in 1997, and have converted this impres-

Welcome to Town Country Bistro and Bar, Llanrhidian, Gower Swansea SA3 1EH Tel: 01792 390015.

sive 18th century stonebuilt establishment into a distinguished bistro. They offer all their guests a warm welcome and a high standard of quality and service. The interior is comfortable and cosy, the atmosphere always relaxed and quiet. There's an open fireplace, and attractive pictures adorn the walls. One interesting and unusual feature is the bar front, taken from the Kardomah coffee house, a renowned establishment here in South Wales before it was destroyed during the Second World War. Sheila does all the cooking, and as befits a past winner of the All Wales Top Cook award, she provides a range of delicious choices, including vegetarian options. The changing, innovative menu boasts such dishes as halibut under a herb crust, smoked duck breast, game ragu and fillet of Welsh beef. The desserts are also superb, with tempting delights such as mixed nut fudge flan and chocolate and chestnut gateau well worth leaving room for. Open Tuesday to Saturday, lunch and evenings.

OXWICH MAP 2 REF F8
12 miles SW of Swansea off the A4118

One of the prettiest Gower villages, Oxwich is huddled along one lane at the west end of a superb three miles of sand. Once a small port exporting limestone and also a haven for smugglers, today it is a marvellous holiday area with safe bathing from a clean beach, wind-surfing and water-skiing.

The village boasts some picturesque cottages in traditional Gower style, including a cottage once occupied by John Wesley. Oxwich's **Church of St Illtud** lies half-hidden by trees but is worth seeking out. It is thought that its ancient font was brought to the church by St Illtud himself.

Oxwich Castle

For walkers there are plenty of footpaths to explore. The walk to **Oxwich Point** in particular provides some magnificent views of Gower. Just back from Oxwich's beach is part of the **Oxwich Nature Reserve**, home of many rare species of orchid as well as other plant life. There are many species of bird, too, to delight amateur ornithologists.

PORT EINON   MAP 2 REF F8
13 miles W of Swansea off the A4118

The road to this lovely hamlet leads down a steep hill. Regarded as something of a surfing centre, Port Einon offers some rather spectacular coastline from where the coasts of Somerset and Devon can be seen.

SCURLAGE   MAP 2 REF F8
13 miles W of Swansea off the A4118

Scurlage is a picturesque village just inland from Port Einon. **The Countryman** is a large establishment built in 1971 and owned and personally run for the past 10 years by Alex Williams and Mary Davies. Located within picturesque and popular Gower, this attractive public house/restaurant and nightclub offers a wonderful range of amenities and facilities. Visitors can quench their thirst with a fine selection of ales (up to six different ones) and enjoy a meal in the excellent restaurant. The atmosphere throughout is warm and welcoming, as young and old, locals and visitors mix freely. The hospitality on offer is, in short, first-class. In the evenings there's a variety of entertainments on offer - including cabaret nights at weekends, and children's entertainment on Saturdays and during school holidays. The separate Waves Nightspot is open Thursday-Saturday from 10 p.m.-2.30 a.m. in season, Friday and Saturday 10-2.30 in winter. Pub/restaurant open all day every day.

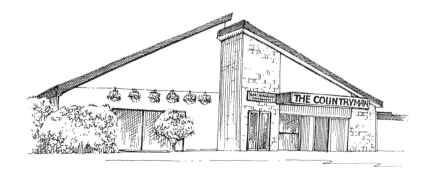

The Countryman, Scurlage, Gower, Swansea SA3 1AY
Tel: 01792 390597.

KNELSTON
MAP 2 REF F8
12 miles W of Swansea off the A4118

This attractive village has a ruined 12th century church and, to the north, is **Arthur's Stone**, a large burial chamber capstone. Traditionally the Stone is said to be the pebble King Arthur removed from his shoe when on his way to the Battle of Camlann in AD 539. The story goes that the King threw it over his shoulder and it lies where it landed. Up until the late 19th century local girls would enact a ritual here to discover whether their lovers were true or not. At midnight on a night when the moon was full, they would place a honey cake soaked in milk on the Stone, then crawl under the Stone three times. At this point, if their lovers were true, they would join them.

RHOSSILI
MAP 2 REF E8
16 miles W of Swansea off the B4247

Rhossili is a delightful and very pretty village overlooking Rhossili Bay with its outstanding beaches. **The Cafe Rendezvous** occupies a handsome building dating back to the early 19th century. Owners Andrew and Denise, a former financial controller and director of nursing respectively, opted for a complete change in careers and took over these charming, traditional tea rooms in 1992. They have developed them into a superior licenced restaurant and coffee house. The interior is cosy and inviting; there is also a lovely rear garden area suitable for fine days and warm

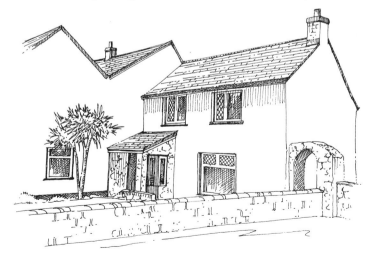

Cafe Rendezvous, New Park Cottage, Rhossili, Gower SA3 1PL
Tel: 01792 390645.

evenings. The separate lunchtime and evening menus offer a good range of choices, from steaks, fish and chicken dishes to jacket potatoes, salads and sandwiches and other light meals. The cream teas are a speciality. In the evenings the excellent choices of cuisine are augmented with additional specials, making for at least eight main-course options, of which three will feature fresh locally caught fish. All are served amid an atmosphere of friendly hospitality. Booking advised. Open Easter-end October daily, weekends in winter.

At the westernmost tip of the Gower Peninsula lies **Worms Head**, a spectacular spindly island connected to the mainland by a low tide causeway. Windy Worms Head is reached from this clifftop village, which looks out over a huge, sandy, west-facing beach popular with surfers. It was also described by Dylan Thomas as *'miles of yellow coldness going away into the distance of the sea'*. In the sturdy little church here is a memorial plaque to a Gower man, Edgar Evans. Better known perhaps as Petty Officer Evans, he died in the tragic expedition to the Antarctic led by Captain Scott in 1912.

LLANGENNITH   MAP 2 REF E8
16 miles W of Swansea off the B4271/B4295

Rhossili is a small, quiet and rural village overlooking Rhossili Down. Here stands the largest church on the peninsula, which dates from the 12th century. It was built on the site of a 6th-century priory founded by St Cenydd but sacked by Viking raiders in AD 986. The grave inside is thought to be that of St Cenydd. The church tower has a saddle-back roof, an excellent example of fortified architecture that was once typical in the area. A great number of surfers come to this part of the Gower peninsula because of the excellence of the local surf and facilities.

The Kings Head pub, a very old country inn standing opposite the ancient Norman church, is, without a doubt, the hub of the pretty coastal

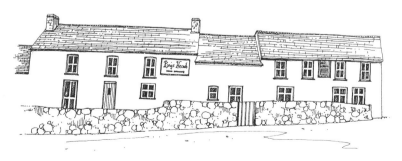

**Kingshead, Llangenwith, Gower, Swansea SA3 1HX
Tel: 01792 386212.**

village of Llangennith. Ownership of this lovely inn can be traced back to 1790 and, long before that, it was a farm and brewery dating back to the settlement of St Cenydd, the Cornish saint. Today, Anna and Paul Stevens serve the finest real ale and superb food, with delicious pizzas made to order and a specials board including local seafood and a selection of Thai and Oriental specialities as well as traditional home cooking. The beach below the village is three miles of the finest sand with Rhossili Downs rolling away to the east, making this a delightful place to while away an afternoon.

Llangennith Post Office, which offers bed and breakfast accommodation, provides an ideal centre for exploring the magnificent beaches of the Gower Peninsula and for visitors to enjoy some of the best walking country in the region. This area attracts a great many surfers, ramblers, cyclists and caravanners, who come to enjoy the tranquillity and relaxation it

The Post Office, Llangennith, Gower, Swansea SA3 1HU
Tel/Fax: 01792 386201 email: jan@llangennithpo.demon.co.uk

offers. As the name suggests, this handsome and welcoming establishment was built in the 1920s as a post office and telephone exchange. Now adorned with hanging baskets, it still operates as the Post Office combined with the Village Store and Tea-room. The interior is decorated and furnished to a high standard of taste and comfort with three attractive and comfortable guest bedrooms. The large new conservatory affords wonderful views over the sea. WTB 2 Stars.

LLANMADOC   MAP 2 REF F8
15 miles W of Swansea off the B4295

Climbing **Llanmadoc Hill** is worth the effort for the fine views it affords
of the Gower. On its lower slopes **The Bulwark** is an Iron Age hillfort.

SWANSEA VALLEY

CLYDACH   MAP 2 REF G8
5 miles NE of Swansea off the A4067

Formerly two cottages dating back to the mid-19th century, **The Carpenters Arms** in Clydach offers first-class service and comfort and excellent
food and drink. Tenant Mark Rushton was chef here for four years before
taking over the tenancy in 1996. Open all day every day, meals are available Tuesday-Sunday. The comprehensive menu (lunches noon-2; evenings
7-10 p.m.) and specials board offer a minimum of 12 main courses. Guests
can eat in the lounge, bar, or dedicated restaurant area. The changing spe-

**Carpenters Arms, High Street, Clydach, Swansea SA6 5LN
Tel: 01792 843333.**

cials include Chinese Pork, Leek/Potato/Cheese bake, fish platter, chicken
chasseur, minted lamb chops, sausage and mash and many others, all home-
cooked and expertly prepared. There are always at least three ales available
including Worthington Best and Tetley Smooth, as well as a range of lagers
and spirits, and a superb wine list. Booking is advised for the restaurant for

Friday and Saturday evenings and Sunday lunch. The atmosphere is always relaxed and friendly in this superior pub.

LOUGHOR
MAP 2 REF F8

7 miles NW of Swansea off the A4070

The Globe Inn dates back to the 1700s. One intriguing fact about this distinguished public house is that, back in the 1960s, it was the last public house in South Wales to admit women. It has now been in the same family since 1962, owner Jamie Cook being the third generation of his family to run the premises. It boasts a magnificent interior, with lots of bygone memorabilia including many original paintings of the pub, the village and

**The Globe Inn, 85 Glebe Road, Loughor, Swansea SA4 6QD
Tel: 01792 516176.**

local landmarks over the years, and a large horse collar, taken from the last dray horse to deliver ale to the inn. Another interesting feature is its ultraviolet pool table, the first such in South Wales. It is open all day every day, offering hot and cold snacks and meals. To wash them down, Buckleys Best Bitter, Dylans Bitter plus a changing guest ale, Guinness, Carling and Stella lagers, Strongbow ciders and a selection of spirits and wines are available. Most evenings there are entertainments or quizzes, adding to the lively and friendly atmosphere of this outstanding old inn.

NEATH

Neath has a long industrial history, going back to the late 16th century when the first copper smelter in South Wales was built here by Cornishmen. The town itself dates from Roman times and there are some remains of Roman Nidum close by the ruins of 13th century **Neath Abbey**. Founded by Richard de Granville on land seized from the Welsh in around 1130, the abbey was converted into a mansion for Sir John Herbert in the 16th century. Later, it was used for copper smelting with workers being housed in the mansion. As well as founding the abbey, de Granville also built **Neath Castle** in the mid-12th century round which the town grew. Unfortunately, little more than the outer face of the gateway remains today.

Housed in the Old Mechanics Institute, **Neath Museum** has permanent displays on the history of the town from prehistoric times through to the Act of Union of 1535.

Situated in Pen-Y-Dre near to Neath Rugby Union Club and just across the road from the Neath Canal, **The Star Inn** is the oldest pub in Neath - the present owners have dated it back to 1790 but it may well be even older. A Free House since 1984, owner Alan Gibbon, a local man, bought the premises in 1986. He and his wife Rosemary have turned the pub into a very popular place indeed. Recently refurbished with character and charm, it is stylish and comfortable. This is a true traditional Welsh pub - no music, no fruit machines, pool table or jukebox, just superb real ales, light snacks and a friendly, homely atmosphere, and it features in every edition of the *Good Beer Guide*. Alan is very keen on providing a good selection of real ales; many brews can be sampled here, including draught Bass, kept in tip-top condition. Also on hand is Hancocks HB Bitter and numerous other real ales, changed regularly. One feature of this outstanding pub are the original handpumps, dating back to the 1940s. Open every day, 12.30-11 p.m. Sundays midday-2.30 and 7-10.30 p.m. Snacks served all day.

**The Star Inn, 83 Pen-y-dre, Neath SA11 3HF
Tel: 01639 637745/769645.**

THE VALE OF NEATH

CYNONVILLE
MAP 2 REF G8

5 miles SE of Neath off the A4107

Afan Forest Park is a wilderness of over 9,000 acres of forest. There are trails for cycling or walking (in summer visitors can hire mountain bikes) and an informative visitors' centre. At the **Welsh Miners Museum** onsite, exhibits illustrate the life of a typical miner, with pit gear and mining equipment on display and genuine coal faces to explore.

ABERDULAIS
MAP 2 REF G8

2 miles NE of Neath off the B4434/A4109

Since as early as the 1500s the power generated by the magnificent National Trust-owned **Aberdulais Falls** has been harnessed for a number of industries including copper smelting and tinplate. An antique waterwheel is still in use, now generating electricity.

Situated right next door to Aberdulais Falls, and built as an ale house back in the 16th century, and later a coaching inn and post inn, **The Dulais Rock Inn** is an impressive and friendly public house and restaurant. Open all day every day, with meals available daily from noon until 9.30 p.m., it features a separate restaurant area seating up to 30 people. Ales on offer include Worthingtons and Whitbread, as well as guest ales and a range of lagers, ciders, Guinness, wines and spirits. On Friday evenings there's a

**The Dulais Rock Inn, Aberdulais Road, Aberdulais, Neath SA10 8EY
Tel: 01639 642449.**

guest organist in the lounge, playing sing-along tunes. Adjacent to the bar area there's a full-sized old-fashioned skittle alley. The restaurant/lounge area has comfortable seating and is decorated with taste and style, with interesting memorabilia adorning the walls. The bar area makes a feature of the stone fire surround and is embellished with brasses and brass ornaments. The menu offers a range of steaks and grill dishes, as well as jacket potatoes, sandwiches and other traditional favourites.

CILFREW   MAP 2 REF G8
2½ miles N of Neath off the A465

Penscynor Wildlife Park offers visitors the chance to see a wonderful range of animals - meerkats, tropical birds, parrots, over 25 species of monkey - in a delightful setting. A chairlift offers rides to the clifftop - the descent is by bobsleigh!

CRYNANT   MAP 2 REF G7
5 miles N of Neath off the A4109

Cefn Coed Colliery Museum stands in one of the most beautiful and unspoilt valleys in the South Wales coalfield. Here visitors can discover what it was like for miners who worked underground. Photographs, maps, galleries and exhibits bring to life the tradition and legacy of mining. The well-stocked souvenir and gift shop has one of the best selections of genuine and reproduction miners' lamps in South Wales, together with a good selection of books on the coal industry.

DYFFRYN CELLWEN   MAP 2 REF H7
10 miles NE of Neath off the A4109

Formerly a house and shop, **The Dyffryn** public house was converted in 1939 to a club; this closed in 1992 and stood vacant until Lyn and Christine Williams purchased it in 1994. They have gradually refurbished the premises and now have a fine, comfortable and very welcoming inn on their hands. A real family-run premises, Lyn and Christine are ably assisted by their daughters Jessica and Lauren, Christine's sister Jacqueline and barmaid Helen.

The excellent well-kept ales include Worthington and Buchanans, plus Rupert Tetlow Mild, and a good range of lagers, cider and Guinness. The bar snacks available include pasties, sandwiches and filled rolls. The lovely paved beer garden is just the place to relax; it is enclosed and safe for children, who are provided with a Wendy house to play in. Open Monday-Friday evenings from 7 p.m., Saturday from 2 p.m. and Sunday from midday.

The Dyffryn, 58 Main Road, Dyffryn Cellwen, Onllwyn
Neath SA10 9LA Tel: 01639 700577.

The attractive and large function room seats up to 130 people and is popular for private parties and functions. On Saturday nights there's entertainment provided - soloists, duos, bands or a disco.

PORT TALBOT

Well known for its steel industry, Port Talbot was named after the Talbot family, who developed the docks in the 19th century. Now called the Old Docks, this area saw significant expansion again in the 1960s when, together with British Steel, the British Transport Docks Board built a modern deep-water harbour that was opened by HM the Queen in 1970.

Coal-mining has taken place in the area for centuries, during which time many superstitions have grown up. In 1890, the miners at **Morfa Colliery** nearby reported seeing ghostly images in and around the colliery. *'The Red Dogs of Morfa'*, as they were known, were said to be fierce hounds who would run through the streets; their appearance was marked by a sweet, rose-like scent filling the mine shaft. Such were the number of eerie manifestations that on the morning of 10th March 1890, nearly half the morning shift failed to report for work. Later that day there was an explosion in the colliery - 87 miners were killed.

AROUND PORT TALBOT

MARGAM MAP 2 REF G8
5 miles SE of Port Talbot off the A48

Margam Country Park includes the ruins of the 13th century **Margam Abbey** and is formed from land originally belonging to the Abbey. Following the Dissolution of the Monasteries, the estate passed to one Sir Rice Mansel, who built a mansion here in 1537. Today the Country Park is a huge recreational area covering some 800 acres and including an informative Visitor Centre, waymarked walks, a farm trail, the largest maze in Europe, deer herds and a classical 18th century orangery.

Margam Abbey Church is all that remains of the Cistercian house founded by Robert, Earl of Gloucester, in 1147. Following a violent revolt by the lay brothers, the house went on to become one of the wealthiest in Wales. The adjacent **Stones Museum** is home to an important collection of inscribed and sculpted stones from Roman and Celtic times through to the Middle Ages.

LLANGYNWYD MAP 2 REF H8
10 miles E of Port Talbot off the A4B4282/A4063

Llangynwyd is a pretty village perched on a hill in the Llynfi Valley. The village has an imposing tall-towered church and the oldest thatched inn in Wales. Llangynwyd is also associated with the 'Mari Llwyd', an ancient Welsh custom practised at Christmas time.

The **Ogwr Ridgeway Walk** is a 13-mile cross-country path through mountainous terrain. Offering superb views, it runs from the hills around Llangynwyd to Mynydd y Gaer in the east.

Corner House Inn stands in this small peaceful village, opposite a village memorial to Wil Hopkin. He was a local thatcher who was renowned for his singing, poetry, and doomed love for one Ann Thomas, whose mother refused to accept their love and forced Ann to marry another. It is a popular public house for its welcoming atmosphere and traditional ales. Located in a handsome stonebuilt building dating back to the 16th century, the interior boasts exposed stone walls, beamed ceilings and a large open fireplace. Horse brasses and a collection of prints and memorabilia adorn the walls. There are four real ales on offer, including Brains and three changing guest ales. Owners Andrew and Sandra Cox are a warm and friendly young couple enjoying their first venture into the pub trade - they have been at the pub since mid-1998. Hearty hot and cold meals are served throughout the day. There's live music every Thursday and Sunday night.

**The Corner House, Llangynwyd, Nr Maesteg, CF34 9SB
Tel: 01656 732393.**

BRIDGEND

Known in Welsh as Pen-y-Bontar Ogwr (the crossing of the River Ogmore), Bridgend was once regarded as so vital a route that two castles we constructed, one either side of the river. The surviving remains of one of these 12th century fortifications can be found on the west side of the river in the area known as **Newcastle**. The surviving rectangular tower, richly carved Norman gateway and massive curtain walls are still extant. **Coity Castle** was once the stronghold of a Norman lordship. Strengthened over three centuries, it withstood attack by Owain Glyndwr but was finally abandoned in the late 16th century.

AROUND BRIDGEND

COYCHURCH   MAP 2 REF H9
1 mile E of Bridgend off the A473/B4181

The 13th century church here in the village of Coychurch has several unusual features including a blank bay before the crossing; a cinque-foiled clerestory in the nave and lobed quatrefoil windows in diamond-shaped frames. The tower collapsed in 1877 and destroyed the south transept as well as shattering one of the two Celtic crosses here.

EWENNY
MAP 2 REF H9
2½ miles S of Bridgend off the A48/B4524

The medieval church here, which appears to be fortified, was founded by William de Londres of Ogmore Castle in the early 12th century. His son, Maurice, founded **Ewenny Priory** in 1411. It is one of the finest fortified religious buildings in Britain. Its precinct walls, with their towers and gateways, give the priory its unlikely military character, though experts believe they were put up for reasons of prestige rather than defence. There is a working pottery close by.

Slightly north of the village visitors will find **Bryngarw Country House and Park**, with formal gardens, ornamental lakes, woodland walks and a Japanese garden.

OGMORE
MAP 2 REF H9
3 miles SW of Bridgend off the B4524

This pretty village lies at the mouth of the Ogmore River. Guarding a ford across the River Ewenny, a tributary of the River Ogmore, are the ruins of **Ogmore Castle**, a stronghold of the Norman de Londres family. The ruins of the castle include a three-storey keep, a dry moat surrounding the inner ward and a surviving 40 foot wall. The grounds are said to conceal buried treasure, guarded by a ghost known as Y Ladi Wen (the White Lady).

The nearby River Ogmore is supposed to be haunted by the tormented spirits of misers who died without disclosing where they had hidden their wealth. Legend has it that these spirits will be released from their misery only when their hoards are found and thrown into the river, downstream of the castle.

MERTHYR MAWR
MAP 2 REF H9
3 miles SW of Bridgend off the A4106/B4524

Merthyr Mawr is a delightful village of thatched cottages bordered by meadows and woodlands. Close by is **Merthyr Mawr Warren** - Europe's largest dune system and Site of Special Scientific Interest.

The ruins of **Candleston Castle** are surrounded by the huge dune system of Merthyr Mawr. Here at the edge of the dunes, Candleston Castle was once a 15th-century fortified manor that children in the area believe to be haunted. The biggest mystery of Candleston is the lost village of Treganllaw (Welsh for 'the town of a hundred hands'). We have no way of telling what happened to the village, but most believe it was engulfed by dunes.

SOUTHERNDOWN

MAP 2 REF H9

5 miles SW of Bridgend off the B4524

This is a quiet village on the tranquil coast road from Bridgend. Fine views can be had from this attractive village over the sea to Devon. Nearby can be found the remains of the seaside gardens of the entirely demolished Dunraven Castle. There are some fine walks by the cliffs over the sands and rock pools, and around to the fragmentary remains of an Iron Age promontory hill fort above the sea.

The Glamorgan Heritage Coast Centre at Dunraven Bay, Southerndown, has information and fine displays outlining the history and status of this wonderful 14-mile stretch of protected coastline.

Occupying an enviable position near the sea, **Three Golden Cups** is a relaxing and friendly public house. Built as a farmhouse in the 1600s, the interior of this handsome stonebuilt establishment features two open fire-

**Three Golden Cups, Southerndown, Nr Bridgend CF32 0RW
Tel: 01656 880432.**

places, beamed ceilings, and an interesting variety of memorabilia, including items from a shipwreck of a Portuguese vessel that sank off the coast. A hub of the local community, it is frequented by surfers, long-time patrons, the local cricket club and visitors alike, who come to enjoy its excellent atmosphere and great range of real ales. There is a hearty menu of fish and seafood dishes, steaks, burgers and more, as well as a good choice of vegetarian dishes. Specialities include home-made pork in cider, apple and cream sauce, and beef and ale pie. Landlord Russell Jones has been here since 1995, and is a jovial and welcoming host. There's a delightful beer garden and outdoor children's play area.

PORTHCAWL   Map 2 ref G9
7 miles SW of Bridgend off the A4106/A4229

This popular seaside resort was once a busy coal exporting port which declined in the face of competition from Barry and Port Talbot. It continues to go from strength to strength, with broad sandy beaches, well placed golf club, fairground, fishing from the pier and what is said to be the largest caravan park in Wales. The west side of the harbour is more tranquil.

Porthcawl Harbour features an historic harbourside warehouse, old-fashioned lighthouse, watchtower and new lifeboat station with shop. At **Porthcawl Museum** visitors will find memorabilia of old Porthcawl, housed in the old Police Station.

Bob Lewis has owned and run the distinguished **Atlantic Hotel** since 1986. Located on the seafront, within a few minutes of the picturesque harbour, town centre and Royal Porthcawl golf club, this handsome hotel has 18 rooms and a large restaurant. There is a lift to the first floor bedrooms. Tastefully decorated and furnished throughout, it has earned 3 Stars and 4 Crowns from the AA. Some rooms have four-poster beds; all

Atlantic Hotel, West Drive, Porthcawl CF36 3LT
Tel: 01656 785011 Fax: 01656 771877.

are comfortable and welcoming, bright and well decorated, many with recently refurbished bathrooms. The restaurant enjoys a first-class reputation for its fine cuisine. The Austrian chef brings a wealth of experience and care to preparing a range of delicious and tempting dishes. There is also a comfortable lounge bar, and an attractive conservatory which looks out onto the seafront. The friendly and efficient staff offer a high standard of service and quality to all guests.

The resort boasts some of the cleanest beaches in South Wales at Sandy Bay, Trecco Bay and the quieter Rest Bay. Visitors can enjoy a stroll along the Promenade or hop on the 'Promenade Princess', a road train which runs from Coney Beach to Rest Bay and back. At the more tranquil western side of the resort, visitors can amble across grassy Lock's Common or explore the secluded sands and rock pools. The headlands above Rest Bay are home to the famous Royal Porthcawl Golf Club.

Here in the seaside town of Porthcawl, in a small terraced shop, **The Huw Thomas Gallery** is a haven for those interested in a gift with a difference. Huw Thomas, having trained as a wildlife illustrator, opened this Gallery in 1996. Here he displays the work of many local artists and crafts-

The Huw Thomas Gallery, Lias Road, Porthcawl, Bridgend Mid-Glamorgan CF36 3AH Tel: 01656 773727.

men. Perhaps one of the most impressive displays in the shop is that of Welsh lovespoons which are a unique and ideal gift for anyone visiting Wales. Although there is certainly a Welsh bias to the items on sale, it is not to the exclusion of items of other ethnic origins. Huw's interest in both art and nature can clearly be seen in the pictures, shells, crystals, fossils and carvings in both wood and stone from around the world. While in the area, make a point of dropping in; Huw will always find something to interest you, and there's certainly plenty to see and choose from.

On the outskirts of Porthcawl, the charming village of **Newton** has an imposing church, historic well and a traditional village green. Close by in the village of **Nottage** lies **The Farmers Arms** public house. A Grade II listed building, it is the oldest pub in Nottage, dating back to the 14th century. It is a whitewashed, stonebuilt building which is large and welcoming. There is a handsome beamed and ivy-clad ceiling in the restaurant area, exposed stone walls and attractive lantern lighting. Owner Guy Bowen

Farmers Arms, Lougher Row, Nottage, Porthcawl
Mid-Glamorgan CF36 3TA Tel: 01656 784595.

has over 30 years experience in the hotel and catering trade. He is a lively and gregarious host, with a great love of music. With his partner Glenys Llewellyn he offers a warm welcome to all guests. This lively pub offers entertainment on most nights. The menu is extensive and reasonably priced. All food on offer is home-made, available at lunch and dinner. The menu includes pies, curries, fish and meat dishes, as well as vegetarian options. The three-course Sunday lunch is a real treat, boasting a choice from among three different roasts. There is a wide range of beers on offer, including Wolverhampton/Dudley, Bass, Whitbread, Carlsberg/Tetley and Scottish/Courage. There are also real ales, including two changing guest beers at all times.

KENFIG   MAP 2 REF G9
7 miles W of Bridgend off the M4

Only a few minutes drive from Porthcawl, **Kenfig National Nature Reserve** is one of the most important sites in Britain for nature conservation.

It stands on a medieval town buried beneath the sands, only the castle keep is now visible. The legend of Kenfig Pool has it that, on a quiet day, when the water is clear the houses of the buried town can be seen at the bottom of the lake and, if one listens carefully, the bells of the old church can be heard ringing, always, before a storm.

CARDIFF

Wales' capital city is a delightful place with an unexpected beauty, grace and style. The history of the city, the administrative and commercial heart of Wales, reaches back some 2,000 years. Cardiff's Civic Centre is an architectural masterpiece. White-stone buildings of classical design, **The National Museum & Gallery** and the **City Hall** among them, are set in wide, tree-lined avenues and green parklands. The overall effect is quite stunning and it is easy to see why this collection of buildings is regarded as one of the world's most accomplished examples of civic architecture.

The National Museum is in Cathays Park and has interactive displays and exhibits on a wealth of themes, including such diverse ones as prehistoric sea monsters, coins, ceramics and more. The east wing houses a fine collection of paintings, including a superb collection of Impressionist works. There is also an excellent area devoted to the evolution of the Welsh landscape.

Close by is **Cardiff Castle**, set in 400 acres of parkland yet alongside the magnificent Civic Centre. It has Roman walls, a Norman keep and exuberant 19th century state apartments, all open to the public. This unique three-in-one historic site began life as a Roman fort, evolved into a medieval castle and was transformed into a lavish mansion, in the 19th century, by the Marquess of Bute. The old city centre is near the Castle; Capability Brown's 18th century landscaped park lies between the Castle and the river.

The story of Cardiff is in no small part the story of the Bute family. They controlled the docklands and, as Cardiff boomed as a coal exporting port, the family made a vast fortune. Some of this wealth was poured back into the wholesale reconstruction of Cardiff Castle, a no-expense-spared exercise for which the architect and so-called 'eccentric genius' William Burges was employed. Burges' flamboyant imagination was allowed to run riot, the result being a glittering, opulent set of rooms that have to be seen to be believed. The castle also preserves its links with its more distant past, for the grounds contain a well-preserved medieval keep and stonework dating from Roman times.

In the area once known as Tiger Bay - Cardiff's historic dockland - one of Europe's most exciting waterfronts is rapidly emerging. The Cardiff Bay Development Area has been and continues to be an ambitious redevelopment plan for the city's Inner Harbour and Docklands. As well as the high-tech Visitors' Centre, the area also boasts the **Welsh Industrial and Maritime Museum** in Bute Street. This museum offers a thorough exploration of Welsh industrial and maritime development, housed in five former dockland buildings. One gallery has ancient trams and cars, another various industrial engines (many of which can whirr, clank, thud or grind noisily into life), another locomotives (full size and model), another for ships and shipping, and there's an extensive area outdoors.

Another museum in this rejuvenated part of town goes by the name of **Techniquest**. Located in Stuart Street, it is a fascinating hands-on science centre, with a huge selection of exhibits and activities, together with a planetarium. Other features of this superb new waterfront development include the **Norwegian Church Arts Centre**, a former church for Norwegian seamen (author Roald Dahl was baptised here) now restored as a cultural and arts centre, and **Lightship 2000**, a restored Helwick Light Vessel LV14 now serving as a cafe.

Equally impressive is the city's mixture of old and new - for example the canopied Victorian arcades close to the up-to-the-minute **St David's Shopping Centre** and its marvellous covered market, which has one of the best fresh fish stalls anywhere. There's a fine pedestrianised area, one of several in the city, around the superb church of **St John the Baptist**.

Cardiff is also home to a shrine of rugby football, the **Arms Park**, where the emotional pre-match singing can bring a lump to the throat of even the most hardened cynic. This part of Cardiff also boasts other musical associations: Ivor Novello was born near the ground. Two of his most memorable songs were the evocative *We'll Gather Lilacs in the Spring* and *Keep the Home Fires Burning*.

A mile or so from the city centre stands **Llandaff Cathedral**, a beautiful building set in a grassy hollow beside the **River Taff**. The Cathedral suffered severe bomb damage during the Second World War. Part of its restoration includes a controversial modern sculpture entitled *Christ in Majesty* by Sir Jacob Epstein, which dominates the interior. Inside, visitors will also find some delightful medieval masonry, a marvellous modern timber roof and some works of art by members of the Pre-Raphaelite movement. This towering, uncompromising piece is still the source of much discussion and comment.

AROUND CARDIFF

TONGWYNLAIS   Map 3 ref I9
6 miles N of Cardiff off the M4

Castell Coch has fairytale spires peeping through the woods to the north of Cardiff. Built on the site of a 13th-century 'Red Castle' by the third Marquis of Bute and the eccentric architect William Burges, it was created as a companion piece to Cardiff Castle in the 19th century. The attention to medieval-style details is impressive, while the interior is truly opulent.

Castell Coch, Tongwynlais

ST FAGANS   Map 3 ref I9
4 miles W of Cardiff off the A4232

On the outskirts of Cardiff, St Fagans is home to the **Welsh Folk Museum**, one of the first of the new breed of open-air museums. Old buildings from all over Wales have been brought here and reconstructed, stone by stone, timber by timber, in a beautiful parkland setting of over 100 acres. There are farmhouses, workers' cottages, a tollhouse, a cock-pit, a mill, a tannery and a chapel. There are regular demonstrations of traditional crafts. Great attention has been paid to detail, for example in the old schoolhouse which comes complete with old-fashioned desks and blackboard.

PENARTH   MAP 3 REF I9
5 miles S of Cardiff off the A48

Penarth is a popular and unspoilt seaside resort of Victorian and Edwardian character and great charm. Attractions for those in need of fresh sea air include the 19th-century pier, the Esplanade, the views of the Bristol Channel and the seafront formal gardens and parks. The broad sweep of the Esplanade and clifftops are ideal for a leisurely walk. **Windsor Gardens**, the seafront park, offers the perfect vantage point.

Now a branch of the National Museum of Wales, the **Turner House Art Gallery** was built in 1888 by James Pyke Thompson to show his own personal collection. The gallery now shows selections from the National Museum's collection.

Penarth Pier has been restored to its former glory, and now once again ranks as one of the finest piers in Wales. **Penarth Marina**, built in the lee of Penarth Head, is a new harbour village with attractive waterfront houses and shops; yachts moored in the harbour add to the grace and distinction of this part of the resort.

To the south of the town lies the **Comeston Lakes Country Park and Medieval Village**. The Park offers over 200 acres of lakes, woodlands and meadows. From a derelict quarry, a haven of peace and natural beauty has been encouraged to flourish here, providing a habitat for wildlife and rare plants. As well as the usual attractions, including a visitors' centre, picnic areas and a cafe, the Park also has a re-creation of a medieval village (from about the 14th to 15th century) complete with farm buildings, bakehouse, peasants' cottages and domestic animals that would have been seen at the time. One of the most fascinating archaeological discoveries in Wales, here visitors can see excavated buildings, and costumed 'villagers' going about the farming and livestock rearing as they would have in the Middle Ages.

In 1897, **Lavernock Point**, to the southeast of Comeston Lakes Country Park, was the site of Marconi's early experiments in radio transmission and the scene of the historic reception of the words, 'Are you ready?' that were transmitted from the island of Flat Holm some three miles away.

BARRY ISLAND   MAP 3 REF I9
8 miles SW of Cardiff off the A4050

The coast around here, like its countryside, is full of contrasts. Barry Island, for example, is a bright and breezy traditional seaside resort where children enjoy all the fun of the fair. Yet close by there are spectacular views from towering cliffs looking out across the Bristol Channel to the Devon coast.

Barry grew as a centre for the coal industry. Remains of a 13th century castle stand here. The **Welsh Hawking Centre** has over 200 birds of prey, and features regular flying demonstrations. There are also animals to pet and an adventure playground.

ST NICHOLAS   MAP 3 REF I9
8 miles W of Cardiff off the A48

Dyffryn Gardens form part of the Dyffryn Estate. The impressive manor house was built in 1893, though the estate dates back to the 14th century. The superb gardens were landscaped in the 19th century. Though the house is not open to the public, the gardens are, offering a series of broad sweeping lanes, formal beds, shrubberies, water features and various outdoor 'rooms'. Each room is enclosed within clipped yew hedges and each has its own distinct character. There is an arboretum, vine walk, round garden, paved court, rose and kitchen garden, Pompeiian garden, and Theatre Garden (where open-air plays and concerts are staged). Dyffryn is a must for all those who appreciate fine landscaping and natural beauty. The double-sided herbaceous borders, over 100 yards long are a particular treat.

HENSOL   MAP 3 REF I9
9 miles W of Cardiff off the M4

Llanerch Vineyard is the largest in Wales, producing award-winning Welsh Wines estate-bottled under the CARIAD label. Here visitors will find 6 acres of vines on south-facing slopes overlooking the Vale of Glamorgan. This modern vinery is set in converted old farm buildings; at the visitor centre there are wine-tastings, refreshments and a wine and gift shop. The extensive grounds include a 10 acre country park of woodlands and lakes, as well as a children's play area.

PENMARK   MAP 3 REF I9
10 miles SW of Cardiff off the B4265

Close to this village is the ruined castle of **Umfrevilles** and the superb Norman **Church of St Mary**, one of the largest in the Vale of Glamorgan. How the village got its name is uncertain, but a colourful story provides one explanation. It is suggested that Penmark is the Anglicised version of 'Pen March', the horse's head. In King Arthur's time, a prince of North Wales owned a very strong and very swift horse, which was used to carry messages to the King's court in Somerset. On one occasion the horse was galloping so fast it slipped and, in falling, was decapitated, at a place called

Cefn March, 'the horse's ridge', near **Gilfach Reda** in Cardiganshire. Its head, however, travelled on until it fell, and the place where it fell became known as 'Pen March'.

ST HILARY   MAP 3 REF H9
12 miles SW of Cardiff off the A48

Beaupré Castle (pronounced bewper), an Elizabethan country house cum fortress, is set in peaceful countryside southeast of the town. One of the charms of Beaupré is its location, a little way off the road, accessible by a footpath across green fields. A particularly attractive feature worth look-ing out for is the beautifully carved outer porch, dated 1586. It bears the arms of the Bassets, the family linked with Beaupré since medieval times, and their motto (on the arms in Welsh) means 'Better Death than Shame'. Memorials to the family lie in the Norman **Church of St Hilary**, just out-side the town.

The ruins of **St Quentin's Castle**, with its 14th century gateway, stand close to the town's walls. Started by Gilbert de Clare, the castle was never finished as the owner died during the battle with the Scots at Bannockburn in 1314.

COWBRIDGE   MAP 3 REF H9
13 miles W of Cardiff off the A48

Cowbridge is a handsome, prosperous town with an historic status as the capital of the Vale of Glamorgan. The town is centred around its long main street, where there is an appealing selection of shops selling every-thing from local crafts to books.

Cowbridge has been a busy meeting place for many centuries. It has been a market town for nearly 1,000 years and is surrounded by historic sites. This elegant market town is known as the capital of the rural Vale, and its busy main street is lined with fashionable shops and delightful inns and restaurants. The **Old Wool Barn Craft Centre** is a craft studio where visitors can see craftspeople at work and examine or buy many of their creations.

Some 3 miles south of Cowbridge, **Plas Llanmihangel** is a 16th cen-tury Elizabethan manor house with some parts dating back to the 12th century. Guided tours are available.

TRERHYNGYLL   MAP 3 REF H9
14 miles SW of Cardiff off the A48

The **Jane Hodge Resort Hotel** has been offering a high standard of service and comfort to all its guests since 1991. Manager Derek Evans, Deputy

**Jane Hodge Resort Hotel, Trerhyngyll, Nr Cowbridge
Vale of Glamorgan CF71 7TN
Tel: 01446 772608 Fax: 01446 775831.**

Manager Rhian Jenkins and their courteous, efficient staff offer a warm welcome to all their guests. Catering for people with disabilities, their carers, and able-bodied guests, the hotel has 30 ensuite rooms. Its setting in this quiet village just outside the ancient market town of Cowbridge, also near the sea and the major cities of Cardiff and Swansea, makes it an ideal base from which to explore the many sights and attractions of the region. Brickbuilt under a tiled roof, it has extensive grounds and gardens, all immaculately maintained and includes a landscaped lake and fountain, extensive leisure club facilities and a swimming pool. The hotel is spacious and modern in design, and is cheerfully and tastefully decorated throughout. Private car park. 4-Crowns Highly Commended by the Welsh Tourist Board. Registered charity number: 212463.

LLANTWIT MAJOR   MAP 3 REF H9
15 miles SW of Cardiff off the B4265

Llantwit Major is perhaps the Vale of Glamorgan's most historic place. This delightful little town of narrow medieval streets, cosy inns and quaint old dwellings grew up around an ancient seat of Christian learning, the oldest of its kind in Britain. It was here that the Kings of Morgannwg were brought to be buried.

In a sheltered hollow below the town's crooked old streets stands a huge church of cathedral-like proportions. The imposing **Church of St Illtud** was, in fact, a religious site which in many ways had the stature of a cathedral. It was founded in around AD 500 by St Illtud, an influential early Christian figure, and St David, Wales' patron saint, is known to have studied here. Missionaries would travel from here through Wales, Cornwall and Brittany to spread the early Christian teachings. In medieval times the church grew to its present dimensions though, in reality, it is two churches in one, since it is a combination of an early Norman and late

13th-century church. It houses a fine collection of Celtic crosses and the pillars are inscribed with the most intricate designs.

Llantwit Major has examples of period architecture from several different centuries, including a Roman Villa, Medieval Grange and a Tudor Mansion.

NASH POINT   MAP 3 REF H9
18 miles SW of Cardiff off the B4265

Nash Point is a headland with two lighthouses and the remnants of an Iron Age fort. The cliffs along this part of the coast are made up of huge slabs of limestone which have weathered in a peculiar way to resemble giant building blocks. Nearby is **St Donat's Castle**, the home of the Atlantic College in which first Lord Mountbatten and now the Prince of Wales have taken great interest and given their support. The castle, which dates from about 1300, was owned by American newspaper magnate William Randolph Hearst, who spent huge sums restoring and furnishing the historic building. His guests here included film stars and VIPs from all over the world. The castle now houses the United World College of the Atlantic, the world's first international sixth form school with students from many countries. **St Donat's Art Centre** is a lovely art gallery and concert venue housed in a converted tithe barn.

6 The Valleys of Southeast Wales

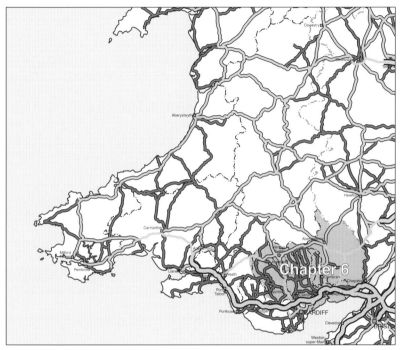

History, ancient and more modern, abounds in this part of South Wales. The region boasts several distinguished castle remains, and of course tells the story of Wales' industrial heritage better than any other part of the country.

The Wye Valley and Vale of Usk offer some truly magnificent scenery and breathtaking sights such as Tintern Abbey and the time-ravished fortresses of the Welsh borderlands. The Wye Valley Area of Outstanding Natural Beauty provide endless opportunities for outdoor pursuits, including walking, superior fishing, cycling, canal-cruising, golf, canoeing and gliding. The towns of the Wye Valley, such as Abergavenny, Monmouth, Newport and Chepstow offer wonderful shopping, historic architecture and scenes of tranquil beauty.

But visitors should not overlook the other picturesque valleys of the region - including the Monnow, Llanthony, Dare, Cynon and Rhondda -

for they have much to offer both in scenic beauty and in the attractions of their principal towns, including Merthyr Tydfil, Caerphilly, Pontypridd and Pontypool. Among this region's many delightful castles are the strategic Three Castles of Gwent - Grosmont, Skenfrith and White Castle - built to protect the Welsh Marches.

The Valleys of Southeast Wales are known the world over for their culture, heritage and warm welcoming atmosphere. They offer many attractions found nowhere else - unexpected beauty, vistas, country parks and forests, scenic footpaths, a proud history and a wealth of sights, sounds and experiences available to the visitor.

THE COUNTY OF MERTHYR TYDFIL

MERTHYR TYDFIL   MAP 3 REF I7
24 miles N of Cardiff off the A470

The A645 in this part of Wales acts as a dividing line: to the south are the historic valleys once dominated by coalmining and the iron and steel-making industries, while to the north are the untouched southern uplands of the Brecon Beacons National Park. This rigidly observed dividing line is explained by geology. The coal-bearing rocks of the valleys end along the line of this road, giving way to the limestone and old red sandstone rocks of the Beacons.

Geology also explains the growth of industry in these parts. The iron-smelting which accompanied the coalmining was a result of the fact that limestone, a key part of the smelting process, was easily quarried locally. Iron ore was also to be found nearby. These ingredients all came together in the most productive way at Merthyr Tydfil, the former 'iron and steel capital of the world'.

Cyfarthfa Castle Museum is by no means the only monument in Merthyr Tydfil to times gone by. It is situated in the state rooms of Cyfarthfa Castle, which was built by the Crawshay family of ironmasters in 1825 to overlook their ironworks, then the largest in the world. The family moved out in the 1890s; in 1909 the Borough Council bought the Castle and grounds, principally to use as the town's grammar school. With the support of a group of local collectors and enthusiasts, a museum and art gallery were established and a professional curator was employed by the Borough until 1920.

By way of a contrast, the living conditions of the workers are also remembered at **Joseph Parry's Cottage**. Parry was a famous 19th century composer. He wrote the haunting hymn *Myfanwy,* which is a favourite performance piece with male-voice choirs. He was born in this tiny terraced cottage, now renovated and open to the public, almost within the shadow of the grand Cyfarthfa Castle.

Nearby there's another reminder of Merthyr Tydfil's former industrial pre-eminence, the **Ynysfach Engine House**. Originally opened in 1801, it was the first furnace to use steam power and was soon producing more iron than furnaces at Cyfarthfa. It suffered as steel production replaced that of iron, and by 1879 was closed. It was saved from total ruin by the Merthyr Tydfil Heritage Trust in 1989 and opened as a Heritage Centre for the Iron Industry in the area.

DOWLAIS

MAP 3 REF I7

2 miles E of Merthyr Tydfil off the A465

Once one of Merthyr's busiest districts, the blast furnaces and foundries of Dowlais (on the hillside above the centre of town) turned out metal for world markets as far apart as the Russian Steppes and South America. In the 19th century, the skies were bright day and night from the glow of the ironworks. Dowlais has seen tremendous changes since its industrial hey-day. The **Dowlais Viaduct** is an impressive sight.

PONTSTICILL

MAP 3 REF I7

3 miles N of Merthyr Tydfil off the A465/A470

The **Brecon Mountain Railway** runs on a short but very scenic line from the northern end of Merthyr Tydfil to a lakeside terminus just beyond Pontsticill. This charming narrow-gauge line was created with much sweat and toil by enthusiasts of the Age of Steam on the course of an old British Rail route from Merthyr to Brecon. The views from the lakeside terminus, which look out across the waters towards the peak of **Pen-y-fan**, the highest summit in South Wales, are marvellous. At Pant Station there is a display of various engines including vintage locomotives and others from around the world.

THE COUNTY OF BLENAU GWENT

EBBW VALE

MAP 3 REF I7

25 miles N of Cardiff on the A4046

This old steelmaking town, whose member of Parliament was once the formidable Aneurin Bevan, was transformed for the 1992 Garden Festival. The area where this was held continues to thrive, with a wealth of lakes, gardens, wetlands and woodland. The project is progressing to become an ambitious garden village. There are pleasant trails and walks, interesting exhibitions and some extraordinary sculptures, one of which is made from 30,000 individually modelled clay bricks. There is also a factory shopping outlet in the town.

TREDEGAR   MAP 3 REF I7
3 miles NW of Ebbw Vale off the A465

Tredegar was the birthplace of fiery orator and social reformer Aneurin Bevan, founder of the National Health Service. It was in Tredegar too that the novelist A J Cronin worked as a doctor and collected the background material for his work, *The Citadel*, later made into both a feature film with Robert Donat and a television film starring Ben Cross.

On the outskirts of Tredegar there is a fine example of the way in which the old industrial valleys are changing for the better. **Bryn Bach Park** is a 600 acre stretch of grassland and woodland ranged around the centrepiece of a manmade lake. In its Visitor Centre displays show how the park has been reclaimed from derelict and neglected wasteland and transformed into a most attractive area with fishing, walking and plenty of wide open spaces.

THE COUNTY OF RHONDDA CYNON TAFF

PONTYPRIDD   MAP 2 REF I8
13 miles NW of Cardiff off the A470

The friendly valley town of Pontypridd comes alive especially on Wednesday and Saturdays, when the streets are packed with stalls and shoppers who come from far and wide for market day.

The town is justly proud of its past. An old chapel near Pontypridd's historic stone bridge across the River Taff is the home of the **Pontypridd Historical and Cultural Centre**. In the town's attractive **Ynysangharad Park** there are two statues commemorating Evan and James James, a father-and-son songwriting team responsible for composing the words and music of the Welsh National Anthem, *Hen Wlad fy Nhadau*. Wales' 'Land of Song' reputation is at its strongest in these parts. Pontypridd and the surrounding area have produced an amazing trio of world-famous singers: opera stars Sir Geraint Evans and Stewart Burrows (born in the same street) in nearby Clifynydd, and Tom Jones.

LLANTRISANT   MAP 3 REF I9
4 miles SW of Pontypridd off the A4119/A473

Llantrisant is an old town which takes its name, Three Saints, from saints

Illtud, Gwyno and Dyfod, to whom the originally Norman church is dedicated.

Along with other parts of this region of South Wales, this town has attracted a great deal of new industry. Major manufacturers have large factories here. One big employer is the Royal Mint; a display of coins from across the ages can be seen at the **Model House** in the town centre.

Standing in the town's Bull Ring is a statue of a figure dressed in a fox skin head-dress. This is, in fact, the town's memorial to Dr William Price, an amazing character who lived from 1800 to 1893. Dr Price espoused many causes which scandalised straight-laced Victorian Britain. He was a vegetarian who believed in free love, nudism and radical politics. His most famous (considered infamous at the time) deed was his attempt, in 1884, to cremate his illegitimate son Iesu Grist (Jesus Christ), who had died in infancy. As a result of the controversy and the ensuing court case, cremation became legal in Britain.

TREHAFOD   MAP 3 REF I8
2 miles NW of Pontypridd off the A4058

The **Rhondda Heritage Park** in Trehafod is dedicated to telling the story of South Wales' coalmining past. Only a handful of pits now survive in the Welsh valleys, where once there were hundreds. It is a fallacy to think of modern South Wales in terms of heavy industry. Miners now account for only a tiny percentage of the workforce, yet the strong traditions of the mining valleys are proudly upheld and rightly cherished. The Heritage Centre is an ongoing project which will tell future generations of an industry that shaped South Wales, even though it is now coming to an end. Machinery and mining equipment are on display, and visitors can see an imaginative 'Black Gold' presentation. An excellent underground tour illustrates what it might have been like to work a shift - the heat, sounds and smells are very realistic. More unusual features include an art gallery, an exhibition on the role of women in the history of mining, and an authentic Valley chapel.

ABERDARE   MAP 3 REF H8
10 miles N of Pontypridd off the A4059

This friendly town lies at the northern end of the Cynon Valley. The valleys are now famous for their male-voice choirs; singing has a strong tradition in South Wales and musicians are revered. Aberdare is no exception in this respect. It must be the only town in Britain which has for its main monument a statue of a choir conductor, Griffith Rhys Jones (1834-97), baton in hand, conducting the traffic in **Victoria Square**.

Although Aberdare's roots began in the Industrial Revolution, there is little coalmining in the area today. The surrounding valleys are green again thanks to ambitious land reclamation and environmental improvement schemes which have transformed the region in the last 30 years or so. Just a stone's throw from Aberdare's busy town centre is **Dare Valley Country Park**. Created on former colliery land, this wooded park has trails that tell of the natural and industrial history of the area.

LLANWONNO

MAP 3 REF H8

12 miles N of Pontypridd off the B4275

This lovely little hamlet nestles in the forested hills between the Cynon and Rhondda Valleys. A minor mountain road leads to this delightful spot, which consists of no more than an old church, pub and row of cottages. It seems a world removed from the tightly packed terraces of the villages below, yet it is only a short drive from the main road.

Llanwonno is associated with the strange tale of Guto Nyth-Bran, the 18th-century long-distance runner whose speed became legendary in this part of Wales. According to legend, he ran across the mountain to fetch yeast in the time that it took his mother to boil a kettle of water. Guto's grave (his real name was Gruffydd Morgan) is in the village churchyard here.

RHIGOS

MAP 3 REF H7

15 miles NE of Pontypridd off the A4061/A4109

New Inn is a comfortable and welcoming pub and restaurant located near the quiet village of Rhigos. Owners Maureen and Gwyn Thomas are a hard-working, conscientious couple who have taken great care and expended a lot of energy on attaining and maintaining the reputation this fine restaurant now enjoys. They offer a high standard of service to all

New Inn, Smiths Avenue, Rhigos, Nr Hirwaun
Mid-Glamorgan CF44 9YU Tel: 01685 811071.

their customers. Here in this tranquil village close to some of the few remaining working mines in Wales, this traditional stone-built building boasts
an extensive lawned garden area. The interior is tasteful and attractive,
combining modern features with traditional comfort and embellished with
handsome photographs, artwork and the restaurant's ever-expanding porcelain chicken collection! Lunch is served from noon-2 p.m., evening meals
from 7 p.m. There are no fewer than three sittings for the popular Sunday
lunch. Chef Colin uses only the freshest ingredients in preparing a good
range of home-prepared and home-cooked favourites. Bar snacks are also
available. The restaurant area is non-smoking. Occasionally there is live
evening entertainment on offer.

THE COUNTY OF CAERPHILLY

CAERPHILLY   MAP 2 REF I8
8 miles N of Cardiff on the A469

Right in the middle of Caerphilly there is a castle of incredible proportions. **Caerphilly Castle** is one of Britain's largest castles and amongst the
greatest surviving examples of medieval military architecture in Europe.
Often overlooked by visitors to the region, this alone merits a trip to Caer-

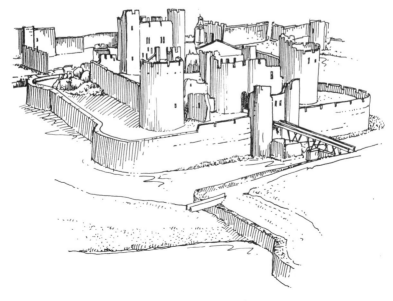

Caerphilly Castle

philly, which also offers superb shopping. This fortress was built largely in the late 13th century by the Norman Lord Gilbert de Clare. He created a mighty 'stone and water' system of concentric defences which can still be seen today, together with a formidable gatehouse rising above the waters of the moat. The castle also has a leaning tower which manages to out-lean Pisa's world famous one!

Denehurst Guesthouse in an extensive and very attractive bed and breakfast in St Martin's Road in Caerphilly. Owner Margaret Hall has been running this comfortable establishment since 1985; she is ably assisted by her daughter Nicola. Attracting a varied and international clientele, it ben-efits from its proximity to the cen-tre of Caerphilly. The Castle is just a short distance away, as are the town's excellent range of shops and other attractions. The three guest bed-rooms are cosy, comfortable and tastefully decorated. They feature all the conveniences guests have come to expect. The large, well-kept garden is just the place to relax on fine days. The breakfasts (either full English or Continental) are home-prepared and home-cooked, and make use of the

Denehurst Guesthouse, 16 St Martin's Road, Caerphilly, Mid Glamorgan CF83 1EJ Tel: 01222 883724.

freshest local ingredients. Here in this charming and welcoming establish-ment, Margaret and Nicola, your friendly and knowledgeable hosts, make every effort to ensure that their guests have a relaxing and enjoyable stay, maintaining a high standard of service and efficiency.

NANTGARW   MAP 3 REF I8
2 miles SW of Caerphilly off the A470

For a period in the early 19th century, Nantgarw produced some of the finest porcelain in the world. At **Nantgarw China Works** they continue to make exquisite pots and clay pipes. Visitors can watch the craftspeople at work.

MAP 3 REF I8
YSTRAD MYNACH
5 miles NW of Caerphilly off the A472

The 16-arched **Hengoed Viaduct**, built in 1857, once catered for one of the busiest stretches of railway in the area.

MAP 3 REF I8
NELSON
7 miles NW of Caerphilly off the A472

Llancaiach Fawr is a wonderfully entertaining and very well laid out living history museum. This handsome Elizabethan manor brings the days of the Civil War to life with costumed guides who are accurate down to the tiniest nuance of 17th century speech. No stuffy stately home this, all the exhibits are very hands-on. Visitors can try on historic clothes, handle armour or even spend a spell in the stocks. There are also special events held throughout the summer.

THE COUNTY OF TORFAEN

MAP 3 REF J8
PONTYPOOL
19 miles NE of Cardiff on the A4042

This valley prides itself on being the earliest place in Britain successfully to produce tin plate. That was in 1720; today the town's past industry is celebrated at the **Valley Inheritance Centre** in Pontypool Park.

In fact, industry in the town goes back a lot further, to 1425 when the first forge began operating here. The first ironworks followed in 1577 and it is said that the first forge in America, opened in 1652, was built by Pontypool emigrants.

Canals too, have played an important part in the development of Pontypool. This legacy is recalled at **Junction Cottage**, a tollkeeper's cottage of 1814 at the junction of the Monmouthshire and Brecon Canal and the River Lwyd.

At **Llandegfedd Reservoir**, just a few miles east of Pontypool, all thoughts of industry seem totally misplaced. Llandegfedd is a popular recreation area with the local folk. Visitors can buy permits for trout fishing, and sailing is permitted on the lake. Nature lovers will enjoy birdwatching here, especially in the winter months when the area is a haunt for wildfowl.

AROUND PONTYPOOL

BLAENAFON   Map 3 ref J7
6 miles NW of Pontypool off the A4043

The **Big Pit Mining Museum**, just outside Blaenafon, gives its visitors an authentic insight into South Wales' industrial past, for the pit was a working colliery before becoming a museum of the mining industry. Visitors, accompanied by guides who are former miners, descend 300 feet underground, with safety helmets and cap lamps, to experience for themselves the working life of generations of Welsh miners. There's also plenty to see on the surface, including workshops, an engine house, pithead baths and an exhibition of mining techniques.

South Wales' metal-producing past is also remembered at Blaenafon, for just across the valley from the Big Pit there are the **Blaenafon Ironworks**, an early industrial site which has been preserved and is open to the public.

Blaenafon Ironworks

CWMBRAN

MAP 3 REF J8

4 miles S of Pontypool off the A4043

A new town built in the old industrial valleys of South Wales, Cwmbran was once dominated by heavy industry. The mines and large works have disappeared, forests have been planted and major environmental improvement schemes have taken away the old eyesores.

Just to the south of town, at **Llantarnam**, is a modern abbey built on the site of a 12th century Cistercian house, the gateway of which survives.

One mile west of town, **Greenmeadow Community Farm** was founded to protect this extensive green area. There are a wide range of animals here, including rare breeds, and a deer enclosure, craft workshops and lovely bluebell wood.

The Bush Inn occupies a very picturesque location commanding superb views of the surrounding valley. Among the many natural and man-made features to explore in the neighbourhood there is a mountain trail behind the pub, a reservoir, old coal mine workings, and an old burial ground. Attracting a mixed clientele of walkers, pony-trekkers, Morris dancers, local choir member and police cadets from the local training college, as well as visitors and holiday-makers, this remains a quiet, relaxing pub.

**The Bush Inn, Graig Road, Upper Cwmbran, Gwent NP44 5AN
Tel: 01633 483764.**

There is a lively atmosphere at weekends when the pub hosts a regular disco. This charming whitewashed establishment was built around 1800 as two stone cottages. It was once a mine shop and subsequently a public house. Interior features include the welcoming open fire, flagstone floors and a collection of pictures, plates and teapots adorning the walls. The lounge is small and very cosy, resembling an old-fashioned sitting room in decor and ambience. Bar snacks are available. The pub serves real ales including two from a local brewer. Tenants Rob and Theresa Lewis offer a friendly welcome to all their guests.

THE WYE VALLEY

NEWPORT   MAP 3 REF J8
12 miles E of Cardiff on the A48

Wales' third largest conurbation after Cardiff and Swansea, Newport has its own particular gem: the **Newport Museum and Art Gallery**. The well-presented and imaginatively displayed exhibits cover a wide range of themes including the substantial Roman influence in this part of Wales, represented by an exquisite Roman mosaic floor depicting the four seasons. The town's industrial and maritime history is also recalled here, together with its strong links with the Chartist Movement of the 19th century, which campaigned for electoral reform.

The town boasts a good selection of quality shopping and entertainments. Newport's **St Woolos Cathedral**, crowning a prominent hill above the shopping streets, is well worth a visit. It stands on a site which has seen religious worship since the 6th century, and has at its entrance an ancient little chapel.

Just off exit 28 of the M4 to the west of Newport, **Tredegar House and Park** was home to one of the great Welsh families - the Morgans - for more than 500 years. Now restored, it is an outstanding example of 18th-century architecture and landscape design. The Great Kitchen and Gilt Room are among the highlights of this impressive stately home. In the park, carriage rides, boating and an adventure playground provide plenty to see and do. The Edwardian Sunken Garden, Orangery and a series of walled gardens complete the scene.

ROGERSTONE   MAP 3 REF J8
2 miles W of Newport off the M4/A4048

The Jolly Roger is a very pleasant and comfortable restaurant, public house and inn here in the quiet village of Rogerstone on the outskirts of Newport. Landlord Michael Smithson and his wife Jacqueline are new to the

**Jolly Roger, 68 Tregwilym Road, Rogerstone, Newport NP1 9EJ
Tel: 01633 892377.**

trade, having come here from Jersey in 1998, but they bring a wealth of
enthusiasm and vitality to their new venture, offering guests a warm and
friendly welcome and a high standard of quality and service. This impressive stonebuilt hotel and public house dates back to the 19th century.
Built as a hotel, it has retained a traditional charm and ambience. The
interior is tastefully decorated, with a large open fire adorned above with a
collection of brass plates. It is very spacious, with a relaxed and informal
atmosphere. The lounge is comfortable and cosy, with attractive pictures
on the walls. This pleasant inn attracts a loyal local following and also
many visitors from further afield, who come for the welcoming atmosphere and great food and ales. The meals are wholesome, home-cooked
and reasonably priced. For those wishing to extend their stay in this lovely
part of South Wales, there are four guest bedrooms.

CAERLEON
2 miles N of Newport off the B4236

MAP 3 REF J8

The Romans established a major garrison town called Isca at what is now
Caerleon. In fact, this area hides a wealth of Roman remains. Along with
Chester and York, Caerleon was one of the Romans' most important mili-
tary bases in Britain. The elite of the Roman army were based here, in

what became a large Roman town. For entertainment the soldiers had a 6,000-seat amphitheatre and a huge bathhouse complex (the Romans' equivalents to the leisure centres of today!). The extent of the remains here are impressive: the amphitheatre is still here and the fortress baths and the foundations of barrack lines and parts of the ramparts, as well as the remains of the cookhouse and latrines, have been excavated and are open to the public. The excellent **Legionary Museum** displays many of the finds.

PENHOW   MAP 3 REF J8
5 miles NE of Newport off the A48

Penhow is home to a fascinating historic site which claims to be Wales' oldest lived-in castle. Visitors are offered a self-guided tour using a personal stereo together with recorded commentary telling of the 850-year history of the fortress. **Penhow Castle** is endowed with a 15th-century Great Hall, complete with minstrels' gallery, and is very impressive.

REDWICK   MAP 3 REF J8
5 miles SE of Newport off the M4

The Rose Inn is a distinctive and attractive public house built in the 1870s and located in the quiet and serene village of Redwick, distinguished by an impressive and historic stone-built 15th-century church. Only three miles

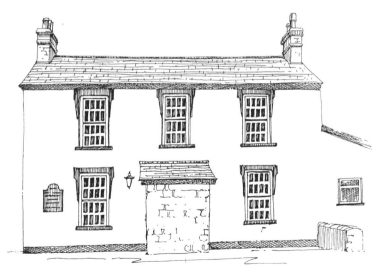

The Rose Inn, South Row, Redwick, Nr Magor NP6 3DU
Tel: 01633 880501.

from the busy M4, yet only 10 minutes from the sea wall, this charming retreat maintains its peaceful, rural atmosphere. Owners Denise and Mick Connolly have been running the pub since 1995. They are jovial and friendly hosts. The pub boasts a number of original features, including the bare stone walls and large open fireplace with wood-burning fire. The walls are adorned with an extensive brass collection, Toby jugs and pretty plates. The excellent meals are served Monday-Saturday noon-2 and 6-9 p.m., and Sundays noon-9 p.m. The menu features a good range of tempting starters and main courses, including sirloin steaks, lamb and pork chops and other hearty favourites, as well as a good selection of curries. All the food is home-cooked. To wash your repast down there's a variety of beers, lagers, wines and spirits to choose from, including Bass and HB traditional beers and a guest traditional beer, changed fortnightly.

CAERWENT
Map 3 ref K8
8 miles E of Newport off the A48

Parts of the Roman walls remain in Caerwent, some still 15 feet high in places, where extensive Roman buildings have been excavated, including the town hall, forum, temple, public baths, houses, shops and inns.

In the tranquil and picturesque village of Caerwent, **The Coach & Horses Inn** dates back to 1712. This traditional stonebuilt inn and hotel is situated at the Eastgate of the Roman city of Venta Salurum - the only Roman civil town built in Wales. Owners Glyn and Margaret Davies have

**Coach & Horses, Caerwent, Newport, Monmouthshire NP6 4AX
Tel: 01291 420352.**

been here since 1991, and are very jovial and welcoming hosts. This fine inn is popular with walkers, fishermen and golfers - it makes an ideal base for the golf enthusiast, as there are four local golf courses, two of which are championship standard. The inn is also convenient for Chepstow Race Course and the Wye and Usk Valleys. There's a friendly, relaxed atmosphere in this Free House, where a wide selection of real ales, beers, wines and spirits are available. The restaurant boasts an extensive and varied menu; the three-course Sunday Lunch is the house speciality. From the large beer garden/children's play area to the rear there are wonderful views across the surrounding countryside. The six newly refurbished guest rooms offer a high standard of comfort, with excellent amenities.

CALDICOT   MAP 3 REF K8
9 miles E of Newport off the M4/A48

Caldicot has a well-preserved **Castle** dating back to the 12th and 14th centuries. It was restored for use as a family home in the 1880s, and was occupied right up until the mid-1970s. It is now a local museum, set in the grounds of the attractive surrounding country park.

THE VALE OF USK

USK   MAP 2 REF J8
8 miles N of Newport on the A472

This is a delightful small town set on the banks of the river from which it takes its name. Like Monmouth, Usk has the remains of a castle (in private ownership) and a fine square. Fishing is excellent locally, as the Usk is a fine salmon-fishing river, attracting angling enthusiasts from far and wide.

Just 5 minutes' walk from the market town of Usk, opposite a very pleasant river walk, **Glen-Yr-Afon House Hotel**, now it its 25th year, occupies an impressive and elegant Victorian house which retains many of its original features yet is also modern in its level of comfort. Managers Alex Brown and Tim strong are welcoming and conscientious hosts, who have, with owners Jan and Peter Clarke, been running the hotel for over 10 years with flair and efficiency. They offer genuine hospitality to all their guests. The 26 large ensuite rooms are graciously appointed and decorated with taste and style. The oak-panelled restaurant's extensive a la carte and table d'hote menus include beef, pork and salmon dishes, all expertly prepared and presented. The wine list is excellent. With facilities for fishing, golfing, gliding, croquet and grass skiing nearby, this fine hotel makes a very good base from which to explore the many sights and attractions of the area. Open all year.

Glen-Yr-Afon House Hotel, Pontypool Road, Usk
Gwent NP5 1SY Tel: 01291 672302 Fax: 01291 672597

The **Gwent Rural Life Museum** in New Market Street has displays of the country's rural past with exhibits dating back to around 1800, including wagons, craft tools and vintage machinery. All of these are housed in a renovated 17th-century barn which has an adjacent Victorian cottage.

LLANSOY   MAP 3 REF J8
5 miles E of Usk off the A449

Brecon Court Deer Farm and **Cwrt-Y-Brychan Vineyard** are two wonderful attractions in this handsome village. The Farm is renowned for its fine stags and European bloodstock. The vineyard has 8 acres planted with a variety of vines; free wine-tastings are offered.

BETTWS NEWYDD   MAP 3 REF J7
2 miles N of Usk off the B4598

This is a quiet and picturesque village very close to the River Usk. Fishing rights on the river are owned by a village syndicate which includes the owner of the local Black Bear Inn.

Owner Stephen Molyneux has been a chef for 20 years, and has owned the **Black Bear Inn** since 1994. Stephen's fame - he has worked in restaurants in Bordeaux, Cologne, Papillion and Toulouse, as well as serving a stint as chef on Freddie Laker's yacht- has spread far and wide since his days of running a successful and prestigious enterprise on the Isle of Man.

This superb establishment has featured in *Egon Ronay's Pubs and Inns* as 'offering outstanding cuisine'. The menu boasts a variety of innovative

Black Bear, Bettws Newydd, Nr Usk, Monmouthshire NP5 1JN
Tel: 01873 880701 Fax: 01873 880701.

dishes, including fish and seafood, saddle of Welsh Roe-deer, breast of duck and steaks. His style is imaginative, creative and always a triumph. Stonebuilt and dating back to the 16th century, this fine traditional pub boasts beamed ceilings, large open fire and quarry-tiled flooring. It is decorated with taste and restraint, with handsome pictures adorning the walls and a collection of horse brasses near the fireplace. Intimate and informal, evenings see it filled to capacity.

LLANGYBI   Map 3 ref J8
3 miles SE of Usk off the A449

Built in the 12th century for Cistercian monks, **The White Hart** is a distinguished inn situated in the beautiful Usk Vale, on the quiet Usk to Caerleon Road, famous for its Roman encampment. The building was taken over by Henry VIII as part of Jane Seymour's wedding dowry, and is also reputed to have been used by Cromwell as his Gwent headquarters. The interior boasts the original 12th-century fireplaces, amid a wealth of other interesting features, including 11 remaining 17th-century windows, a priest hole, and a great many exposed beams. The decor is tasteful and in keeping with this magnificent old building's history. The heart of the local community, this popular inn is the meeting place for the local hunt and is also a fa-

**The White Hart, Llangybi, Gwent NP5 1NP
Tel: 01633 450258.**

vourite of ramblers, anglers and other visitors. The inn serves a good range of real ales, bar snacks and a full a la carte menu in the restaurant. The menu is extensive, specialising in seasonal dishes. There are also two attractive guest rooms (1 twin, 1 double).

MONMOUTHSHIRE

CHEPSTOW   Map 3 ref K8

17 miles E of |Newport off the A466

Built on the banks of the River Wye, Chepstow has the distinction of being based around the first castle in Britain to be constructed of stone. The well-preserved **Chepstow Castle** occupies a crag overlooking the river. It was founded just after the Norman Conquest by William FitzOsbern, and later belonged to the Norman Strongbow, one of the powerful Marcher Lords (and the man who 'conquered' Ireland in the 12th century). Opposite the castle is a museum of local history.

Medieval town walls enclose Chepstow's narrow streets, and the main road is straddled by the battlemented 13th century town gate which adds further to the town's charming historic character. At the same time, Chepstow is a bustling modern town with many interesting shops to browse around. **Chepstow Racecourse**, on the northern approaches to the town, is the largest in Wales.

Chepstow Castle

TINTERN PARVA   Map 3 ref K8
4 miles N of Chepstow off the A466/B4228

This riverside village, which nestles amongst the wooded slopes of the lovely Wye Valley, is a most beautiful place. In fact, the entire valley, from Chepstow to Monmouth, is an officially designated Area of Outstanding Natural Beauty. The village, of course, is famous for the ruined **Tintern Abbey** as well as it glorious woodlands (particularly breathtaking in the autumn). The Cistercian abbey, now a majestic ruin, was founded in 1131 by Walter de Clare and was active until the Dissolution of the Monasteries enacted by Henry VIII. It is easy to see why this abbey, in its splendid setting, inspired poetry from William Wordsworth and was painted by Turner.

Tintern's former railway station is now a **Visitor Centre** and a good source of information on what to see and where to walk in this lovely valley. There is a model steam railway in operation on summer weekends and a changing programme of exhibitions. Opposite the Old Station visitors will find **Wye Valley Herbs**, which produces culinary, medicinal and dyer's herbs of all kinds.

Tintern Abbey

WOLVESNEWTON
MAP 3 REF K8
5 miles NW of Chepstow off the B4293

This village takes its name from a Norman family of the 13th century named Lupus (wolf) of Lovel, who were lords here. A quarter of a mile west is believed to have been the site of the manor house, which may have been built on the site of a more ancient dwelling situated as it is on a mound of about an acre and a half, surrounded by a moat to the west.

The hills around the village are an ideal retreat, undisturbed by any signs of hustle and bustle, a perfect place to visit and stay. **The Model Farm Museum** is a collection of unique farm buildings built by the Duke of Beaufort in the 18th century, with views overlooking some breathtaking countryside. Children and adults love the Quiz Trail which leads around the museum. There are also farm animals to pet, a craft shop selling memorabilia and a workshop where craftspeople work making toys such as rocking horses can be observed.

LLANDOGO
MAP 3 REF K8
6 miles NW of Chepstow off the A466

There are fine views of the Wye Valley from Pen-y-Fan, a wooded hill above Bigsweir Bridge. One of the last maypoles in Gwent was sited here, although nowadays it is down in the valley. This attractive village also has a wealth of craft, antique and book shops.

MONMOUTH   MAP 3 REF K7
16 miles N of Chepstow on the A466

This prosperous market town is an excellent touring base for the **Wye Valley** and has many good hotels. Charles I is said to have stayed at the Kings Head - although if it had had this name then he probably would have thought twice about it!

Monmouth Castle was the birthplace of Henry V in 1387. A statue in the aptly-named Agincourt Square commemorates this historic link, and of course serves as a reminder of the king's famous victory over the French in 1415. Founded in around 1068, the castle was rebuilt by Henry V's grandfather, John of Gaunt, in the late 1300s. **Great Castle House** was built in 1673 by the 3rd Marquess of Worcester from the ruins of the castle; he used the town house while his other homes, Badminton and Troy House, were being rebuilt.

Another interesting place in Monmouth is the 14th century **St Mary's Church**. Its belfry has eight bells, allegedly recast from a peal Henry V brought back from France. The story goes that as Henry was leaving Calais the ringing of bells was heard and he was told that the French were celebrating his departure. He immediately turned back and liberated the bells for presentation to his native town.

Another famous son of Monmouth, Geoffrey of Monmouth, was Prior of St Mary's and later bishop of the cathedral of St Asaph in North Wales. It was probably in Monmouth that Geoffrey wrote his massive work, *A History of the Kings of Britain*, with its legends of Merlin and Arthur. Look out for the elaborately carved Geoffrey's Window in the building (now a Youth Hostel) along the street leading northwards from Agincourt Square.

Three rivers meet at Monmouth: the Wye, Monnow and Trothy. All are noted for their fishing. The Wye is crossed by a five-arched bridge built in 1617. The Monnow, however, boasts the most noteworthy bridge of all. The three-arched **Monnow Bridge** has a sturdy fortified gatehouse, the only one of its kind in Britain, which dates from medieval times.

In the town's Glendower Street is the **Monmouth Museum** with its exceptional collection of items relating to Lord Admiral Nelson. His connection with the town was slight but the memorabilia was donated by Lady Llangattock, mother of Charles Stuart Rolls, pioneer airman, motorist and co-founder of Rolls Royce. A statue of Rolls himself stands in front of the Shire Hall in Agincourt Square. The museum has the very telescope which Nelson raised to his eye at Copenhagen.

The Naval Temple, opened in the early 19th century to commemorate Britain's victories at sea, stands on the hill known as **The Kymin** overlooking the town. The views from the top of this 840-foot high hill looking across the Wye and Monnow Valleys are truly superb. In the 18th century, a group of men known as the Kymin Club met here once a week and, in 1794, built their own pavilion, the Round House. This was followed by the Naval Temple, which is decorated with plaques commemorating 15 admirals and their most famous battles. This impressive spot is managed by the National Trust.

SKENFRITH   Map 3 ref K7
6 miles NW of Monmouth off the B4347

To the north of Monmouth the **Monnow Valley** forms something of a gap in the natural defences of the Welsh Marches between the river cliffs of the Wye Valley and the mountains further west. It was here that the Normans built the Three Castles of Gwent: Skenfrith, White, and Grosmont.

Skenfrith Castle stands with its church and village beside the Monnow. Built in the 13th century by Hubert de Burgh, the castle is noted for its fine round tower keep and its well-preserved curtain wall. Once the troubled domain of medieval warlords, this border region is today peaceful and undisturbed, a perfect place for relaxed, unhurried exploration.

GROSMONT   Map 3 ref J7
9 miles NW of Monmouth off the B4347

This is another very attractive hillside village with a 13th-century church. French-speakers will have guessed by now that this village's name derives from 'gros mont', meaning 'big hill'. The first castle here was little more than a steep earthen mound topped by timber defences. **Grosmont Castle** was later rebuilt in stone. An Arabic 'faience jar' found here is a relic of the Crusades.

Considering the modest size of this village, the church here is generously large. This is explained in part by the fact that the village was a borough up until the mid-19th century.

LLANTILIO CROSSENY   Map 3 ref J7
8 miles W of Monmouth off the B4233

This attractive village offers a marvellous view of the 13th century church from the former moat of Hen Gwrt, nearby. The remains of the White Castle northwest of the village are the most substantial of the trio of moated castles Hubert de Burgh built to defend the Welsh Marches.

LLANVETHERINE   Map 3 ref J7
9 miles NW of Monmouth off the B4521

Walkers who are making the **Three Castle Walk** will pass through Lower Green Farm on their approach to the third of the three castles, **White**

Castle, near the village of Llanvetherine. This isolated castle gets its name from the time, centuries ago, when its walls were covered with white plaster. All that has now gone, but other features of note include the massive round towers, curtain walls and steep moat, which may be crossed by a wooden bridge.

The Three Castles were always kept under the strict control of the Crown to prevent them being used against the reigning monarch. Built in about 1180, with 13th-century additions, the White Castle was never tested in war and, following the Welsh retreat in 1277, it became an administrative centre, collecting tithes, taxes and levies from the residents of the surrounding countryside.

White Castle also has the dubious distinction of being home, briefly, to Rudolf Hess, Hitler's deputy, who fled the Third Reich under mysterious circumstances and is said to have spent his time here feeding the swans in the castle moat.

ABERGAVENNY   MAP 3 REF J7
12 miles W of Monmouth off the A465

Abergavenny's origins go back beyond the Normans to Roman times, when it was the site of a modest fort, Gobannium. The town makes a good touring base both for the **Brecon Beacons National Park** and for all points here in the southeast. This market town welcomes many visitors, particularly in the summer months. Abergavenny hasn't always enjoyed such a hospitable reputation, however. One chilling story of old Abergavenny relates how, in 1176, the Norman knight William de Breos invited the Welsh lords to dine at his castle and then murdered the lot while they were disarmed at table.

Today visitors to the remains of the 12th to 14th century Abergavenny Castle can be assured a much more cordial welcome. Walls, towers and the rebuilt gatehouse can be seen. The early 19th-century keep and an adjoining house now contain a good local history museum. The museum boasts a fascinating collection of old prints, a Welsh kitchen and a saddlery. The church has a remarkable collection of memorials.

Here in the busy market town, Rita Graham has been running the attractive and welcoming **Ivy Villa Guest House** since 1980. This handsome 19th-century stonebuilt establishment offers a high standard of comfort, and is a convenient base from which to explore Abergavenny, the Brecon Beacons National Park and many other of the sights and attractions of the area. Here guests can enjoy a quiet, relaxed atmosphere. There are five guest rooms - two family rooms, one twin room, and two singles - all tastefully decorated, homely, spotless and very comfortable. The home-cooked breakfasts are hearty and sure to see guests off with a good start to

**Ivy Villa Guest House, 43 Hereford Road, Abergavenny
Monmouthshire NP7 5PY Tel: 01873 852473.**

the day. Pets welcome. Tea-making facilities and TVs in all rooms.

There are some attractive ancient buildings in Nevill Street and particularly Market Street. Visiting Abergavenny for its twice-weekly (Tuesday and Friday) market is well worthwhile. Farmers with their sheep and cattle come to the town on Tuesdays, as stallholders set up shop in the open air, creating a lively and friendly atmosphere. Antiques and craft fairs have grown into popular Market Hall attractions.

GILWERN   MAP 3 REF J7
17 miles W of Monmouth off the A4077

The **Monmouthshire and Brecon Canal** run south to Pontypool and northwest to Brecon. It lies within the often spectacular scenery of the Brecon Beacons National Park, which is especially beautiful in spring and autumn.

UPPER LLANOVER   MAP 3 REF J7
13 miles SW of Monmouth off the A4042

Owners Ann and John Cullen have been running **The Goose & Cuckoo** public house since 1984. This traditional pub attracts both locals and guests from all over the world, including walkers, riders, cyclists - all coming to sample the delights and breathtaking views of the surrounding countryside. At 900 feet above sea level, this warm and welcoming public house is a haven of comfort. It began life in the late 18th century as a cider house,

The Goose & Cuckoo, Upper Llanover, Nr Abergavenny
Monmouthshire NP7 9ER Tel: 01873 880277.

occupying what was then the drovers' road from Cwmouon to Abergavenny. Traditional features of the handsome interior include an open fireplace with woodburning stove and a Victorian monks' bench. The windows in the lounge look out upon beautiful bucolic scenes over the open countryside. This charming pub offers a fantastic range of 60 malt whiskies, as well as real ales from Wales, Scotland and England. All food is home-cooked - the 13-bean soup is famed far and wide - including the breads and ice-creams, and make use of local produce where possible.

CWMYOY   MAP 3 REF J6
14 miles NW of Monmouth off the A465

Cwmyoy Church makes a most unusual sight. Built on the side of a hill, it has been the victim of subsidence to such an extent that everything appears to be leaning over on the point of collapse. The tower itself appears to be leaning at a far greater angle even than that of the tower at Pisa, Italy. The Llanthony Valley, in which Cwmyoy sits, has a proliferation of religious sites, including Llanthony.

LLANTHONY   MAP 3 REF J6
17 miles NW of Monmouth off the A465

Gerald of Wales, the monk who wrote of his medieval travels around Wales, described Llanthony as a place truly calculated for religion and more adapted to the canonical discipline than all the monasteries of the British Isles. He was referring to **Llanthony Priory**, which was built on a spot which has links with the earliest glimmerings of Christianity in Wales. During the Age of the Saints in the 6th century, Llanthony was chosen by St David for a cell. In the 11th century the Norman warlord William de Lacy found it and was so struck by its peace and sanctity that he built a hermitage which later became the Priory of Llanthony. Its remains may still be seen here.

Finally, Father Ignatius tried to establish another religious house further up the Llanthony Valley but the project came to naught early in the 20th century. The valley's beauty also brought the poet Walter Savage Landor and the designer Eric Gill to live here. For walkers, part of the **Offa's Dyke Path** runs along the ridge of wild hills above Llanthony.

RAGLAN   MAP 3 REF J7
6 miles SW of Monmouth off the A40

Raglan Castle has a handsome, decorative appearance. This castle may look less sturdy and imposing than some of Wales' earlier, more robust fortresses, but it must have been strong enough, for it withstood the longest siege of the Civil War from June to August 1646. It was built in the more settled late Middle Ages of the 15th and 16th centuries, when greater consideration would have been given to decoration and home comforts. Raglan's most outstanding feature is its Great Tower, which stands surrounded by a water-filled moat separate from the rest of the castle.

Clytha Park House was built in the 1820s for William Jones, whose uncle had earlier built **Clytha Castle**, a folly designed by John Nash, in memory of his wife. The Castle was lived in as a gamekeeper's cottage until 1949; the entire estate was acquired by the National Trust in 1979. The House is open to the public, while the Castle is leased to the Landmark Trust and is available only for holiday lets.

TOURIST INFORMATION CENTRES

Centres in **bold** are open all the year around.

Aberaeron Tourist Information Centre
   The Quay, Aberaeron SA46 0BT
   Tel No: 01545 570602

Abergavenny Tourist Information Centre
   Swan Meadow, Monmouth Road, Abergavenny NP7 5HH
   Tel No: 01873 857588 Fax No: 01873 850217

Aberystwyth Tourist Information Centre
   Terrace Road, Aberystywyth SY23 2AG
   Tel No: 01970 612125 Fax No: 01970 626566

Barry Island Tourist Information Centre
   The Triangle, Paget Road, Barry Island CF62 5TQ
   Tel No: 01446 747171

Brecon Tourist Information Centre
   Cattle Market Car Park, Brecon, Powys LD3 9DA
   Tel No: 01874 622485 Fax No: 01874 625626

Builth Wells Tourist Information Centre
   Groe Car Park, Builth Wells, Powys LD2 3BT
   Tel No: 01982 553307

Caerleon Tourist Information Centre
   5 High Street, Caerleon NP6 1AG
   Tel No: 01633 422656

Caerphilly Tourist Information Centre
   Lower Twyn Square, Caerphilly CF8 1XX
   Tel No: 01222 880011 Fax No: 01222 860811

Cardiff Tourist Information Centre
Cardiff Central Railway Station, Cardiff CF1 1QY
Tel No: 01222 227281 Fax No: 01222 239162

Cardigan Tourist Information Centre
Theatr Mwldan, Bath House Road, Cardigan SA43 2JY
Tel No: 01239 613230

Carmarthen Tourist Information Centre
Lammas Street, Carmarthen SA31 3AQ
Tel No: 01267 231557 Fax NoL 01267 221901

Chepstow Tourist Information Centre
Castle Car Park, Bridge Steet, Chepstow NP6 5EY
Tel No: 01291 623772 Fax NoL 01291 628004

Crickhowell Tourist Information Centre
Beaufort Chambers, Beaufort Street, Crickhowell, Powys NP8 1AA
Tel No: 01873 812105

Elan Valley Tourist Information Centre
Visitor Centre, Rhayader, Powys LD6 5HP
Tel No: 01597 810898

Fishguard Town Centre Tourist Information Centre
The Square, Fishguard
Tel No: 01348 873484 Fax No: 01348 875246

Fishguard Harbour Tourist Information Centre
Passenger Concourse, The Harbour, Goodwick, Fishguard SA64 0BU
Tel No: 01348 872037

Haverfordwest Tourist Information Centre
Old Bridge, Haverfordwest SA61 2EZ
Tel No: 01437 763110 Fax No: 01437 767738

Hay-on-Wye Tourist Information Centre
Craft Centre, Hay-on-Wye, Hereford HR3 5AE
Tel No: 01497 820144

Knighton Tourist Information Centre
Offa's Dyke Centre, West Street, Knighton, Powys LD7 1EW
Tel No: 01547 528753

Llandarcy Tourist Information Centre
BP Club, Llandarcy, Neath SA10 6HJ
Tel No: 01792 813030 Fax: 01792 322451

Llandeilo Tourist Information Centre
Crescent Road Car Park, Llandeilo SA19 6HN
Tel: 01558 824226 Fax No: 01558 824252

Llandovery Tourist Information Centre
Heritage Centre, Kings Road, Llandovery SA20 0AW
Tel/Fax No: 01550 720693

Llandrindod Wells Tourist Information Centre
Old Town Hall, Memorial Gardens, Llandrindod Wells, Powys LD1 5DL
Tel No: 01597 822600

Llanelli Tourist Information Centre
Public Library, Vaughan Street, Llanelli SA15 3AS
Tel No: 01554 772020 Fax No: 01554 750125

Llanwrtyd Wells Tourist Information Centre
Ty Barcud, The Square, Llanwrtyd Wells, Powys LD3 4RB
Tel/Fax No: 01591 610666

Magor Tourist Information Centre
First Services & Lodge, Junction 23A/M4, Magor NP6 3YL
Tel No: 01633 881122 Fax No: 01633 881985

Merthyr Tydfil Tourist Information Centre
14a Glebeland Street, Merthyr Tydfil CF47 8AU
Tel No: 01685 379884 Fax No: 01685 350043

Milford Haven Tourist Information Centre
94 Charles Street, Milford Haven SA73 2HL
Tel No: 01646 690866 Fax No: 01646 690655

Monmouth Tourist Information Centre
Shire Hall, Agincourt Square, Monmouth NP5 3DY
Tel No: 01600 713899 Fax No: 01600 772794

Mumbles Tourist Information Centre
Oystermouth Square, Mumbles, Swansea SA3 4DQ
Tel No: 01792 361302 Fax No: 01792 363392

Newcastle Emlyn Tourist Information Centre
    Market Hall, Newcastle Emlyn SA38 9AE
    Tel/Fax No: 01239 711333

Newport Tourist Information Centre
    Museum & Art Gallery, John Frost Square, Newport, Gwent NP9 1HZ
    Tel No: 01633 842962 Fax No: 01633 222615

Newport (Pembs) Tourist Information Centre
    2 Bank Cottages, Long Street, Newport SA42 0LT
    Tel No: 01239 820912

New Quay Tourist Information Centre
    Church Street, New Quay SA45 560865

Pembroke Tourist Information Centre
    Visitor Centre, Commons Road, Pembroke SA71 4EA
    Tel No: 01646 622388 Fax No: 01646 621396

Pembroke Dock Tourist Information Centre
    The Guntower, Front Street, Pembroke Dock SA72 6JZ
    Tel No: 01646 622246

Pontneddfechan Tourist Information Centre
    Nr Glynneath SA11 5NR
    Tel No: 01639 721795

Pontypridd Tourist Information Centre
    Historical & Cultural Centre, The Old Bridge, Pontypridd CF37 3PE
    Tel No: 01443 409512 Fax No: 01443 485565

Porthcawl Tourist Information Centre
    Old Police Station, John Street, Porthcawl CF36 3DT
    Tel No: 01656 786639

Presteigne Tourist Information Centre
    Shire Hall, Broad Street, Presteigne, Powys LD8 2AW
    Tel No: 01544 260650

Rhayader Tourist Information Centre
    The Leisure Centre, North Street, Rhayader, Powys LD6 5BU
    Tel No: 01597 810591

St David's Tourist Information Centre
City Hall, St David's SA62 6SD
Tel/Fax No: 01437 720392

Sarn Tourist Information Centre
Sarn Park Services, Junction 36 M4, Nr Bridgend CF32 9SY
Tel No: 01656 654906 Fax No: 01656 646523

Saundersfoot Tourist Information Centre
The Barbecue, Harbour Car Park, Saundersfoot SA69 9HE
Tel No: 01834 813672 Fax No: 01834 813673

Swansea Tourist Information Centre
Singleton Street, Swansea SA1 3QG
Tel No: 01792 468321 Fax No: 01792 464602

Tenby Tourist Information Centre
The Croft, Tenby SA70 8AP
Tel No: 01834 842402 Fax No: 01834 845439

INDEX OF TOWNS AND VILLAGES

A

Aberaeron   45
Aberarth   48
Abercrave   33
Aberdare   163
Aberdulais   141
Abergavenny   182
Abergorlech   101
Abergwesyn   16
Abergwili   114
Aberporth   59
Aberystwyth   38
Ammanford   109
Amroth   72

B

Barry Island   154
Begelly   73
Bettws Newydd   175
Black Mountain   21
Blaenafon   168
Boncath   97
Borth   41
Brecon   21
Brecon Beacons   19
Brecon Beacons National Park   19
Bridgend   145
Broad Haven   82
Bronllys   25
Bronwydd   114

Brynamman   109
Builth Wells   13
Burry Port   121

C

Caerleon   171
Caerphilly   165
Caerwent   173
Caldey Island   72
Caldicot   174
Canaston Bridge   84
Capel Betws Lleucu   53
Capel Dewi   63
Cardiff   151
Cardigan   57
Cardigan Island   61
Carew   75
Carmarthen   113
Carregwastad Point, Nr
    Fishguard   89
Carregwastad Point, Nr Strumble
    Head   92
Castle Morris   92
Cefn March   156
Cenarth   113
Chepstow   177
Cilfrew   142
Cilgerran   62
Cilgwyn   96
Ciliau Aeron   48
Cilmery   15

Cilycwm   101
Clydach   138
Clyro   18
Cowbridge   156
Coychurch   145
Cribyn   57
Crickhowell   33
Croes Goch   92
Crossgates   7
Crosswell   95
Crynant   142
Cwmbran   169
Cwmdu   36
Cwmyoy   184
Cwmyoy Church   184
Cynonville   141

D

Dale   77
Dale Peninsula   78
Defynnog   31
Devil's Bridge   53
Dinas Cross   97
Dinas Head   97
Dinefwr Park   105
Doldowlod   13
Dowlais   161
Dryslwyn   107
Dyffryn Cellwen   142

E

Ebbw Vale   161
Eglwysfach   40
Elan Village   4
Erwood   17
Ewenny   146

F

Felinfach   26

Fforest Fawr   19
Fishguard   88
Foelgastell   111

G

Gateholm Island   77
Gilfach Reda   156
Gilwern   183
Glasbury   18
Golden Grove   106
Goodwick   90
Gorslas   111
Gower Peninsula   130
Groesffordd   27
Grosmont   181
Gwaun Valley   95
Gwbert-on-Sea   61

H

Haverfordwest   79
Hay-on-Wye   18
Hensol   155
Heol Senni   30
Howey   11

K

Kenfig   150
Kidwelly   120
Knelston   135
Knighton   10

L

Lampeter   54
Langland Bay   130
Laugharne   117
Libanus   30
Llanarth   51
Llanarthney   108

Llanbadarn Fawr   41
Llanbister   6
Llanddewi Velfrey   84
Llanddewi-Brefi   57
Llandegley   7
Llandeilo   103
Llandogo   179
Llandovery   100
Llandrindod Wells   4
Llandybie   108
Llandysul   62
Llanelli   122
Llanelwedd   14
Llanfarian   43
Llanfihangel-Nant-Melan   8
Llangadog   102
Llangammarch Wells   15
Llangattock   35
Llangennith   136
Llangolman   95
Llangorse   29
Llangorse Lake   29
Llangrannog   58
Llangybi   176
Llangynidr   30
Llangynin   116
Llangynwyd   144
Llanina   51
Llanmadoc   138
Llannon   119
Llanon   44
Llanrhidian   131
Llanrhystud   44
Llansoy   175
Llansteffan   118
Llanthony   184
Llantilio Crosseny   181
Llantrisant   162
Llantwit Major   157
Llanvetherine   181
Llanwnnen   56

Llanwonno   164
Llanwrthwl   4
Llanwrtyd Wells   16
Llechryd   62
Llywernog   45
Llywyn-teg   119
Loughor   139
Lovesgrove   42

M

Manorbier   72
Margam   144
Marloes   77
Marloes Peninsula   78
Martletwy   85
Merthyr Mawr   146
Merthyr Tydfil   160
Milford Haven   75
Monmouth   179
Mwnt   61
Mynydd Preseli   95

N

Nantgarw   166
Narberth   84
Nash Point   158
Neath   139
Nevern   96
New Quay   49
New Radnor   8
Newcastle Emlyn   111
Newport   96, 170
Newton   150
Nolton Haven   80
Nottage   150

O

Ogmore   146
Old Radnor   8

Oxwich   133

P

Painscastle   17
Parkmill   131
Pembrey   121
Pembroke   73
Pen-y-Cae   32
Penarth   154
Penbryn   59
Pendine   119
Penhow   172
Penmaen   131
Penmark   155
Pennant   49
Pontargothi   115
Pontarsais   116
Ponterwyd   45
Pontfaen   93
Pontrhydfendigaid   53
Pontsticill   161
Pontypool   167
Pontypridd   162
Port Einon   134
Port Talbot   143
Porthcawl   148
Porthgain   92
Preseli Hills   95
Presteigne   8
Pumsaint   101
Pwll   122

R

Raglan   185
Ramsey Island   87
Redwick   172
Rhayader   2
Rhigos   164
Rhossili   135

Rhydlewis   60
Rogerstone   170
Rosebush   94

S

Sandy Haven   78
Saundersfoot   72
Scurlage   134
Sennybridge   31
Simpson Cross   80
Skenfrith   181
Solva   88
Southerndown   147
St Clears   116
St David's   85
St Dogmaels   61
St Fagans   153
St Florence   70
St Govan's Head   74
St Harmon   3
St Hilary   156
St Ishmaels   78
St Nicholas   155
Strumble Head   92
Swansea   126

T

Talgarth   23
Talley   101
Talybont-on-Usk   29
Talyllyn   28
Tenby   66
The Mumbles   127
The Rhos   80
Tintern Parva   178
Tongwynlais   153
Trapp   106
Trecwn   94
Tredegar   162

Tregaron   51
Trehafod   163
Trerhyngyll   156
Tresaith   59
Tretower   35

U

Upper Killay   130
Upper Llanover   183
Usk   174

V

Vale of Usk   174

W

Whitland   117
Whitland Abbey   117
Whitney-on-Wye   19
Wolfscastle   82
Wolvesnewton   178
Wye Valley   170, 180

Y

Ynyslas   41
Ystradfellte   19, 32
Ystradgynlais   32

INDEX OF PLACES TO STAY, EAT, DRINK & SHOP

		Page No	Map Ref

Accommodation

CHAPTER 1: SOUTH POWYS

Beacons Edge	Bronllys	25	3I6
Caebetran Farm	Felinfach	26	3I6
Dolycoed	Talyllyn	28	3I6
George Hotel	Brecon	22	4I6
Gliffaes Country House Hotel	Crickhowell	33	4I7
Holly Farm	Howey	12	3I5
Liverpool House	Rhayader	3	4H4
Maeswalter	Heol Senni	30	3H7
The Lion Hotel	Llanbister	6	3I4
The Lion Hotel	Builth Wells	14	4I5
The Pines Caravan Park	Doldowlod	13	3H5
The Usk Inn	Talybont-on-Usk	29	3I7
Three Wells Farm Country House	Howey	11	3I5
Ty Clyd Guest House	Llandrindod Wells	5	4I5

CHAPTER 2: CEREDIGION

Llwyn-Yr-Eos	Rhydlewis	60	2E5
Llys Aeron	Aberaeron	47	2F5
Neuaddlas Guest House	Tregaron	52	2G5
Pantycelyn Guest House	Llanwnnen	56	2F5
Plas Dolau	Lovesgrove	42	2G4
The Barn House	Llanon	44	2F4
The Black Lion Royal Hotel	Lampeter	55	2F5

CHAPTER 3: PEMBROKESHIRE

Fourcroft Hotel	Tenby	69	1D8
Glendower Hotel	Goodwick	91	1C6
Grove Hotel	St David's	87	1B6
Hallsville Hotel	Tenby	68	1D8
Heywood Mount Hotel	Tenby	70	1D8
Ivybridge	Goodwick	90	1C6
Skerryback	Sandy Haven	78	1C7
The Cartref Hotel	Fishguard	89	1C6
The City Inn	St David's	86	1B6

		PAGE No	MAP REF

Accommodation (Cont.)

The Mariners' Inn	Nolton Haven	80	1C7
The Old Post Office	Rosebush	94	1D6
Wendy Brandon Handmade Preserves	Boncath	97	1D6
West Hall	St Florence	71	1D8
Wolfscastle Country Hotel	Wolfscastle	83	1C6

CHAPTER 4: CARMARTHENSHIRE

Coed Llys Uchaf	Llangynin	116	2E7
Derlwyn Arms	Brynamman	110	3G7
Ffynnon Rhosfa Farm	Llannon	119	2F7
Swyn Yr Afon	Pontargothi	115	2F7
The Castle Hotel	Llangadog	102	2G6

CHAPTER 5: GOWER PENINSULA & THE HERITAGE COAST

Atlantic Hotel	Porthcawl	148	2G9
Jane Hodge Resort Hotel	Trerhyngyll	156	2H9
The Post Office	Llangennith	137	2E8
Three Cliffs Bay Caravan Park	Penmaen	131	2F8

CHAPTER 6: THE VALLEYS OF SOUTHEAST WALES

Coach & Horses	Caerwent	173	3K8
Denehurst Guesthouse	Caerphilly	166	2I8
Glen-Yr-Afon House Hotel	Pontypool	174	2J8
Ivy Villa Guest House	Abergavenny	182	3J7
Jolly Roger	Rogerstone	170	3J8
The White Hart	Llangybi	176	3J8

Pubs, Inns & Wine Bars

CHAPTER 1: SOUTH POWYS

George Hotel	Brecon	22	4I6
The Farmers Arms	Cwmdu	36	3I6
The Lion Hotel	Llanbister	6	3I4
The Lion Hotel	Builth Wells	14	4I5
The Three Horseshoes	Groesffordd	27	3I6
The Usk Inn	Talybont-on-Usk	29	3I7

CHAPTER 2: CEREDIGION

Brynhoffnant Inn	Llandysul	62	2E6
The Black Lion	Aberaeron	45	2F5
The Black Lion Royal Hotel	Lampeter	55	2F5
The Penrhiwllan Inn	New Quay	50	2E5
The Royal Oak	Llanfarian	43	2F4

		PAGE NO	MAP REF

Pubs, Inns & Wine Bars (Cont.)

CHAPTER 3: PEMBROKESHIRE

The Atramont Arms	Croes Goch	93	1C6
The City Inn	St David's	86	1B6
The Evergreen	Tenby	67	1D8
The Mariners' Inn	Nolton Haven	80	1C7
The Old Post Office	Rosebush	94	1D6
The Watermans Arms	Pembroke	73	1C8

CHAPTER 4: CARMARTHENSHIRE

Derlwyn Arms	Brynamman	110	3G7
The Black Lion	Abergorlech	101	2F6
The Bunch of Grapes	Newcastle Emlyn	111	2E6
The Castle Hotel	Llangadog	102	2G6
The Red Lion Hotel	Llandybie	108	2F7

CHAPTER 5: GOWER PENINSULA & THE HERITAGE COAST

Carpenters Arms	Clydach	138	2G8
Farmers Arms	Nottage , Nr Porthcawl	150	2G9
Kingshead	Llangennith	136	2E8
The Corner House	Llangynwyd	144	2H8
The Countryman	Scurlage	134	2F8
The Dulais Rock Inn	Aberdulais	141	2G8
The Dyffryn	Dyffryn Cellwen	142	2H7
The Globe Inn	Loughor	139	2F8
The Railway Inn	Upper Killay	130	2F8
The Star Inn	Neath	140	2G8
Three Golden Cups	Southerndown	147	2H9
Vincent's	The Mumbles	129	2F8
Welcome to Town Country Bistro & Bar	Llanrhidian	132	2F8

CHAPTER 6: THE VALLEYS OF SOUTHEAST WALES

Black Bear Inn	Bettws Newydd	175	3J7
Coach & Horses	Caerwent	173	3K8
Jolly Roger	Rogerstone	170	3J8
New Inn	Rhigos	164	3H7
The Bush Inn	Cwmbran	169	3J8
The Goose & Cuckoo	Upper Llanover	183	3J7
The Rose Inn	Redwick	172	3J8
The White Hart	Llangybi	176	3J8

		PAGE No	MAP REF

Restaurants

CHAPTER 1: SOUTH POWYS

George Hotel	Brecon	22	4I6
Gliffaes Country House Hotel	Crickhowell	33	4I7
The Farmers Arms	Cwmdu	36	3I6
The Lion Hotel	Llanbister	6	3I4
The Lion Hotel	Builth Wells	14	4I5
The Three Horseshoes	Groesffordd	27	3I6
The Usk Inn	Talybont-on-Usk	29	3I7
Three Wells Farm Country House	Howey	11	3I5

CHAPTER 2: CEREDIGION

Brynhoffnant Inn	Llandysul	62	2E6
The Black Lion	Aberaeron	45	2F5
The Black Lion Royal Hotel	Lampeter	55	2F5
The Penrhiwllan Inn	New Quay	50	2E5
The Royal Oak	Llanfarian	43	2F4
Y Pantri	Lampeter	54	2F5

CHAPTER 3: PEMBROKESHIRE

Fourcroft Hotel	Tenby	69	1D8
Glendower Hotel	Goodwick	91	1C6
Grove Hotel	St David's	87	1B6
Hallsville Hotel	Tenby	68	1D8
Heywood Mount Hotel	Tenby	70	1D8
Martha's Vineyard	Milford Haven	76	1C7
The Atramont Arms	Croes Goch	93	1C6
The Cartref Hotel	Fishguard	89	1C6
The City Inn	St David's	86	1B6
The Mariners' Inn	Nolton Haven	80	1C7
The Old Post Office	Rosebush	94	1D6
The Watermans Arms	Pembroke	73	1C8
The Wolfe	Wolfscastle	82	1C6
Wolfscastle Country Hotel	Wolfscastle	83	1C6

CHAPTER 4: CARMARTHENSHIRE

Derlwyn Arms	Brynamman	110	3G7
Fanny's Restaurant	Llandeilo	103	2G7
Tafarn Y Sospan	Pwll	122	2F8
The Bunch of Grapes	Newcastle Emlyn	111	2E6
The Castle Hotel	Llangadog	102	2G6
The Red Lion Hotel	Llandybie	108	2F7

		PAGE No	MAP REF

Restaurants (Cont.)

CHAPTER 5: GOWER PENINSULA & THE HERITAGE COAST

Atlantic Hotel	Porthcawl	148	2G9
Café Rendezvous	Rhossili	135	2E8
Carpenters Arms	Clydach	138	2G8
Farmers Arms	Nottage , Nr Porthcawl	150	2G9
Jane Hodge Resort Hotel	Trerhyngyll	156	2H9
Kingshead	Llangennith	136	2E8
Patricks	The Mumbles	128	2F8
The Corner House	Llangynwyd	144	2H8
The Countryman	Scurlage	134	2F8
The Dulais Rock Inn	Aberdulais	141	2G8
Three Golden Cups	Southerndown	147	2H9
Vincent's	The Mumbles	129	2F8
Welcome to Town Country Bistro & Bar	Llanrhidian	132	2F8

CHAPTER 6: THE VALLEYS OF SOUTHEAST WALES

Black Bear Inn	Bettws Newydd	175	3J7
Coach & Horses	Caerwent	173	3K8
Glen-Yr-Afon House Hotel	Pontypool	174	2J8
Jolly Roger	Rogerstone	170	3J8
New Inn	Rhigos	164	3H7
The Goose & Cuckoo	Upper Llanover	183	3J7
The Rose Inn	Redwick	172	3J8
The White Hart	Llangybi	176	3J8

Specialist Shops and Activities

CHAPTER 1: SOUTH POWYS

The Strand Bookshop & Café	Talgarth	24	3I6

CHAPTER 3: PEMBROKESHIRE

The Old Post Office	Rosebush	94	1D6
Wendy Brandon Handmade Preserves	Boncath	97	1D6

CHAPTER 4: CARMARTHENSHIRE

King's Lodge Pottery	Llandeilo	105	2G7
Swyn Yr Afon	Pontargothi	115	2F7

CHAPTER 5: GOWER PENINSULA & THE HERITAGE COAST

Huw Thomas Gallery	Porthcawl	149	2G9
The Post Office	Llangennith	137	2E8

		PAGE No	MAP REF

Tea Rooms, Coffee Shops & Cafes

CHAPTER 1: SOUTH POWYS

The Strand Bookshop & Café	Talgarth	24	3I6

CHAPTER 3: PEMBROKESHIRE

Preseli Country Café	Llanddewi Velfrey	84	1D7
The Old Post Office	Rosebush	94	1D6

CHAPTER 4: CARMARTHENSHIRE

Tafarn Y Sospan	Pwll	122	2F8

CHAPTER 5: GOWER PENINSULA & THE HERITAGE COAST

Café Rendezvous	Rhossili	135	2E8
The Coffee Bean	The Mumbles	127	2F8
The Post Office	Llangennith	137	2E8

INDEX OF PLACES OF INTEREST

A

Abbeycwmhir, Crossgates   7
Aberaeron Golf Club   47
Aberdulais Falls   141
Abergwesyn Pass   16
Aberystwyth Arts Centre   38
Aberystwyth Castle   38
Aberystwyth Electric Cliff Railway   39
Aberystwyth Harbour and Marina   39
Aberystwyth Town Quay   39
Aeron Express, Aberaeron   47
Afan Forest Park, Cynonville   141
Alban Square, Aberaeron   45
Arthur's Stone, Knelston   135

B

Beacons Pottery and Picture Gallery, Defynnog   31
Beaupré Castle, St Hilary   156
Bedd Illtyd, Nr Libanus   30
Big Pit Mining Museum, Blaenafon   168
Bird Rock, New Quay   49
Bishop's Palace, St David's   85
Black Mountain   21
Black Mountains, Nr Brecon   20
Blaenafon Ironworks   168
Borth Animalarium   41
Brecknock Museum, Brecon   22
Brecon Beacons   19
Brecon Beacons Mountain Centre, Libanus   30
Brecon Beacons National Park   19

Brecon Beacons National Park, Abergavenny   182
Brecon Beacons National Park Visitor Centre, Nr Libanus   20
Brecon Castle   21
Brecon Cathedral   21
Brecon Court Deer Farm, Llansoy   175
Brecon Mountain Railway, Merthyr Tydfil   20
Brecon Mountain Railway, Pontsticill   161
Brecon Priory Church of St John the Evangelist   21
Bronllys Castle, Nr Talgarth   24
Bryn Bach Park, Tredegar   162
Bryngarw Country House and Park, Nr Ewenny   146
Burry Port Harbour   121

C

Caben Coch, Elan Village   4
Caer Penhros, Llanrhystud   44
Caerphilly Castle   165
Caldicot Castle   174
Cambrian Woollen Mill, Llanwrtyd Wells   16
Camddwr Bleiddiaid, Abergwesyn   17
Candleston Castle, Merthyr Mawr   146
Canolfan Crefft Cymru, Tregaron   51
Capel Betws Lleucu   53
Capel Betws Pony Centre and Farm Park   53
Cardiff Arms Park   152
Cardiff Castle   151
Cardiff City Hall   151
Cardigan Guildhall   58
Cardigan Island   61
Cardigan Island Coastal Farm Park   61
Cardigan Museum   58
Cardigan Wildlife Park, Cilgerran   62
Carmarthen Bay Coastal Walk   119
Carmarthen Castle   113
Carmarthenshire County Museum, Abergwili   114
Carn Ingli, Nr Nevern   96
Carreg Bica, Llangrannog   59
Carreg Cennen Castle, Trapp   106
Carreg Cennen, Nr Trapp   20
Carregwastad Point, Nr Fishguard   89

Carregwastad Point, Nr Strumble Head   92
Castell Bach, Llanrhystud   44
Castell Collen, Llandrindod Wells   4
Castell Ddu, Nr Sennybridge   32
Castell Mawr, Llanrhystud   44
Castle Mound, Builth Wells   14
Catherine Lewis Gallery, Aberystwyth   39
Cathole Cave, Parkhill   131
Caws Ffermdy Nantybwla Cheesemaking & Museum, Nr Abergwili   114
CC2000, Canaston Bridge   84
Cefn Carn Cafall, Builth Wells   14
Cefn Coed Colliery Museum, Crynant   142
Cefn Sidan, Pembrey   121
Cei Bach, Nr New Quay   50
Ceredigion Museum, Aberystwyth   39
Cerrig Ina, Nr Llanina   51
Chepstow Racecourse   177
Church Cave, Nr Gwbert-on-Sea   61
Church of St Brynach, Nevern   96
Church of St Edmund, Crickhowell   34
Church of St Gwendoline, Talgarth   24
Church of St Hilary, St Hilary   156
Church of St Illtud, Llantwit Major   157
Church of St Illtud, Oxwich   133
Church of St Mary, Penmark   155
Church of St Michael, Penbryn   59
Church of St Teilo, Llandeilo   103
Church of the Holy Cross, Mwnt   61
Cilgerran Castle   62
Clos Pengarreg, Aberaeron   47
Clytha Castle, Raglan   185
Clytha Park House, Raglan   185
Coity Castle, Bridgend   145
Colby Woodland Garden, Amroth   72
Comeston Lakes Country Park and Medieval Village,   154
Coracle Church, Llechryd   62
Cors Caron National Nature Reserve, Tregaron   52
Cors Caron Nature Reserve, Nr Pontrhydfendigaid   53
Craig y Fan Ddu, Nr Talybont-on-Usk   29
Craig y Nos Castle, Pen-y-Cae   32
Craig y Nos Country Park, Pen-y-Cae   32

Craig-y-Cilau Nature Reserve, Llangattock   35
Crickhowell Castle   34
Crickhowell Stone Bridge   33
Crochendy Llanarth Pottery, Llanarth   51
Crug Hywel, Crickhowell   33
Custom House Shop and Gallery, Cardigan   58
Cwm Deri Vineyard, Martletwy   85
Cwm Einion, Eglwysfach   40
Cwmyoy Church   184
Cwrt-Y-Brychan Vineyard, Llansoy   175
Cyfarthfa Castle Museum, Merthyr Tydfil   160

D

Dale Peninsula   78
Dan Yr Ogof Showcaves, Abercrave   33
Dare Valley Country Park, Aberdare   164
Daugleddau, Nr The Rhos   80
Dinefwr Castle   105
Dinefwr Old Castle   105
Dinefwr Park   105
Dolaucothi Gold Mines, Pumsaint   101
Dolauhirion Bridge, Cilycwm   101
Dowlais Viaduct   161
Drefach Felindre   113
Dryslwyn Castle   107
Duke's Arms, Presteigne   9
Dyffryn Bern, Nr Penbryn   59
Dyffryn Cellwen   142
Dyffryn Gardens, St Nicholas   155
Dyfi Furnace, Eglwysfach   40
Dyfi National Nature Reserve, Eglwysfach   41

E

East Nolton Riding Stables   81
Elan Valley Visitor Centre   4
Ewenny Priory   146

F

Fan Llia, Nr Ystradfelte   32

Fan Nedd, Nr Ystradfellte   32
Felinwynt Rainforest and Butterfly Centre, Aberport   59
Festival of the Black Mountains, Talgarth   24

G

Gateholm Island   77
Gerddi Penlan-Uchaf Gardens, Pontfaen   93
Gigrin Farm, Rhayader   2
Gilfach Reda   156
Gilfach, St Harmon   3
Glyn-Coch Studios, Nr St Clears   116
Glynderi Pottery, Sennybridge   32
Glyndwr's Way, Knighton   10
Golden Grove Mansion   106
Gower Peninsula   130
Great Aberystwyth Camera Obscura   39
Great Castle House, Monmouth   180
Greenmeadow Community Farm, Cwmbran   169
Grosmont Castle   181
Guildhall, Carmarthen   114
Gwaun Valley   95
Gwent Rural Life Museum, Usk   175
Gwenwydd Cochion, Nr Llannon   119
Gwili Pottery, Pontarsais   116
Gwili Railway, Bronwydd   114
Gwinllan Ffynnon Las Vineyard, Aberaeron   47

H

Haverfordwest Castle   79
Haverfordwest Museum and Art Gallery   79
Hay-on-Wye Craft Centre   18
Hay-on-Wye Festival of Art and Literature   18
Heatherton Country Sports Park, St Florence   71
Hengoed Viaduct, Ystrad Mynach   167
Heron's Brook Country Park and Wildfowl Centre, Narberth   84
Hive on the Quay, Aberaeron   47
Holy Trinity Church, Llandrindod Wells   4

J

Joseph Parry's Cottage, Merthyr Tydfil   160
Judge's Lodging, Presteigne   8
Junction Cottage, Pontypool   167

K

Kaleidoscope Discovery Centre, Milford Haven   76
Kenfig National Nature Reserve   150
Kidwelly Castle   120
Kidwelly Industrial Museum   121
Kinsley Wood, Knighton   10
Knox Valley Llanstinan Quad Trail, Trecwn   94

L

Landsker, Haverfordwest   79
Langland Bay   130
Langorse Lake, Nr Talgarth   24
Laugharne Glass   117
Laura Place, Aberystwyth   39
Lavernock Point, Nr Penarth   154
Legionary Museum, Caerleon   172
Lightship 2000, Cardiff   152
Little Castle Head lighthouse, Nr St Ishmaels   79
Llanbadarn Fawr Church   41
Llancaiach Fawr, Nelson   167
Llandaff Cathedral, Cardiff   152
Llandegfedd Reservoir, Pontypool   167
Llandovery Heritage Centre   100
Llandrindod Wells and Radnorshire Museum   5
Llanerch Vineyard, Hensol   155
Llanfair Clydogau, Nr Llanddewi-Brefi   57
Llanfihangel-Nant-Melan   8
Llangammarch Wells   15
Llangloffan Farmhouse Cheese Centre, Castle Morris   92
Llangorse Lake   29
Llanmadoc Hill   138
Llansteffan Castle   118
Llantarnam, Nr Cwmbran   169
Llanthony Priory   184

Llewelyn the Last, Cilmery   15
Llyn Llech Owain Country Park, Gorslas   111
Llywernog Silver-Lead Mine Museum   45

M

Maen Madog, Ystradfellte   32
Manorbier Castle   72
Margam Abbey   144
Margam Abbey Church   144
Margam Country Park   144
Marine Life Centre, St David's   85
Market Hall, Llandovery   100
Marloes Peninsula   78
Merthyr Mawr Warren   146
Middleton Hall, Llanarthney   108
Milford Haven Museum   76
Miranda's Preserves, Strumble Head   92
Model House, Llantrisant   163
Monkton Priory, Pembroke   73
Monmouth and Brecon Canal, Brecon   21
Monmouth and Brecon Canal, Crickhowell   34
Monmouth and Brecon Canal, Gilwern   183
Monmouth and Brecon Canal, Talybont-on-Usk   29
Monmouth Castle   180
Monmouth Museum   180
Monnow Bridge, Monmouth   180
Monnow Valley, Skenfrith   181
Morfa Colliery, Port Talbot   143
Museum of Speed, Pendine   119
Museum of the Home, Pembroke   73
Mynydd Epynt, Nr Llanwrtyd Wells   16
Mynydd Illtyd Common, Nr Libanus   20

N

Nantgarw China Works   166
National Coracle Centre, Cenarth   113
National Cycle Exhibition, Llandrindod Wells   5
National Library of Wales, Aberystwyth   39
Neath Abbey   140

Neath Castle   140
Neath Museum   140
Nevern Castle   96
New Quay Bird Hospital   50
New Quay Head   49
New Quay Yacht Club   49
New Radnor Motte and Bailey Castle   8
Newcastle, Bridgend   145
Newcastle Emlyn Castle   111
Newport Museum and Art Gallery   170
Newton House, Nr Dinefwr Castle   106
Noah's Ark, Cribyn   57
Norwegian Church Arts Centre, Cardiff   152

O

Oakwood Park, Canaston Bridge   84
Oceanarium, St David's   86
Offa's Dyke Centre, Knighton   10
Offa's Dyke Path, Knighton   10
Offa's Dyke Path, Nr Llanthony   185
Ogmore Castle   146
Ogof Ffynnon Ddu Caves   20
Ogwr Ridgeway Walk, Nr Llangynwyd   144
Old Cottage, Llanon   44
Old Wool Barn Craft Centre, Cowbridge   156
Open Studio and Gallery, Solva   88
Oxwich Nature Reserve   134
Oxwich Point   134
Oystermouth Castle, The Mumbles   129

P

Palace of the Bishop of St David's, Abergwli   114
Pant Mawr Farm, Rosebush   94
Parc Howard Museum and Art Gallery, Llanelli   123
Parc Le Breos Burial Chamber, Parkmill   131
Paxton Tower, Llanarthney   108
Pembrey Country Park   121
Pembroke Castle   73
Pembroke Dock   74

Pembrokeshire Candle Centre , Cilgwyn   96
Pembrokeshire Coastal National Park, Amroth   72
Pembrokeshire Motor Museum, Simpson Cross   80
Pen-y-Fan, Brecon Beacons   19
Pen-y-fan, Pontsticill   161
Penarth Marina   154
Penarth Pier   154
Penclacwydd Wildfowl and Wetlands Centre, Llanelli   123
Penhow Castle   172
Penrhos Golf and Country Club, Llanrhystud   44
Penscynor Wildlife Park, Cilfrew   142
Pentre Ifan Cromlech, Crosswell   95
Picton Castle, Nr Haverfordwest   80
Pinners Hole, Knighton   10
Plas Llanmihangel , Nr Cowbridge   156
Pont-y-gwr-Drwg, Devil's Bridge   54
Pontypridd Historical and Cultural Centre   162
Porth-yr-Ogof, Nr Ystradfellte   32
Porthcawl Harbour   148
Porthcawl Museum   148
Powys Observatory, Knighton   10
Preseli Hills   95
Priory Church, Haverfordwest   79

R

Radnorshire Arms Hotel, Presteigne   8
Raglan Castle   185
Ramsey Island   87
Ramsey Island Cruises   87
Red Kite Centre, Abergwesyn   17
Rheidol Railway, Devil's Bridge   53
Rhondda Heritage Park, Trehafod   163
Rhydlewis Fishery   60
Rick Leech, Llanelli   123
River Taff, Cardiff   152
Rock Mills Woollen and Water Mill, Capel Dewi   63
Rock Spa, Llandrindod Wells   5
Royal Society for the Protection of Birds Visitor   100
Royal Welsh Show Ground, Llanelwedd   14
RSPB Ynys-hir Reserve, Eglwysfach   41

S

Sandy Water Park, Llanelli   123
Sea Aquarium and Animal Kingdom Centre, Aberaeron   46
Skenfrith Castle   181
Slate Workshop, Llangolman   95
South Wales Borderers Museum, Brecon   22
St Ann's Head, Nr Dale   77
St Anthony's Well, Llansteffan   118
St Catwg's Church, Llangattock   35
St David's Cathedral   85
St David's Church, Aberarth   48
St David's Church, Llanddewi-Brefi   57
St David's College, Lampeter   54
St David's Lifeboat Station   87
St David's Shopping Centre, Cardiff   152
St Dogmaels Abbey and Water Mill   61
St Donat's Art Centre, Nash Point   158
St Donat's Castle, Nash Point   158
St Govan's Chapel   74
St Govan's Head   74
St Ishmael's Nurseries and Garden Centre   78
St John the Baptist, Cardiff   152
St Justinian's, Nr St David's   87
St Katherine's Church, Milford Haven   76
St Mary's Church, Fishguard   89
St Mary's Church, Hay-on-Wye   18
St Mary's Church, Monmouth   180
St Non's Chapel, St David's   86
St Non's Well, St David's   86
St Quentin's Castle, St Hilary   156
St Woolos Cathedral, Newport   170
Stack Rocks, St Govan's Head   74
Stepaside Heritage Project, Saundersfoot   73
Stones Museum, Margam   144
Strata Florida Abbey, Nr Pontrhydfendigaid   53
Swansea Castle   127
Swansea Maritime and Industrial Museum   126
Swansea Maritime Quarter   126

T

Taff Trail, Brecon   23
Talley Abbey   101
Talybont Reservoir   29
Techniquest, Cardiff   152
Teifi Bridge, Cardigan   57
Tenby Castle   68
Tenby Museum   68
The Arch, Devil's Bridge   54
The Boat House, Laugharne   117
The Brynamman Walk, Ammanford   109
The Bulwark, Llanmadoc   138
The Glamorgan Heritage Coast Centre, Southerndown   147
The Kymin, Monmouth   180
The Model Farm Museum, Wolvesnewton   179
The National Museum & Gallery, Cardiff   151
The Naval Temple, Monmouth   180
The Nectarium, Solva   88
The Old Smith, Cenarth   113
Theatr Mwldan, Cardigan   58
Thousand Islands Expeditions, St David's   87
Three Castle Walk, Llanvetherine   181
Tintern Visitor Centre   178
Tower Bridge, Talgarth   24
Towy Bridge, Llandeilo   103
Traeth Gwyn, Nr New Quay   50
Trapp Art and Crafts Centre   107
Tredegar House and Park, Newport   170
Tretower Court and Castle   35
Tudor Merchant's House, Tenby   67
Turner House Art Gallery, Penarth   154
Twm Sion Cati's Cave, Cilycwm   101
Twyn y Gaer, Nr Libanus   30

U

Umfrevilles, Penmark   155

V

Vale of Rheidol Light Railway, Aberystwyth   39
Valley Inheritance Centre, Pontypool   167
Victoria Square, Aberdare   163

W

Walled Garden of Pigeonsford, Llangrannog   59
Welsh Folk Museum, St Fagans   153
Welsh Gold Centre, Tregaron   51
Welsh Hawking Centre, Barry Island   155
Welsh Industrial and Maritime Museum, Cardiff   152
Welsh Miners Museum, Cynonville   141
Welsh Royal Crystal, Rhayader   2
Welsh Whisky Distillery and Visitor Centre, Brecon   23
Welsh Wildlife Centre, Cardigan   58
White Castle, Llanvetherine   181
Whitland Abbey   117
Wildfowl Centre, Amroth   72
Windsor Gardens, Penarth   154
Wolfscastle Pottery   83
Woollen Mill, Solva   88
Wooltrack Point, Nr Marloes   77
Worms Head, Gower Peninsula   136
Wye Valley   170, 180
Wye Valley Herbs, Tintern   178
Wyeside Arts Centre, Builth Wells   14

Y

Y Gaer, Nr Brecon   20
Y Garn Goch, Ystradgynlais   32
Y Goeden Fach Bonsai, Foelgastell   111
Y Pigwn, Trecastle   20
Ynysangharad Park, Pontypridd   162
Ynyscedwyn Arms   33
Ynyscedwyn Ironworks   33
Ynysfach Engine House, Merthyr Tydfil   161

THE HIDDEN PLACES
Order Form

To order any of our publications just fill in the payment details below and complete the order form *overleaf*. For orders of less than 4 copies please add £1 per book for postage and packing. Orders over 4 copies are P & P free.

Please Complete Either:

I enclose a cheque for £ .... made payable to Travel Publishing Ltd

Or:

Card No:

Expiry Date:

Signature: ....

NAME: ....

ADDRESS: ....

....

....

POSTCODE: ....

TEL NO: ....

Please send to: Travel Publishing Ltd
7a Apollo House
Calleva Park
Aldermaston
Berks, RG7 8TN

THE HIDDEN PLACES
Order Form

Regional Titles	Price	Quantity	Value
Cambridgeshire & Lincolnshire	£7.99	....	....
Channel Islands	£6.99	....	....
Cheshire	£7.99	....	....
Chilterns	£7.99	....	....
Cornwall	£7.99	....	....
Devon	£7.99	....	....
Dorset, Hants & Isle of Wight	£7.99	....	....
Essex	£7.99	....	....
Gloucestershire	£6.99	....	....
Highlands & Islands	£7.99	....	....
Kent	£7.99	....	....
Lake District & Cumbria	£7.99	....	....
Lancashire	£7.99	....	....
Norfolk	£7.99	....	....
Northeast Yorkshire	£6.99	....	....
Northumberland & Durham	£6.99	....	....
North Wales	£7.99	....	....
Nottinghamshire	£6.99	....	....
Peak District	£6.99	....	....
Potteries	£6.99	....	....
Somerset	£6.99	....	....
South Wales	£7.99	....	....
Suffolk	£7.99	....	....
Surrey	£6.99	....	....
Sussex	£6.99	....	....
Thames Valley	£7.99	....	....
Warwickshire & West Midlands	£7.99	....	....
Welsh Borders	£7.99	....	....
Wiltshire	£6.99	....	....
Yorkshire Dales	£6.99	....	....
Set of any 5 Regional titles	**£25.00**	....	....
National Titles			
England	£9.99	....	....
Ireland	£8.99	....	....
Scotland	£8.99	....	....
Wales	£8.99	....	....
Set of all 4 National titles	**£28.00**	....	....
		———	———
		———	———

*For orders of less than 4 copies please add £1 per book for postage
& packing. Orders over 4 copies P & P free.*

THE HIDDEN PLACES
— Reader Comment Form —

The *Hidden Places* research team would like to receive reader's comments on any visitor attractions or places reviewed in the book and also recommendations for suitable entries to be included in the next edition. This will help ensure that the *Hidden Places* series continues to provide its readers with useful information on the more interesting, unusual or unique features of each attraction or place ensuring that their stay in the local area is an enjoyable and stimulating experience.

To provide your comments or recommendations would you please complete the forms below and overleaf as indicated and send to: The Research Department, Travel Publishing Ltd., 7a Apollo House, Calleva Park, Aldermaston, Reading, RG7 8TN.

Your Name:

Your Address:

Your Telephone Number:

Please tick as appropriate: Comments ☐ Recommendation ☐

Name of *"Hidden Place"*:

Address:

Telephone Number:

Name of Contact:

THE HIDDEN PLACES
—— Reader Comment Form ——

Comment or Reason for Recommendation:

....

....

....

....

....

....

....

....

....

....

....

....

....

MAP SECTION

The following pages of maps encompass the main cities, towns and geographical features of South Wales, as well as many of the interesting places featured in the guide. Distances are indicated by the use of scale bars located below each of the maps

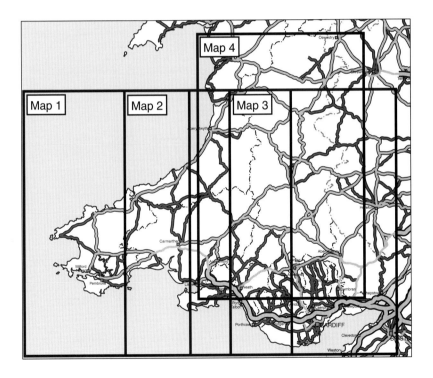

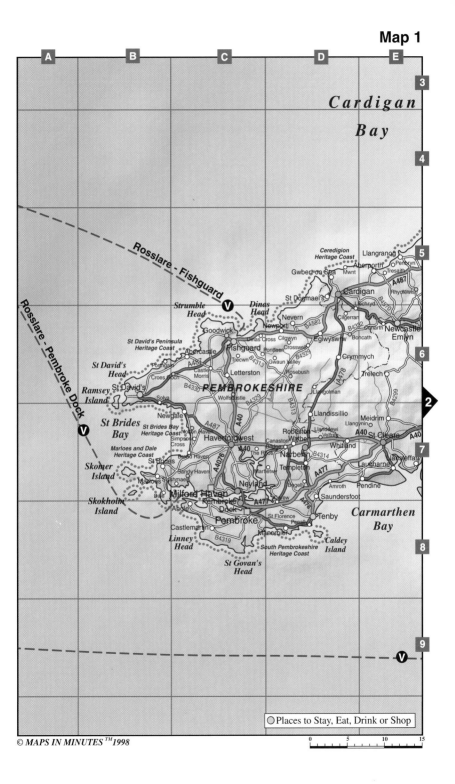

Map 1

○ Places to Stay, Eat, Drink or Shop

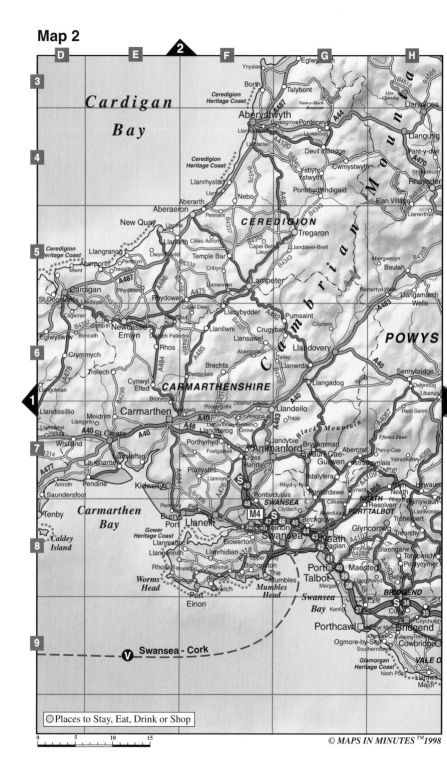

Map 2

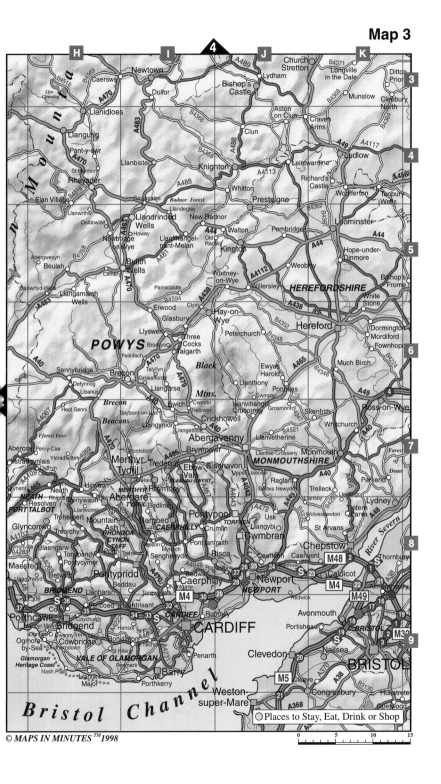

Map 3

© MAPS IN MINUTES ™ 1998

○ Places to Stay, Eat, Drink or Shop

0	5	10	15

Map 4

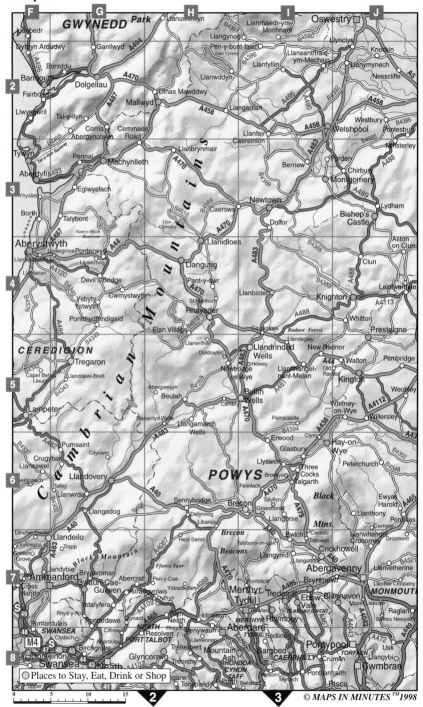

○ Places to Stay, Eat, Drink or Shop